Mark McNeal

The Faith

Mark McNeal

The Faith

ISBN/EAN: 9783741164248

Manufactured in Europe, USA, Canada, Australia, Japa

Cover: Foto ©Andreas Hilbeck / pixelio.de

Manufactured and distributed by brebook publishing software (www.brebook.com)

Mark McNeal

The Faith

THE FAITH.

BY THE

REV. MARK McNEAL

LONDON:
R. WASHBOURNE, 18, PATERNOSTER ROW.
DUBLIN: J. DUFFY. GLASGOW: H. MARGEY.

1880.

THIS WORK, ENTITLED

THE FAITH,

IS DEDICATED WITH AFFECTION

TO THE MEMORY OF THE

VERY REV. CANON O'NEAL,

WHO WAS FOR MANY YEARS

VICAR-GENERAL

IN THE LONDON DISTRICT,

AND ALSO IN THE ARCH-DIOCESE.

THE GOOD WHICH HE EFFECTED

IS ALONE KNOWN TO HIM

WHOM HE SO LONG

AND SO ZEALOUSLY SERVED.

PREFACE.

It is admitted among eminent Protestant divines, whose candour has enhanced the value of their erudition, that there can be only one Church, which must be necessarily conceded, since what is of Divine institution is identified with Truth, which is One, and must continue to be so to the end of time, the same to-day as yesterday. A celebrated Protestant prelate,* in his fervid persuasions as to the above, thus conclusively expresses himself—"Seeing," as he as rationally as emphatically remarks, the "controversies of religion in our times are grown in number so many, and in nature so intricate, that few have time or leisure, fewer have strength of understand-

---

* Dr. Field on the Church.

ing, to examine them, what remains for men desirous of salvation in things of such consequence but diligently to seek out *which among all* the societies of men is that blessed company of holy ones, that household of truth, that spouse of Christ, the Church of the Living God, the pillar and the ground of truth, that so they may embrace her communion, follow her direction, and rest in her judgment?" This has been, it may be deemed, fully responded to in the following pages, in the manifestation of a Church which Infinite Wisdom could alone have framed and Infinite Power could alone have preserved. It is designated Catholic, which comprises the faith of the Apostles, which they so zealously propagated, which the martyrs prized beyond life itself, and which enabled the saints, in the assurance of its promised bliss, to feel but little the startling severities which they practised.

This faith, which constitutes the Christian's victory, triumphed over the might that held the world in thraldom, and now, in the most enlightened, enterprising, and resolute of periods, when all appears to cede to human persistence, she continues her intrepid step in the march of Providence, that leagued nations must make way for, as once the rivers of the earth. Upon those who have but a very limited control over their importunate passions, in whose hush alone the voice of reason can be very well heard, the subject-matter of the following pages will make little impression and realise little influence. But those who seek to find under the impulse of a soul's surety will find, as possessing the pledge of Heaven so to do, the truth, on which the Catholic Church is founded. Thrice happy are they when within the security of her Divine build " in following her direction" and "in resting in her judgment."

CONTENTS.

SECTION I.

Enlightenment of the present age—Modern spread of Catholicism parallel to that of Christianity in the early ages—Diffusion of truth the source of multitudinous heresies—Origin, nature, and development of heresy in general, and of Arianism in particular—Imperial patronage its principal support—Necessary dependence of heresy on secular aid—Athanasius the great opponent of Arianism—Failure of all attempts at compromise or conciliation—The persecution of emperors and the assaults of heresiarchs alike unable to subvert the truth—The Macedonian, Nestorian, and Eutychian heresies successively condemned—Immense fertility of heresy at all times—Mutual hostility of the various sects—Appeal of each to Scripture and antiquity in support of its tenets, and denunciation of all who differ from them—Opinion the sole basis of their several systems—Contrast between the Catholic Church and heresy—Stability, unity, and unchangeability of the Church—Identity of her doctrine at all times and in all places—Her internal harmony and charity . . . . p. 1

SECTION II.

Teaching of the Fathers on controverted points—Witness of eminent Protestant divines to the truth of Catholic doctrines—Clear language of inspiration on such points—The Seven Sacraments vouched for by Scripture, taught in the writings of the Fathers, and assented to by the reformers themselves—Refusal of some Anglicans to accept this testimony as conclusive—Their desire for a Convocation to settle disputed points—Unavoidable failure of such a scheme—Private judgment, the basis of Protestantism, antagonistic to dogmatic teaching—The religious system of Rome—The Church's unity a note of her Divine origin—Sanctity another note of the true Church—The imperfections of individuals no invalidation of the Church's claim to sanctity—The moral writings of Protestantism no sufficient stimulus to piety—Superiority of the spiritual works of Catholicism—The zeal of her children a witness to the Divine origin of the Church—Desirability and necessity of rites and ceremonies—The Church accused of excess in ceremonial, and of idolatry and superstition—Falsity of such accusations . p. 50

Section III.

Justification of the Church's method in educating her priests—Use of the Breviary—The spirit of the Church exemplified in the lives of the saints as contained in the Divine office—Extreme care with which the process of canonisation is conducted—Sanctity of life demanded by the office of an Apostle—Absence of this requisite in the case of the so-called reformers—Charges brought against religious orders—Imitation of their external practices by Protestants in our own day—Refutation of the generally received opinion respecting the Jesuit system of morality—Impossibility of the Church's ever countenancing deceit—Absurdity of the statement that the confessional promotes vice—Salutary nature of the influence it exercises—Requirements for confession—The use of confession sanctioned by the formularies of the Established Church, but repudiated by it in practice—Protestants not without certain virtues—Their strict observance of Sunday, and ready response to benevolent appeals—Heroic virtue unknown to them—Loss of the spirit of Catholicism—The Catholic Church no enslaver of the intellect—Her office in restraining its licence and promoting real progress—Honest research must lead to conviction of the truth—Charges of cruelty and tyranny brought against the Church—The Inquisition—The due exercise of ecclesiastical authority not to be confounded with tyrannical oppression—Submission to the existing Government invariably inculcated by the Church—Pacific conduct of Pius IX. . . . . p. 100

Section IV.

The Church's claim to Catholicity—Meaning of this term—Catholicity exclusive of sectarianism, and therefore inapplicable to Protestants—Apostolicity of the Church—The possession of an unbroken succession from the Apostles indispensable to the infallibility of her decisions, and the maintenance of her spiritual supremacy—Testimony of the Fathers on this point—Inability of heresy to counterfeit these four notes, viz., Unity, Sanctity, Catholicity, and Apostolicity, or to deny them to the Church—Their presence is declared to be fortuitous—Disunion existing in the Anglican body—The power of deciding on controverted points disclaimed by its rulers and prelates—Denial of the fundamental truths of religion, the result of rejecting the authority of the Church—Absurdity of the Protestant position—Difference of opinion distinct from diversity of belief—The tractarian movement—Wrong done to the Church by the misrepresentations of her adversaries—Catholicism alone meets the exigencies of human nature . . . . p. 165

xi

Section V.

Catholic Christianity the completion and fulfilment of Judaism—Testimony of history to the successive victories of the Church over every fresh persecution—A similar outcome of the present struggle in Germany may be anticipated—Germany indebted for her Christianity and civilisation to the very religion she now seeks to suppress—The policy of her Government towards the Church aggressive, not defensive—Overthrow of the Papal supremacy its ultimate object—The temporal power an integral part of the constitution of the Church—The training of ecclesiastics a better preparation for ruling than the education ordinarily given to princes—Character of the late Pontiff . . *p.* 229

Section VI.

The Catholic Church only opposes the secular power when it infringes on the spiritual domain—Relative position of Church and State—Limits of ecclesiastical jurisdiction—The infallibility of the Pope renders him a supreme teacher, not an absolute monarch—Respect for the throne never long survives reverence for the altar—State of affairs in Italy—Precedent afforded by the French Revolution—Heresy never permitted to hold sway in France—Catholicism the Christianity of antiquity—Her Founder at all times the chief object of infidel hatred—Weakness of the morality of philosophers in comparison with the maxims of the Gospel—Testimony of Freethinkers to the sublimity and consistency of the Church's doctrines, and the elevating nature of her ceremonies—The principles of Atheism and Deism degrading to humanity and prejudicial to society—Powerlessness of oppression to stamp out the vitality of Catholicism—Proof afforded by the history of Ireland—The revival of the faith in England in a great measure the work of Irish and French refugees—Recent conquests of the Church, as received by Protestants—Invective and misstatement the only resource of the latter . . . . *p.* 256

Section VII.

Effect produced by the proclamation of the dogma of the Immaculate Conception—The definition of dogma an occasion for heresy to take a definite form—Heresy at all times the offspring of pride and the parent of confusion—Contrast between the multiplicity and diversity of Protestantism and the unity, dignity, and unchangeability of Catholicism—Failure of the Conference of Worms, owing to the disunion of its members—

Conduct of Cranmer—His character contrasted with that of the Venerable Bede—Meaning of the terms Saint and Father of the Church—The rejection of tradition and authority by Protestants makes a chaos of Christianity—The fixity of Catholic doctrine and the indestructible vitality of the Church due to her upholding of order—Ancient MSS. attest the identity of her teaching—The use of Latin a valuable aid to the Catholic Church—The Greek schism—The maintenance of faith intact excludes the possibility of compromise with error—The authority of the Sovereign Pontiff the corner-stone on which the edifice of Catholicism rests . . . . p. 308

Section VIII.

Immense power of journalism—It is seen to contend in vain against the Divinely established Church—The hostility of public opinion lessened by the conversion of some of the Church's most inveterate foes—Testimony of Macaulay and Chateaubriand to the indestructibility and beauty of the Catholic Church—The Church a promoter of intellectual and artistic progress, and the mainstay of social order—The means of grace indispensable to the spiritual life supplied by her alone—Relation of grace to free will—This doctrine clearly defined and expounded by the Church only—Charges of obstructiveness and intolerance continually brought against the Church—The obedience she demands from her children not inconsistent with true liberty—Acceptation of the doctrines, but repudiation of the authority of Rome by the Ritualists—Their position illogical and untenable—Their isolation from the body to which they belong—Probable withdrawal from them of State protection . . . . . . p. 344

Section IX.

The confessional and the use of the Cross invariably awaken hostility—Reason why this is so—Freedom of the Church's teaching on these, as on all other points, from novelty or contradiction—Canon Ryle upon Catholicism—Agreement of the varying sects on one point, viz., to denounce as preposterous and absurd the received belief of millions in all ages—The Catholic Church alone merits the confidence of mankind—The assertions of Protestants create prejudice against her clergy, but fail to disprove her celestial origin, or the high virtues she inculcates—Exultant speech of the Archbishop of Canterbury at the Church Congress—Witness of Luther to the truth of the Catholic religion—Test applied by Henry IV. of France . . . . p 380

Section X.

Catholicism not, like Protestantism, obnoxious to change, or subject to human caprice—Indifference or infidelity the logical outcome of Protestantism—Eulogy of the Church of God—Discordant views of Protestants respecting the Scriptures—Victory of the faith, though oppressed, persecuted, and arraigned before tribunals—The preponderance of evidence in favour of Catholic claims—The decision of upright judges would necessarily be on her side were her cause debated in a Court of law—Strong argument against itself afforded by the internal discord of Protestantism—Faith mystified, morality undermined, order overthrown, and error multiplied by the reformers—Impossibility that there can be more than one Divinely appointed way of salvation, one Divinely established Church upon earth—Infallible result of honest, prayerful research in leading inquirers to the one true fold—Peace of conscience in life, and serenity at the hour of death, found in the Catholic Church alone—Conclusion . . . . *p.* 405

ERRATA.

Page 71, lines 16 and 17, *for* Apollos *read* Apollo.
Page 188, line 24, *for* made *read* make.
Page 229, line 11, *for* if *read* it.
Page 235, line 21, *dele* the success you [expect will not always be yours.
Page 240, line 26, *for* enfeebled *read* too enfeebled.

THE FAITH.

SECTION I.

It is almost impossible to consider what is effected by man at the present time without a deep impression that if he does not equal the Antediluvian in a longevity of centuries, he could hardly have been surpassed by him in the mightiness of his works. Assisted by the mechanical powers under a manifold variety of improvements, we behold him accomplishing undertakings as vast as perilous, with rapidity and facility. In vain does Nature place the most stupendous obstacles in the way of his projects. In vain does she guard her treasures with rivers, rocks, and mountains. In vain does she arm herself with all the violence of winds and floods to arrest the victorious progress of one whose enterprise is scarcely bounded by the atmosphere which gives him life. She is forced to yield to a strength which ingenuity has multiplied into that of the giants of ancient mythology who tore up mountains by their roots, and when she is most refractory on account of the magnitude of man's designs, her obstinacy only makes his persistence the more surprising and his triumph the more distinguished. When we turn to the productions of the human mind, the wisdom which they exhibit, the knowledge which they unfold, the argument which they present, the description which they furnish, vividly image forth to us the far-advanced excellence of man in his grand characteristic of a thinking being. All concur, whether in reference to the unfoldings of science or the productions of art, to display his expanded knowledge and his inexhaustible invention, and in no country is this more felicitously and marvellously evinced, either as to science or art, than in a land in which a Bacon and a Stephenson first drew their breath. Here science and art have indeed progressed to a perfection which, if a century ago it had been predicted to the wisest of our forefathers, would have been deemed by them as including all the improbability of romance and the extravagance of fable. It is within this enterprising and influential Empire that that religion is now so steadily spreading which the Ambroses, the Austins, the Jeromes, the Gregories, and the Justins professed, and the Apostles taught—the religion which has for ages preserved her broad marks of authority intact, and which have shone brighter from the very efforts made to efface them—the religion which has sacrificed nations to the integrity of her unity, yet has ever had a wide compensation in the almost immediate acquisition of diversified and distant countries—the religion, in fine, which has her vitality and influence from the presence of truth that pervades every part of her as Omnipresence the Creation, enchants the understanding in proportion as the understanding more extensively comprehends her excellence, and inflames the heart in the same degree as the understanding is ennobled by a more intimate acquaintance with her worth. She is the religion therefore, as thus definitely set forth, which " is all fair and without spot," and, " which," says Frasynous, " fears not the most profound discussions, fearing only prejudice and passion, being well assured of triumph provided that people bring to the discussion an unbiassed mind and honesty of intent." Kingdoms term this religion Catholic, and the pious headings of the legislative acts of ancient rulers witness to the antiquity of the creed as well as its universality.

In the continuous progress of the above belief in this land, from which once it was nearly extirpated, where once it was universal, circumstances present themselves not dissimilar to those that gave prominence to the rabid and merciless days of Pagan resistance to the diffusion of Christianity. At the first confrontings of inspiration, the world was rife with philosophical schools of a manifold character. Learning and eloquence, absurdities and follies, were equally conspicuous in their conflicting and assiduous teachings. They possessed emperors and senates for their auxiliaries, and what the passions most revelled in was not without a sanction in the deeds of the divinities before which man prostrated and adored. Iniquity was in supremacy. The demon that was successful in Eden was now triumphant on every side among the descendants of the banished and the fallen. Victory was left for Omnipotence alone. The standard of the Cross was finally raised in the land that error as well as conquest had made so renowned throughout the world, and forwarded amid conquering legions and dire anathemas upon its humiliations and denials. It prevailed over every sense, passion, and interest " that combated," says Bossuet, " for idolatry which was made for pleasure, and from whose mysteries every sign of modesty was sedulously excluded." It eventually surmounted the diadem, and what was at one period most despised and contemned ennobled what was most honoured and prized. Well might the most exalted of diadems, when first dignified by the Cross, have been encircled with these inspired words, "There is nothing impossible or difficult to

God." The philosophers eventually, of almost innumerable and quaint denominations, who had so often, like the *ignis fatuus*, led their toiling yet sanguine disciples through multiform perplexities into final and inextricable difficulties by a false show of prospective comfort, began closely to federate with a faith which possesses the Providence that overthrew the confronting Dagon, and regulates the periods for the rise and fall of empires—a faith which glimmering reason, with all its unlimited exercise and unceasing helps, could never have framed nor have well understood without the blending of the illuminating ray of the apostle.

Like unto this wide diffusion of Christianity among a multitude of mutually denouncing and self-confiding teachers in the past, is, as just alluded to, the broad propagation of Catholicity at the immediate period within this Empire, amid innumerable sectarian parties differing as much in their religious tenets, which have their respective Bible vouchings of certitude to lead to the bliss of heaven, as the olden philosophers of pagan times in their contradictory teachings, that were severally pledged, on the soundest of principles, to conduct men to the *summum bonum*, or the chief good on earth. Providence, indeed, in connection with the foregoing seems exceptionally to have permitted this country, that partakes so largely of the triumphs and domination of ancient Rome, freely to aid and advance every variety of creed that the pride of the intellect or the sensuality of the heart could possibly devise, in order to manifest the impotence of heresy, as also idolatry, whilst in their golden age of liberty and patronage of learning and genius, against the eventual sway of truth. And here, as to heresy, it may not be inopportune before proceeding further to enter into some details.

Heresy—now scarcely admitted to have an existence, or at least not well understood in its full purport by the majority of sects that have had so protracted and robust a life in this empire—has her origin and continued being in a deliberate and persistent denial of some portion of revealed and confirmed truth. Whilst apostles taught, this subsequent perverter of nations commenced the formation of her party, and audaciously maintained her controversies, even in the presence of the inspired. Whether it was the unrestrained indulgence of desire or the pride of distinction that first gave rise to this pre-eminent iniquity, or the calamitous union of both which made the guilt and ruin of Eden, is a problem which must await the universal manifestation of consciences for its indisputable and final solution. This, however, may be readily said, that as they conjointly gave rise to sin in Paradise, they, under one or other of the above respects, without the forfeited abode of innocence, produced the second great woe of disobedient man. Thus, if it was not the unrestrained impulse of desire that stimulated some among the children of Adam first to innovate, it was the coveting of a chief and independent position that made them refractory outcasts of a religion which was instituted to repair the evils that sprung from the pride and concupiscence of the unfaithful progenitors of the human race. Heresy, this adroit adept in perversion, to attain her end, commonly makes her advances in the fervid utterance of the language of Scripture, like Satan in giving his assurances to Eve from among the flowers of Paradise, hoping thereby to add to her influence. Sometimes she seeks to sway the many by a display of sanctity and austerity, combined with a cautious reserve upon doctrinal changes; at other times she strives for the suffrages of the many by a liberal concession of doctrinal freedom, and by a broad countenancing of opposition to every control of spiritual authority, especially that which is exercised and enforced by Catholicity. "Against this authority," says a celebrated writer, "she is ever in conspiracy, and this vicious and dogged insubordination has affected thrones as well as altars, for heresy, in adding to her party, has always increased the number of rebels "—ever affecting the zeal of a Mathathias as to all that is truly evangelical, nevertheless, seldom failing to be in contradiction with herself in what has been advanced as such by her own absolute and hardy constructions, which she is constantly revising, and this revising is generally founded on a yet greater departure from ancient fathers and ancient councils, so that down to this present period she strictly responds to the concise description given of her in primitive ages by Tertullian—" that she never ceases to innovate, her progress being like unto her origin." Thus, whilst Catholicity, which is identified with orthodoxy, and is manifested to be so by displaying within herself the unchangeable attributes of truth, conserves her simple and unique character, heresy, the fell production of a fallen humanity, and grotesque in form, is never permanent in her creeds, ever varying, ever reforming. Every attempted doctrinal decision augments her confusion, and each crafty defence adds to bewilderment, so that the very labours of heresy, in preparing her professions of faith, make her inconsistencies more obvious, multiply dissent, and deepen confusion on every side. Heresy may proclaim sundry Christian doctrines, yet she is to be classed with Paganism, that had as many deities as passions; and as with heresy and her teachers, as many judgments upon fundamentals as differing schools. "He that will not hear the Church, let him be unto thee as a heathen or a publican" (Matt. xviii. 17). It is not unfrequently, as the present period testifies, that heresy, in progressing in extravagance, glides finally into infidelity, a more unrelenting and enduring foe to Catholicity than herself, in not admitting a belief in anything divine. But in the further development of the above important matter, what a startling contrast does not Catholicity present herself to Protestantism (an indefinite term which best favours heresy in all her incongruities, generalities, and delusions), by so complete and continued an accordance in all her teachings! Definition with her is elucidation, not confusion; it silences contention, and does not admit of a dissenting murmur among her members.

However, heresy, with all her inconsistencies and averments that go to make of Christianity a chaos, has never been wanting in powerful auxiliaries to promote her vague and despotic pretensions. But it was in vain that the most celebrated of her defenders, at an early as well as a later period, declaimed, argued, and battled for her edicts. Her cabals, with their worldly astuteness, their religious parade, and supported by an imperial abetting, could never effectively prevail against those sacred œcumenical councils which were determined in their decisions "by what was taught in all places and in all times." Widely successful at intervals indeed in kingdoms heresy has been, it must be conceded, and in the very first ages of faith, in disseminating her pernicious and subtle novelties. Catholicity seemed at periods, in a few of her once earnest and orthodox lands, to be on the very verge of extinction. In them a lamentable counterpart to the almost universal worship of Baal in Judea presented itself, as to an expanded domination of error, and so strikingly to be seen in the broad calamitous spread of Arianism. This apparent imminent peril of Catholicity, was, however, but that of her Divine Founder, who has shown forth her future trials in himself, when hurried on to the edge of the precipice. A God-man, in his all-wise designs, permitted on this memorable occasion his fanatical and infuriated assailants, who were not to be convinced of the holiness of his mission by wisdom or miracle, to exercise a wild dominion over His sacred Person, and savagely to hurry Him on to a contemplated and frightful death. The exultation of the motley crowd that with execrations surrounded truth and sanctity itself, increased as their dire purpose appeared to be nearer to its consummation, but no sooner did the Divine feet, that stood firmly on the pinnacle of the stately Temple, reach the made for and steep boundary than they turned and wended their way through the dense and frantic throng, as when they advanced after the resurrection through every intervening obstacle into the midst of the persecuted and drooping Apostles. Again we read that the Redeemer had listening multitudes around Him, fascinating them by His exposition of the inspired pages, and eliciting from the very emissaries of the prejudiced and malignant the enthusiastic praise of " Never did man speak like this man." Thus deadly error by her artful plans may seem for a brief moment to have brought truth under subjection, but the might of the Lord remains with her as with Samson, though in bonds, and often with the exulting shouts of her enemies commences her freedom and her triumph. "A thousand sects, and a thousand heresies," says a profound orator, already quoted, "have gone out from the bosom of the Catholic Church, and have elevated themselves against her, but if she has seen them so elevate themselves according to the prediction of Jesus Christ, she has also seen them fall according to His promises, though having for their auxiliaries emperors and kings." [1]

But under this consideration in first referring to Arianism, just spoken of, the most subtle, insidious, and calamitous of impious devisings recorded in early Christian history, what a combination of deep plot-

---

[1] Bossuet.

tings and formidable alliances does not this heresy unfold, so well adapted to bring about a vast spiritual ruin! It had a man for its wily contriving, who possessed the lineaments of piety, but without the sentiments; the gait of humility, but without the submission; the eloquence of the fathers, but without the unction; over whom a too confiding charity had spread her anointed hands, that a discriminating zeal had refused to countenance in his sanctimonious pretensions. This man of execrable memory, who made the most strenuous efforts to attain to high episcopal rule, dared, within the holy edifice that was upraised to advance the glory of the Divine Founder of Christianity to deny His con-substantiality with God the Father. At first the astounding declaration, which anathematised the fervent adorations of every foregoing saint and martyr, horrified the believing world. But she who is the watchful, the exact and uncompromising guardian of those dogmas that are confided to her keeping, who neither changes them, adds to them, nor takes from them, with her characteristic promptitude solemnly sent forth her condemnation through her convened prelates congregated in a General Council, an assembly which some professing Protestantism have not as yet been so monstrously alienated from the feelings and discipline of a Catholic ancestry as totally to disrespect and to little heed. Arianism and its author heard with the sullen determination of thwarted blasphemy their formal condemnation, in the detailed reasons for which was clearly evinced the constant and unvarying belief of the Catholic Church in the Divinity of the Sacred Reformer and Redeemer of mankind, which is as fixed and immovable as that eternal heaven from whence the Second Person of the most Blessed Trinity descended to take upon Himself the nature of man. In vain did Arianism with its chieftain strive, as many subsequent heresiarchs and their abettors have striven, by the most ambiguous professions of credence in what had been authoritatively put forth, to retain their position with the children of Catholicity, that they might thereby more effectually succeed in spreading their subverting fictions in lieu of an Apostolic faith. But "the Catholic Church," to adopt in substance the language of a sensible writer upon the foregoing immediate matter, "by her precise and accurate formularies of belief, to which the most solemn and unequivocal assent was exacted before any recognition in her holy Communion was allowed of, frustrated every tortuous artifice which a designing and tergiversating heresy could employ. By this plan," continues the same writer, "which has been in salutary use from the foundation of Christianity to the existing time, the Church has preserved the integrity of her tenets and the purity of her morality. Arianism and Nestorianism, the two Goliath heresies of the primitive Church, finally fell before it, which without it might have become the renegade religions of the empires of the earth."

Yet Arianism, partaking of the audacity of the spirit that warred against Omnipotence, and conspired against Infinite Wisdom, boldly but stealthily persisted in her impious purposes. She affected to pay a due deference to the august decisions of the Council, the introduction into its creed of the term consubstantial now alone appearing seriously to disturb her sensitive conscience. In the pages of the inspired writings the term "consubstantial," it was with ostentatious instance urged, was not to be met with, as if its comprehensive and lucid exposition of the aggregate meaning of each scriptural passage expressive of the Divinity of Jesus Christ, could not secure for it the force of actual existence in the inspired word; as if the alleged temerity in employing a term though not met with in the sacred writings, yet rigorously and conclusively embodying the substance of the testimonies therein penned in support of the Divinity of Jesus Christ, was greater than the denial that the Scriptures did comprise positive evidence of the perfect equality of Jesus Christ with God the Father in all things. O conscientious Arianism, and most calamitous of heresies! The assumption of a term that is so pre-eminently suitable to indicate the absolute faith of Catholicity is affectedly recoiled from as not having the Scriptures to warrant its acceptation, and yet, with more than the narrated daring of him who pilfered fire from heaven, the most sophistical advances are made to deprive the inspired volume of one of the most sublime, the most consoling, and the most obvious of its dogmas—a dogma which was haloed by the encircling flames of a Polycarp's pyre, and constituted the majesty of those before whom the ferocity of the forest submissively crouched, which has made man resolute in the face of the most appalling dangers, and serene in the midst of the most excruciating torments, which yields to prayer its chief confidence and to charity its most animating glow. These are some of the principal witnessings to Christianity's foremost and fundamental truth that have furnished to the most gifted among sceptics a theme for the most transporting sentiments, as also to the contemplative Christian a subject for the most enrapturing thoughts.

Whilst persistent and subtle Arianism was insidiously scheming and interweaving sophism with sophism to cheat if possible Christianity into her salutary orthodoxies, the first Christian Emperor expired, and heresy soon after had its first wide imperial patronage in the person of Constantius, on the death of his brothers. Yet if a Constantius was on the throne of the Cæsars, an Athanasius was still in the chair of the patriarchs, and the throne of falsehood was not able to triumph over the chair of truth. Vain were the efforts of a heretical Emperor, as well as those subsequently of an idolatrous Cæsar, to bring about the destruction of that belief to which St. Peter had given such explicit utterance, and for the fervent profession of which the contrite thief had a Divine assurance that on dying he would pass from the writhings of the cross to the ecstasies of Paradise. Some, indeed, there were of the most pronounced influence, on account of their sacred position, general knowledge, and rigid practices, that inclined their ears to the Achitophels of Arianism, and who by their ultimate co-operation rendered the counsels of iniquity so formidable. Futile, indeed, also for an extended period were the efforts and censures of orthodoxy, which appeared proportionably to augment the wilfulness and audacity of the heterodox. Arianism, it was solemnly pledged, should prevail. To effect this the effrontery of assertion was substituted for the testimonies of centuries, the lax concessions of intrigue for the strict enforcements of discipline, and the worst imputations of calumny for the influential statements of truth. The determined and unscrupulous endeavours of a widely countenanced and deadly heresy seemed to have baffled the most authoritative of spiritual positions. Athanasius was compelled for a period to withdraw from a revolting scene of violence and crime, of usurpations and desecrations. The satellites of an Arian ruler pursued him, but the Providence of Elias was with the Catholic patriarch, and furnished him in his retreats, that gave shelter to the reptile and the outcast, with more than the safety of castle walls. Whilst Athanasius was in exile, and orthodoxy was persecuted, Arianism had an ample opportunity for the exercise of its potent and impious sway. Yet the absolute dependence of Arianism upon imperial succour for that position necessarily tended to identify it with the throne, and the amount of royal aid responded to the promptitude of courtly obsequiousness. Thus, as in after ages when regal power is called upon to supplement for the deficiencies in the spiritual administrations of the heretical, a servile pandering to princely wills is looked for, and that cannot long be extended ere the supremacy becomes complete for the monopolising crown over the desecrated mitre. Heresy, apart from secular domination, can never, generally speaking, include a decisive authority within herself, and therefore can hardly make a near approach to any effective administration in her usurped hierarchy. It is certain that she has often affected to do so, and her continued efforts in that direction have been little scared by scruples when opportunity appeared to favour her object. Nevertheless it is useless. The decisions of heresy will never be independent of or succeed against national ordinances being merely human. She has rebelled against a spiritual authority that has God for its appointing, and she will ever eventually be in total subjection to the secular ruling of man. At the present period this has been very prominently shown in most Protestant domains, as to final decisions on Christian matters. On reading this, some, both of the high and inferior of the Protestant clergy, in an experienced conviction of its certitude, may feel a slight suffusion of shame at their degrading and dependent position; nevertheless, it has not led to any of the heroism that now so distinguishes numbers of the German Catholic hierarchy, who prefer a prison to a palace, and poverty to opulence, rather than surrender to imperial rule what exclusively belongs to, and has been exercised for centuries by, the spiritual head of the city and the world.

In taking up again with Arianism it may be said that abilities equal to the Justins and the Irenæuses were not wanting to forward its subtle advances. But there was wanting the clear and obvious suffrages of these Fathers in support of what menaced the very vitality of Christianity itself, and sapped the foundation on which the inspired promises in Scripture rested. From a few and obscure passages in the writings of orthodox and venerated men, Arianism, as busy in intrigue as artful in imparting to falsehood the features of truth, laboured to deduce some favouring for its sedulously propagated and impious tenets, but the precise and lucid expositions of that Œcumenical Council, which had its precedent and the regulations of its form in that convened at Jerusalem by St. Peter, yet remained in vigorous and efficient authority, and manifested, notwithstanding every subtle exposition, the deadly nature of Arianism, whilst subsequent additional impious broachings made this still more obvious. Thus, in the words of St. Vincent of Lerins, "Through these expositions and enlightenments, that which before was simply believed was professed with more exactitude, and that which before was preached without much deliberation was taught with much care." In all this within the Catholic Church there is presented a twofold good, by her making what is false as evident as her own marks of truth, and also in placing the language of unalterable definition as to each controverted point in the mouths of her submissive and united children. Athanasius, whilst abiding, like the worthy of Israel, in den or cavern, as safety might make it expedient, was unceasing in his anathemas upon Arianism. "He was a man," says a historian, cited in Feller, "that was individually contending against the most terrible of heresies, which was armed with all the subtleties of logic as well as the might of emperors, being appointed to such a combat by God, and made equal to such a destination by the gifts both of nature and grace." In him it might be unhesitatingly averred that the characteristic perfections of other saints resided in the same ennobling degree, and which gave him more influence than the broad and glittering badges that princes might bear or confer.

How insignificant do the Eusebiuses of Nicomedia or Cæsarea appear, though so largely possessing natural endowments, literary qualifications, and spiritual power, when contrasted with the outraged and outlawed Athanasius! If complete Arianism was not proved against Eusebius of Cæsarea, he certainly accommodated his mitre to the advantage of an Arian Court by his paternal concessions and his bland intimations that all might be orthodoxly explained. He could composedly dine at a palace when Athanasius awaited his daily bread from the hand of charity within the damp chill of the fetid tomb. Yet though the Arians were in confederate and virulent opposition to Catholicity, this did not prevent them from denouncing each other in their factious wrangles upon what was ultimately to be professed as thoroughly orthodox. Many, with the author of the heresy, affirmed that Jesus Christ, the Son of God, was unlike to the Father in nature and substance; others maintained that He was like unto the Father in substance, yet was not of the same nature with God. As might indeed be readily inferred, it would have been a labour as severe and as interminable as that of the Danaides to prepare such a formula of belief (considering the endless revisions that were made upon the two foregoing principal divisions in Arianism) as would obtain a unanimous assent, or even mitigate the asperity of party invective. Hence the infelicitous toils of Arianism to secure one common subscription to a detailed belief. The clamorous dissent with which each formulary was received upon its publication must have convinced the discerning on either side in opposition to Catholicity of its utter hopelessness, though once perhaps so buoyant, as to eventual agreement, among even the most tractable of the Arian perfectionists. Even when the term " consubstantial," so vehemently objected to by the Arians, was omitted in the formulary drawn up at Rimini, it did not thereby affect its orthodox reading, but only left things more open to dispute and quibble; this did not, therefore, in its omission realise assent and attain peace. It made it, however, evident to the Fathers of the Council who conceded this omission in a conciliatory, if not in a prudent spirit, as also to Christendom at large, that the most sure and lamentable consequences would result from relinquishing terms for the sake of unity and concord that were best fitted to yield conclusiveness upon doctrine without interfering with perspicuity.

Constantius, the defender of a Christianity under the denomination of Arianism, seemed to be more on the alert in accelerating its spread than in securing the safety of the boundaries of his empire. At last he somewhat suddenly died, like the deviser of his belief, after a violent and persecuting career. He passed away without effecting that universal submission to his heretical edicts which his absolute rule and his wily plans, conjoined with the aid of his obsequious prelates, might have induced him to expect. He was as unsuccessful in destroying the foundations of a spiritual edifice as his apostate successor was in laying the foundations of a material temple to falsify the declarations of the Son of God. The perverse and determined endeavours of both Emperors, the one in abetting heresy, and the other idolatry, furnished a lucid testimony of the Divinity of Jesus Christ by their contributing so minutely to the fulfilment of the predictions of the sacred page. "He built His Church upon a rock," says the eloquent and intrepid

St. Chrysostom, "and no effort has been able to overturn it." He overturned the Temple, and no endeavour has been able to rebuild it. "No one can beat down that which God has raised up, and no one can re-raise that which God has cast down." Yet whilst, with regard to Arianism, additional incongruities were continually presenting themselves in her interminable revisions upon symbols of faith, Catholicity, on the other hand, exhibited the reverse in her undeviating features, which did not fail to increase her influence and attractiveness by their majesty and beauty. Her voice, too, in her warnings for the rescuing of those without pilotage from continuous wreck, was ever at intervals to be heard amid the boisterous contentions of a dividing Arianism, which were gradually lessened in their force as contentions multiplied and effected a wider disjunction, till at last they sounded like the feeble mutterings of the departing storm, that appears as it recedes to leave those heavens of order and of light in the possession of an increased clearness and grandeur, whose loveliness and sublimity it had momentarily shrouded and obscured.

In this sequel of Arianism may be readily discerned the concluding counterpart of the most disastrous and determined heresies of the early Church. The Macedonian heresy, which denied the Divinity of the Holy Ghost; the Nestorian, which asserted that there were two persons in Jesus Christ, and that the Son of God was not hypostatically united, but only accidentally, to the Son of Man, in such a manner that He was only the Son of God by adoption, thereby destroying the mystery of the Incarnation; the Eutychian, which confounded the two natures of Jesus Christ, and admitted only one, in affirming that after the hypostatical union the human nature was completely absorbed by the Divine, and became one with it; the Donatist, which declared that God the Son was less than God the Father, and greater than the Holy Ghost, that the Church of Christ had failed, and existed only with them; the Pelagian, which taught that grace was not necessary for the merit of good works, and that original sin did not pass from Adam to his descendants; these most conspicuous offsprings of a rebellion—the contriving of Satan—agitated, they intrigued, they ridiculed, they caballed, they subtilised, they falsified, they anathematised, and they persecuted. They counted thousands among their adherents, made formidable by wealth, titles, learning, and abilities; they possessed themselves of the temples where the voice of unvarying orthodoxy had been reverentially listened to for centuries; they sat even at the foot of thrones, and directed their decrees; and though throughout an extended period (adopting the language of the Puseyite theologians) "they gathered as they went on teaching, with the stammering lips of ambiguous formularies, and inconsistent precedents, and principles but partially developed," they could not succeed against a Church that never hesitates to condemn error in whatever dignity, array, or circumstance of renown she may manifest herself. Within her sanctuary the zeal that once she commended, either for the resolute defence of dogma or the edifying practice of virtue, has invariably forfeited her blessing when that was broached which affected either the testimony of her traditions or the decisions of her Councils. Patriarchal dignity could not prevail with her when in opposition to Apostolical authority upon articles of creed, and whatever glittering or august distinctions have given influence to the suffrages of heretics in support of error, she has nevertheless fearlessly condemned them, as she would even an angel with the radiance of heaven around him if his announcings were not in conformity with what she pronounced as dogma. Macedonius, in a lengthened strife against the Church, signally failed in his impious object, though favoured by power and ability. His endeavours were as unsuccessful as those of the assailing ocean that breaks away from the immovable rock in foaming but useless efforts. Nestorius, who possessed those proprieties of demeanour that engage respect for superiors, whose exalted position was aided by an eloquence that gained the acclamations of cities, after repeatedly denouncing with vehemence the fearful infidelities of others, at the same time studiously parading forth an enthusiastic reverence for the dogmatic expositions of a St. Chrysostom, finally advanced that which was not to be found among the items of a Chrysostom's Creed, nor if it had therein been found would the sanctity of a Chrysostom have hallowed it in the eyes of the Church to which he was so heroically devoted. The tenderness of a mother, which the Church has ever shown towards those even who most broadly swerved from her tenets, were useless in Nestorius's regard. All was in vain. The pride of dignity is often as great an obstacle to the retraction of heterodoxy as the dread of penury. Eutychius came forth to combat the obstinate heresiarch from severe solitudes, where he had forwarded many by counsel and example in the ways of a distinguished piety; however, he soon proved how difficult it is for one, though the assiduous and effective director of others into prompt obedience, submissively to yield where self errs whilst engrossing public attention and applause.

In the midst of specious explanations and unsparing

censures, she to whose ears the voice of truth is so well attuned heard words, however plausibly and confidently put forth, that were not in harmony with orthodoxy, and the austere monk as well as the influential patriarch were alike condemned. An unimpeachable morality could no more exempt from censure than a spiritual position which was next in dignity to that of the successor of St. Peter, when an exact precision in doctrines was not preserved. Though the above were in fierce antagonism among themselves, they were by a respective false teaching equally condemned in their conjoined opposition to the authority of the Catholic Church, and both Eutychius and Nestorius must have arrived at the same conclusion, from the ultimate issue of every endeavour that was made against what possessed the promise, that the rock on which Catholicity was founded was composed of a more sturdy material than the gates of hell. Donatus, in his episcopal rule, with powerful auxiliaries, could not either realise success in his unnatural war against a Divinely protected house, and Absolom's discomfiture was finally the lot of this ferocious and unscrupulous man. Pelagius, from whom, at the closing period of Donatism, the heresy crawled into light which was so especially under the guardianship of sophistry, obtained some attention for his novelties, among many by the known friendly intercourse that subsisted between him and several of the most illustrious Fathers of the then period. But no sooner were these latter apprised of the wide rent which Pelagius's innovations tended to make in the unity of the Catholic Church, than they instantly severed the bonds of friendship, and denounced the most pretentions of men to ascetic practices as an enemy to the declarations of tradition and the definitions of Councils. Others with a somewhat different aspect met with a similar fate. Subtlety may deceive man, but not God, who watches over the orthodoxy of His Church. Whatever may be the character of heresy, whether referring to morals or dogmas, she who ever survives when all appears to concur to certain ruin, is sure, as a succession of centuries testifies, sooner or later to visit it with anathema, and to triumph. Jovinian denied the existence of merit in fasting and works of penance, and, undismayed by the emphatic declaration of an Apostle " who had learnt among angels what he had to teach among men," openly affirmed that the married state was a more perfect state than that of virginity. If there was any studied ambiguity in some of his indulgent averments, that he might more effectively grapple with adverse testimonies and the practices of antiquity, his soft life furnished a sure commentary upon his designing purposes, which made their voluptuous tendings but too obvious, and which were so well calculated to stimulate the tepid in virtue into the active commission of vice. Vigilantius, or rather Dormitantius, exclaims St. Jerome, made his avowals in the same benign form, *par nobile fratrum.* They both, like unto a great innovator, "spoke to the passions, and the passions replied." On morals, as also upon doctrines, they made their wide and iniquitous expositions, which comprised a warrant for every caprice of desire, as well as for every vagary of the intellect, but their chief hope of proselytising was through those allurements that were as the apples in Eden, " fair to the eye, and delightful to behold." As to the seduction of many by a series of concessions that were broad enough for the most sensual epicurean to revel in, the fabled and deadly success of the sirens was theirs in reality. Thousands ardently caroused in the midst of every description of indulgence, with a bloated or feverish satiety alone for a check, yet vainly did Jovinian and Vigilantius devise to lessen the worth of those sterling teachings which constituted the orthodoxy and the perfections of Catholicity. Their utter failure proved that the preservation of the purity of Catholic morals, together with Catholic doctrines, was the sure result of the same sleepless vigilance, and of the same invincible might, which made known the impious intentions of Herod and shattered the confronting idol of the Philistines.

Their formal excommunication indicated the uniform practice of the Church in promptly excluding those from officiating before her holy ark who would as they might list have their unholy gratifications as well as their unorthodox creeds.

From the periods of Nicolas and Ebion, who preached up filthy pleasures as so many preparatory exercises to the raptures of Paradise, to those of Jovinian and Vigilantius—from the periods of Hymenius and Philetus, who strove to be courteous in doctrine, with Christian, Jew, and Gentile, to those of Arius and Pelagius, the Church has ever obtained the guaranteed victories for her faith. As to divisions within, and assaults from without, she has always retained the mastery. But within the above broad spans of strife against each prominent article of Catholic teaching, what a multitude of fantastic forms as to morals and tenets have gambolled before the eyes of the marvelling for a season, and then vanished from the sight, like the arch-quoter of Scripture from the presence of Sanctity and Truth on the mountain's summit! The Catholic Church has not diminished in her tenets, nor lessened in her rites; she still constitutes the chief and unabated interest of history, and though singled out by confederated nations for attack has ever proved herself to be invincible, not less in modern than in ancient times. And what a goodly array of primitive dogma men has she not had in these immediate days of her being to battle with, who have subtly striven through Holy Writ to league every conceit of a heated head, and every desire of a sensual heart, with the emanations of Infinite Wisdom and Infinite Holiness! These are, as enumerated by Hornius, the Lutherans, the Zuinglians, the Carlostadians, the Schivenckfeldians, the Storkonians, the Munsterians, and then the Rotomanites, the Knipperdollingites, the Matthewites, and the Johnites—the Anabaptists, with their divisions of the Mennoites, the Hutterians, the Gabrielites, the Moravians, the Delphites, the Henryites, and the Postilites—the Socinians and the Calvinists, with their divisions of Armenians, the Puritans, and the Brownists, the Separatists, and the semi-Separatists. Hornius terminates this motley catalogue with those who presumptively superseded the foregoing in evangelical perspicacity, the Robinsonians, the Independents, the Waiters and the Seekers. What a melancholy list of wanderings of the human intellect, and what an anomaly in the writer's life that he should have deplored this extreme diversity in Protestantism, and yet not have sided with a Catholic Church, with whose uninterrupted and distinguishing unity no section of sectarianism has ventured to compete! In proportion as these assured sects that Hornius has instanced became more startling in their doctrines, and more licentious in their morals, they pretended to be more familiar with the whisperings of archangels, and more favoured with the graces of the inspired. Thus it is with visionary innovators; the more extravagant they are in their Christian insistences, the nearer they are to Paul and the third heaven. "Since the period," observes another Protestant writer, "when Hornius drew up his genealogy of the errors of the Reformation, it is well known how much the frightful generation has increased. Error since that epoch has been daily begetting error, and fancy and fanaticism producing folly and superstition. Each parent sect has with portentous fecundity generated an offspring too numerous in some instances for industry to reckon, an offspring soon like its parent heresy producing another offspring innumerable as itself, and equally persuaded of its own exceptionable claim to orthodoxy in the righteous exercise of Scriptural interpretation, and thus as it was in ancient times so it is now, that heresy is constant in nothing but its inconstancy"—"each being persuaded," writes Tertullian, "that he is as much empowered to change and remodel that, according to his own judgment, as the author of the sect from whom he received it had to frame it." "And so it will be to the end of the world," declares the learned Bossuet, in his "Variations of Protestantism," "with those who have neither rule nor principle in the constitution of their reformation, and for the same reason as the whole body comprises nothing certain, the doctrines of private persons cannot but be uncertain and contradictory."

This want of rule and principle, by which confusion is reduplicated on confusion, this baneful assumption of a right to private judgment, by which each individual deems himself authorised to adore his own inventions, to consecrate his own errors, and to appeal to God for every thought, has continually aggravated the difficulties, and daily adds to the base admixture, within Protestantism, whilst at the same time it will be found proportionally to manifest in the contrast the purity of the Catholic faith, as it thus affects with still greater alloy that of the Protestant. However, as already alluded to, it is in the inspired volume that each enthusiast, certain of heaven, whether ancient Circumcellion or Messalian, whether modern Jumper or Whirler, has found an incontestable warrant for as many impious averments as throng the pages of the dreamy Koran, or those of the Bible of the licentious Mormonite. Every rambling and preposterous affirmation has had an alleged consecration in some text of Scripture, and the censures that have been pronounced upon a host of flagrant interpretations by the Catholic Church have been perversely construed into formal interdicts against the perusal of

D

the inspired word itself. This has been at periods solemnly insisted upon, on platforms and commons, in tabernacles and churches, that an unswerving and rancorous hatred against Catholicity might be ceaseless. But the Catholic Church has no prohibitions against that which she refers to throughout the year, under suitable and judicious selections, to confirm in faith the Christian, to awe the vicious into duty, and to animate the virtuous to perseverance, in her several places of worship. If the sacred volume, which is readily to be met with on the shelves and to be seen in the shop windows of Catholic booksellers, is not always to be found within Catholic homes, it arises either from a want of education, of means, or of zeal. The interdicts of the Catholic Church have been only directed against those versions of the inspired word that were filled with extravagant distortions, and her censures have been alone visited upon those individuals who, by false constructions upon Scriptural texts, have erected themselves into apostles of error. Well on this does the amiable and judicious Fénélon remark, " that it is necessary that Christians should receive instructions on the Holy Scriptures before they be permitted to peruse them, that they should be so progressively prepared as to be thoroughly habituated to their proper meaning when they did read them, and thus they would be filled with their spirit before they beheld the letter." Had such been the prudential practice on every side from the early propagation of Christianity, "there would not have been so many self-constituted doctors and self-constituted judges, nor so many impieties pertinaciously persevered in under the boasted warranty of the word of God. Christians then would have sought no other sense in the sacred writings than what the Church had attached to them from whose hands they had received them."

However, this reasoning will little prevail with many at the dawn of whose intellect Catholicism has been brought into view under the lineaments of an ogre, and who have grown up with a religious horror of the monster whose eyes in their convictions are constantly glaring around for a straggling prey. *Horribile super aspectu mortalibus instans.* Such early-prejudiced Christians, who are largely comprised in every sect, deem it to be a species of spiritual treason to devote even a momentary investigation as to the absolute nature of Catholicism, and hold as tenaciously to misrepresented Catholic teachings as to their judgments on the inspired word. The more frequently they run through the Divine page the more numerously do they discover reasons to heighten their epithets upon the faith of ages and of their forefathers, from which the selection but of a few is alone necessary in order to read in their aggregate, abomination. This sure result of their penetrating Evangelism, when preaching up in towns and cities their Christian safeties against Popery, stimulates them as occasion may favour to call upon Romanists, with the vehemence and the rapidity of the capering prophets in the days of Elias, to come out from the midst of corruption, and to abide in their Sion of Christian surety and of primitive worship. But as this is the common apostolical summons of all extreme sects, who are as plenteous as blackberries in their genial season of Gospel labour and love, it might be solicitously asked, into what hallowed tabernacle of Sion, in the supposition of some individual farewells to idolatry and mummery, are they solemnly called upon reverentially and thankfully to enter? Whatever absurdities names may indicate, yet the Jumpers, the Shakers, and the Seekers severally deem themselves to be the faithful Abdiels, who, in the midst of prevarications and apostasies, have not bent the knee to what is in opposition to ineffable holiness and an all-saving belief. To hasten and sanctify themselves in one of their pre-eminent yet most simple of Christianities would be the strenuous Evangelical counsel to supposed seceders from Catholicism of each of these sects, the extremes of sectarian aberrations to which those gradually tend who reply with the assurance of inspiration to every doctrinal difficulty that may be propounded, and to every conscientious scruple that may be started through the deified oracle of self. With feelings that have been inherited rather than resulting from recent Gospel expoundings, with shame and indignation in their countenances for the ultimate farcical issues of private judgment and the daring of its preposterous pretensions, the patriarchal sects in the chequered family of Protestantism would, it may be presumed, endeavour to prevent any accession to the ranks of those who, though loudly protesting against Romanism, in the reverse of Herod's expectations with regard to infinite wisdom, clothe religion with the garb of folly, and yet look for its veneration among the multitude. Each, whether Lutheran, Calvinist, or Socinian, would be found in so doing to give pre-eminence to his own Church, that would be affirmed, as of the synagogue of the Jews, in the words of the Redeemer, "to be the sacred abode whence salvation was to come." In this zealous competition for the fellowship of those that have, as is imagined, been induced by some discovery of startling heterodoxy, or more probably by some lively impulse of passion, to step over a boundary as distinct as once was that of Eden from the untilled land which was shaded by no tree of life, the Jumpers, the Shakers, and the Seekers would fiercely resent the contemptuous and dogmatical judgment of men who, whilst they lustily preached up the in-

violability of Gospel liberty, put forth their own
peculiar opinions with as much despotism as they
assigned in such a vasty amount to the triple-
crowned tiara itself. They would at once confidently appeal to the Holy Volume for the sacredness of their tenets and practices, a recourse to
which the most outrageous among the heterodox
ever fly, affirms Tertullian, "as authority for what
they do and for what they teach." Now, with the
conceded right of private interpretation, one of the
distinctive and radical tenets of Protestantism, which
its founder so freely and stoutly exercised in flatly
contradicting an Apostle, and doubtless to prove his
own consistency, did not question the legitimacy of
the great fallen himself as to the exercise of such a
privilege, though no robe of light gave majesty to
his considerate presence, at the Patmos of the heresiarch, the Lutherans, the Calvinists, and the Socinians would find it a something of embarrassment
to deprive the Jumper, the Shaker, or the Seeker
of as good a pretension to orthodoxy through a source
which they apostically claimed for themselves in their
respective arbitrary teachings. In the conviction of
the latter their several Scriptural interpretations under
the asserted aid of Heaven would be set down as the
true sense of the inspired word, and they would be as
much astonished that this should not be as evident

to their opponents as Lutheran, Calvinist, and Socinian would be astounded at the infatuation of those who could believe themselves possessed of the suffrage of a greater wisdom than Solomon's, for such wild conceits and frenetic antics. In this polemical contest with the Jumpers, the Seekers, and the Shakers, what alternative is there for the Lutheran, the Calvinist, or the Socinian but to assume the authoritative tones of Catholicity in the maintaining an absolute and exclusive superiority for their respective Christian beliefs in the assured attainment of the great affair of salvation, by making a consecutive reference to an antiquity that commences with the Apostles, and thus securing a determining influence for the several articles of their creed? For as the idea of Christianity essentially includes something fixed as to doctrines, so the distinguishing tenets which are also implied in the idea of a sect must obviously be put forward by the framer and abettors of this sect as the belief of primitive Christianity. The denial of this would leave them without a fundamental reason for their differing from all other forms of creed, except through the alleged Evangelical privilege of private interpretation.

In necessarily conceding the force of what is just advanced, it also must be necessarily admitted that either the Apostles taught "that man was justified by faith alone, independently of good works," that God predestined some to be damned and others to be saved, and that the Redeemer was not God as well as man, or the reverse. If the Apostles taught any of the doctrines above set forth, whether as respectively upheld by the several founders of Lutheranism, Calvinism, and Socinianism, their vital character as Christian tenets must have made their necessary perpetuity conspicuously prominent, and have ensured their enforcement and their exposition in the churches and theological schools of ancient empires. But vain would the attempt be of the sanguine adherents of Luther, Calvin, or Socinius, in opposition to the pretentious orthodox claims of their confident yet most presumptuous adversaries, obviously to demonstrate the Apostolic worth of the several foregoing distinct teachings through a continuous proof of their identification with the recognised articles of a first Christian belief. It has, indeed, been the anxious endeavour of the most learned, subtle, and systematic of the champions of the Reformation to do so, and thus through such an enhancing medium to impart indisputable orthodoxy to their respective characteristic doctrines, but like the fond and delusive pursuit of the alchemist after the philosopher's stone, that was to give sterling value to the most worthless of metals, it has ever ended in distressing failures and humiliating exposures. Emphatically, indeed, as diverse primitive sects may have denied, through the fear of tongues as brawling as that of Esau, and perhaps of hands as ready to strike, that they ever arrogated to themselves an isolated position in an exclusive orthodoxy, and urbanely courteous as they may have been towards every loose form of Christian profession, yet when constrained, again to be insisted on in substance, by contention as to positive preferences in dogma, to demonstrate a superior illumination over every other affirmed heavenly mission, their negatives upon the vaunted pre-eminent doctrinal claims of their spiritual antagonists, conjoined with the assertions that are made in Apostolical justification of their own peculiar tenets, must, as is readily to be inferred from what has preceded, fashion forth in their regard some description of a distinct Church.

To give it then the visibility of the house on the top of the mountain, even at the period when "the smoke of sacrifice rose from the Pantheon, and when tigers bounded in the Amphitheatre," is also as certainly incumbent on them in this deemed polemical contest as it would be imperative upon those who should professedly uphold their creed to be of a perfect and exclusive nature. This the profound learning of a Le Clerc, disquieted by the consequent necessity of such a manifesting of Apostolic orthodoxy in a contest upon special dogmatical superiority, could not obtain for any influential section of Protestantism; nor could all the astute devisings of a Claude, aided by the indomitable industry of a Jurieu, realise a success under so vital a consideration. No wonder that unto this present time the same result under similar circumstances has attended the efforts of those who have affirmed reason for their sole arbitrator in the rejection or acceptance of mysteries or dogmas, which makes Christianity a mere matter of opinion—opinion that has formed so many systems and engendered so many heresies, that has filled history with delusions, and has proved as fatal to doctrine as morals, and which has induced so many now, as hitherto, among the fervid enthusiasts of the thousand and one Christian sects in eighteen hundred and eighty, solemnly, with upturned eyes to Heaven, to pronounce that to be black which others, in the name of common sense, pronounce to be white. In the midst of all these opposite and vociferously asserted orthodoxies, there cannot be much " rest in the Lord " to the thoughtful, nor much hope to the solicitous to meet with it, in the most brief degree, among endless divisions. No, it is for that Church alone to yield to the reflecting and anxious a solid peace that lays claim to a fixed doctrine and an intact authority throughout foregoing ages, which Infinite Mercy has founded, which Infinite Wisdom directs, and which Infinite Power preserves. Within this Church no individual's name signifies a better believing, nor do there therein subsist " hostile communities frowning defiance on each other." " All within here," says St. Chrysostom, " are united in one creed, and have but one name, which faith has given." The assertion that involves even the most minute infringement upon Catholic teaching, whilst persisted in, continually incapacitates those who hold to self-authority from combating the most heterogeneous in creed, and as fiction, however aged, cannot set up for herself a prescriptive right in a struggle for dominion with truth, so every doctrinal allegement, however lengthened may be its advocacy, is on a par as to worth with the most extravagant or impious of dogmatisings if an entry cannot be found for it in the ancient records of Catholic tenets.

Contentious sects, therefore, for orthodox superiority, in their efforts to secure supposed seceders from a united belief, must compromise one with another, by a fraternal toleration that resolves itself into somewhat of a congregational character, since, proceeding and growing, as they do, out of the same body, like unto the writhing progeny from Medusa's head, their existence would be imminently endangered by a fierce and prolonged snapping among themselves. Every fresh extravagance must defy denunciation in the accepted right, as sacred, of private interpretation, and the Jumpers and Whirlers, in the thorough persuasion of an Evangelical warranty for their doings, must be allowed to stimulate themselves into such a rapidity of movements as would fascinate the most begrimed and grim priests of the temples of the East into ecstatic approbation.

Among such a contrariety of loud pretensions to primitive orthodoxy, that tend to affect the very being of Christianity herself, the deemed seceders from Catholicity could not hope to find rest for their wearied and troubled souls in any of the so-proclaimed Apostolical Churches, except in the one they have so adventurously quitted, which, like the Ark, conserves her integrity amid the severance and dissolution of all that is purely human—a Church which, unlike shifting sectarianism, that can hold to no definition of dogma, not being imbued with truth, identifies herself with a religion that so sublimely demonstrates the order and unity of nature, that acts upon the will with as much empire as the thought, that strengthens and forwards the virtue to which she has given birth, the religion of the heart, whose every precept is a blessing from Heaven, and whose teaching constantly impels man to do good, as ever having in watch over him the eye of a Creator and Father. It is to this Church those must return that have been supposed to have receded from her, to ensure spiritual safety, which sets forth her title to be the designated spouse of the Most High on earth, in the inspired writings, in those sublime and definite words which no one has dared ever to claim and to assume but herself, of being One, Holy, Catholic, and Apostolic. Thanks, in the earnest and grateful words of the Ambroses, the Augustines, and the Chrysostoms, be to Him whose lightnings, at the same instant they illumine, shatter every obstacle which would narrow their spread, that as Catholics we dwell in a tabernacle where there are no contradictions of tongues as to belief, where truth has an evidence as lucid as that which manifested the rectitude of Israel's worship in the distracting darkness of Egypt, and where a repetition of past triumphs under every imaginable woe and assailment whether inflicted by Emperor or proceeding from philosopher furnishes an actual proof of the divineness of the guarantee as to final victories. This Church of the saint, anchorite, and martyr is delineated forth to us by the Redeemer of mankind, " as one fold, under one Shepherd," which at once implies unity in faith, in the absence of which the miracle would fail of its influence. She who declares what among a multitude of her inveterate and traducing enemies will be found to be contumeliously rejected as not Christian, that the saints are to be invocated, and that their remains are to be venerated; that the faithful departed are to be interceded for, and that grievous sins are to be specially confessed; that self-denials are salutary, and that traditions are to be admitted; that representations of what is holy are profitable, and that a spiritual supremacy exists with the successors of St. Peter, receives an harmonious response from her diversified millions, whether they be those that think with animation under a genial sky, or those that range for a precarious subsistence on the frozen confines of existence. The slightest division upon her teachings, which can have no fellowship with anything that does not perfectly correspond with their import, in contrast with those devisings which may be made to amalgamate with everything that is not truth, would be instant separation from her communion.

In each pressing necessity, then, those who unanimously adhere to the defined tenets of Catholicity, whatever may be their climate, their habits, their customs, their laws, or their interests, confidingly lift up their hands to those who, loving what God loves, with the love that inflamed the heart of the Redeemer on the atoning Cross, are filled with an efficacious desire to befriend those who are contending with the like difficulties that once made their solicitudes, and constituted their heroisms—who, though they be in a land where faith is lost in vision and hope in fruition, yet who dwell where that eternal charity abideth that stimulated a St. Stephen to devote his last breath to the cry of pardon for his remorseless slayers, and actuated a Serapion cheerfully to toil with the galling and festering manacles of a slave, that a desponding and an oppressed brother might be made both happy and free. The bodies of those friends of the Most High, endearingly designated by the early piety of Christianity " as the organs of blessed souls, as the tabernacles of holy minds, and as vessels of benediction," have been sacredly prized in the dominions of Catholic faith, from which, as from the garments of the Saviour and His Apostles, a virtue has gone forth and healed. Upon touching the relics of the fervent and heroic in every Christian obligation and practice, the instantaneously cured have become rapturous witnesses of those merited blessings which continue to hallow the saints in their tombs, even as Eliseus in his grave. On every side where Catholicity is the faith, the voice of compassion is heard in supplication for those whose repentant tears cannot now mitigate the intensity of those fires by which some are to be purified, or influence that justice which, in another world, will exact its dues from the imprisoned, even unto the last farthing. It is by the warmth of the prayer which proceeds here from charity, the sun of the other virtues, that the suffering debtors in another world feel the fierceness of their expiatory fires to be gradually diminished. With the Catholic faithful the conviction is unanimous, also, as to the obligation of making special confession of their sins that are of a mortal character. For, however intricate may be the disputes in the schools of theology as to the deadly guilt of many sins, and however extenuating may be the language of numbers who carouse with the prodigal in the broad road of dissipation, yet with all professing Catholicism the conscientious recognition of grievous sins is conjoined with an obligation of their detailed declaration. Abhorrent as mortification is to our corrupt nature, as confession is revolting to unbending pride, yet all within the Church, that defines herself as one, is in agreement as to the great spiritual profit resulting from its ancient and salutary use. With these likewise that constitute the millions of long-existing empires so diverse in habits and usages will be found to subsist tradition, or the unwritten word, which has the force of a rule of faith. The disavowal of any Catholic on this head would be met with a simultaneous anathema. In respect to the veneration of pictures and images of a sacred nature Catholics are in the same conviction with reference to its advantageous legitimacy. As to the spiritual supremacy of the successors of St. Peter, the credence in the affirmative among the children of Catholicity is as undivided as the succession is unbroken.

SECTION II.

In connection with the prominent matters of Protestant controversy spoken of in the preceding pages, and which have so complete a suffrage within the pale of Catholicity, it may be well to remark how beautiful, how pathetic, how forcible, are the expressions of the ancient Fathers. "O martyrs!" cries out St. Asterius,[1] "who animate us by your heroisms and instruct us by your virtues, who prayed to the martyrs before you yourselves became martyrs, avail yourselves of the credit you have with Him in whose honour you have shed your blood, and aid us in our necessities." "Before the venerated bones of the martyrs," exclaimed St. Hilary,[2] "devils tremble, maladies are expelled, and wonders wrought." "Apply the holy mysteries to the dead," exhorts St. Ambrose,[3] in reference to the deceased Valentinian. "Let us with pious earnestness beg repose for his soul. Lift up your hands with me, O people, that at least by this duty we may make some return for his benefits." "To

---

[1] In SS. Martyres.   [2] L. Contra Constant.
[3] S. Ambrose De Obitu Valent.

declare his sin to the priest of the Lord," teaches Origen,[1] "is one of the means by which a sinner may enter into the peace of God, and whence he may derive a remedy for sin." "To those who willingly undertake it, fasting is at all times profitable," says St. Basil.[2] "We must look to tradition," writes St. Epiphanius,[3] "for all things cannot be learned from the Scriptures." James I., as given in Spotwood's "History," p. 530, and referred to by Dr. Milner in his "End of Controversy," Letter 34, thus reproached the Scotch bishops when they objected to his placing pictures and statues in his chapel at Edinburgh: "You can endure lions and dragons (the supporters of the royal arms), and devils, Queen Elizabeth's griffins, to be figured in your churches, but will not allow the like place for Apostles and Patriarchs." "Pictorial representations," says St. Gregory,[4] "serve for the ignorant as the Scriptures for the learned." "Many are the considerations which must keep me in the Catholic Church," affirms St. Augustine[5]—"the assent of nations, her authority first established by miracles, the succession of Pastors from the chair of St. Peter, to whom the Lord hath committed the care of feeding His flock, down to the present Bishop."

With these venerable, explicit, and eloquent

---

[1] Hom. xvii. In Lucam. [2] Hom. 11 de Jejun. Vol. II.
[3] De Hœres. No. 61. [4] Ep. 50. [5] Contra Epist. Fundam.

testimonies upon the orthodoxy of the invocation of saints and the veneration of relics, upon prayers for the dead, and special confession of sins, upon the merits of fasting and the admittance of tradition, upon the honour which is paid to holy pictures and images, and the spiritual supremacy of the successors of St. Peter, what definite agreement is there to be found as to the soundness of these several teachings among approved and influential Protestant divines? "It is confessed," says Thorndyke,[1] "that the lights both of the Greek and Latin Churches have spoken to the saints, and have desired their assistance." "I do not think," avers Whitaker,[2] "those miracles vain which are reported to be done at the monuments of the saints." "The custom of praying for the departed comes," as writes Bishop Forbes, and as St. Chrysostom testifies,[3] "from the Apostles." "Private confession," writes Luther,[4] "is not only useful but necessary." "Arius," exclaimed Hooker,[5] "was worthily condemned for his opposition to fasting." "The observation of the Lord's Day, and sundry other things there are," avows Dr. Feild,[6] "which doubtless the Apostles delivered by tradition." "It is affirmed," says Fulke,[7] "that

---

[1] Epil., Part III., p. 358. [2] Contra Duræum, Lib. x., p. 856. [3] Controv. Con. [4] Tome II., fol. 84. [5] Eccles. Pol. L. v., Sect. 72. [6] Treatise of the Church, Lib. 4. [7] In. L, Ep. Joan.

Paulinus caused images to be painted on the church walls." "The monarchy of the Bishop of Rome is profitable that consent of doctrine may be retained," asserts Melancthon.[1] Such are the responses of the champions of Protestantism in union with the holy and erudite of Catholicity.

In addition to these, many other testimonies might be adduced from equally distinguished Protestant authorities upon the same leading, as well as other prominent controversial points, in conformity with Catholicity, that ever will be found in unison also with Scriptural teachings. But from how many diversified and excited multitudes has not a similar declaration elicited, in varied exclamations of indignation, derision, scorn, and boisterous protestations of dissent? Yet whatever may have been the different influences upon the good by disposition, or the malicious by propensity, whether arising from early prejudices or false interpretations, the interests of party or the spirit of contention, the plain language of the inspired writings is as follows: "The smoke of the incense of the prayers of the saints ascended up before God from the hand of the angel." Rev., c. viii. "There were brought from his (Paul's) body to the sick handkerchiefs and aprons, and the diseases departed from them, and the wicked spirits went out

---

[1] Cent. Epist. Theol., Epist. 74.

of them." Acts, c. xix. "It is a holy and wholesome thought to pray for the dead that they be loosed from their sins." 2 Mach., c. xii. "Many of them that believed came confessing and declaring their deeds." Acts, c. xix. "The men of Nineveh shall arise in judgment with this generation and shall condemn it, because they did penance at the preaching of Jonas." Matt., c. xii., v. 41. "Therefore, brethren, stand fast and hold to the traditions you have learned, whether by word or our epistle." 2 Thess., c. ii., v. 14. "I will speak to thee over the propitiatory, and from the midst of the two cherubim." Exod., c. xxv., v. 22. "I say to thee that thou art Peter, and upon this rock I will build my Church, and the gates of hell shall not prevail against it, and I will give to thee the keys of the kingdom of heaven." Matt., c. xvi., v. 18, 19. These are the most prominent Scriptural authorities that Catholicity advances for her several impugned doctrines—authorities which the most determined and reckless perversity has never been able successfully to withstand, and whose obvious sense has ever constituted the faith of the saints, the faith of ages.

Controverted also as have been her seven sacraments, for them also she has her sacred vouchers. In the Gospels of St. Matthew, c. xxviii., and St. John, c. iii., the sacrament of baptism is announced in these significant words, "Go ye therefore and teach all nations, baptizing them in the Name of the Father, and of the Son, and of the Holy Ghost." "Unless a man be born again of water and the Holy Ghost, he cannot enter into the kingdom of heaven." Confirmation, in Acts, c. viii., is set forth in this clear language, "Then they laid their hands upon them, and they received the Holy Ghost." The Eucharist is established in St. John, c. vi.: "I am the living bread that came down from heaven. If any man eat this bread he shall live for ever. That which I will give is my flesh for the life of the world." The institution of the sacrament of penance forcibly presents itself in the Divine declaration to be found in St. John, c. xx., "Receive ye the Holy Ghost; whose sins you shall forgive they are forgiven them, and whose sins you shall retain they are retained." Extreme unction has its authority in the Epistle of St. James the Apostle, wherein it is said: "Is any man sick among you? Let them bring in the priests of the Church, and let them pray over him, anointing him with oil in the name of the Lord, and the prayer of faith shall save the sick man, and the Lord shall raise him up, and if he be in sins they shall be forgiven him." Holy orders is shown to be a sacrament in these words of St. Paul, 2 Tim., c. i., "I admonish thee that thou stir up the grace of

God which is in thee by the imposition of hands." Matrimony has its conclusive testimony as to its being raised to the dignity of a sacrament in the new law in the great teacher of the Gentiles' Epistle to the Ephesians, c. v.: "They shall be two in one flesh." "This is a great sacrament, but I speak in Christ, and in the Church." Upon each of these sacraments the Fathers have made their lucid professions, and the charitable solicitude they have manifested for the worthy state of the recipients expresses their lively assurance in the several graces they convey. Of baptism, St. Chrysostom [1] declares "that it was instituted by Christ for the spiritual regeneration of man." St. Chrysostom,[2] on confirmation, says, "By our prayers, and the imposition of hands, the Holy Ghost is obtained." St. Cyril of Alexandria,[3] as to the Eucharist, teaches, "We celebrate the unbloody sacrifice in the Church, and by this we approach the mystic benedictions, and are sanctified, being made partakers of the sacred flesh and precious blood of Christ, the Saviour of all." "For if thou thinkest," writes Tertullian,[4] in respect to penance, "that heaven is still closed, remember that the Lord left here the keys thereof to St. Peter, and through him to the Church," and again, "If still you draw back, let

---

[1] Ad. Illumin. [2] Epist. 73. [3] In Epist. ad Nestor. de Excom. [4] Scorpiace n. 10. De Penit. c. xii.

your mind advert to that eternal fire which confession will extinguish." Upon the sacrament of extreme unction Origen [1] has these words, "There is also a seventh remission of sins through penitence . . . in which that also is fulfilled which the Apostle St. James saith, 'If any man be sick among you, let him call in the priests of the Church, and let them impose hands on him, anointing him with oil in the name of the Lord.'" As to holy orders, thus does the martyr St. Ignatius [2] energetically express himself, "I exhort you that ye study to do all things in a divine unanimity—the bishop holding presidency in the place of God, and the presbyters in the place of the council of the Apostles, and the deacons most dear to me, entrusted with the service of Jesus Christ." Finally, in reference to matrimony, St. Augustine [3] declares "that in the marriages of Christians, the sanctity of the sacrament is of more consequence than the fecundity of the womb." Bucer, the courted theologian of the reformers, as well as Illyricus,[4] the unsparing calumniator of a Church whose incessant combats and constant victories prove her to be the all-consoling subject of the Divine promises, have admitted that Protestants in their conferences have assented to the existence of seven

---

[1] Hom. 2. In Levit. [2] Epist. ad Magnes.
[3] De Bono Conjugale, c. xviii. [4] In Adhortatione ad Constantium.

sacraments. "Protestants," says the former, in relation to that held at Ratisbon,[1] "*non gravatim admiserunt septem sacramenta.*"—"Protestants have admitted without much difficulty seven sacraments." Thus, in connection with foregoing Protestant admissions upon the principal controverted points of Catholicity,[2] in which faith it is also conceded salvation may be obtained, a respective corroboration of their doctrinal soundness is to be met with even amongst some of the most learned and distinguished foes of the ancient belief, as well as in the clear declarations of Scripture and the unequivocal evidence of the Fathers.

However, this will prevail but little with those of high, sacred ministrations, who, in the ability to read, admit a capacity to teach, and who have gradually ventured upon advancements and explanations, under the head of Christian assurances, that have ultimately turned religion into a mere matter of convenience, a system that befriends the State and themselves by preserving in some degree a stimulus to conscience and order, and the advantages of opulence and patronage. With the above freethinking yet cultivated ecclesiastical portion of Christianity, who have met every smart remonstrance of a higher spiritual ruling with a prompt complement of defiance,

---

[1] In Actis Colloq. Ratisbon.
[2] By Luther, Melancthon, Chillingworth, &c.

much to the discomfort and dismay of rigid Churchmen, and the satisfaction and hope of the broad philanthropist, many of the alarmed mitred supervisors of a Church, tottering though termed established, have hitherto in vain entreatingly expostulated. So serious, indeed, of late years have been the disputes among Protestants about doctrines that have been registered by primitive reformers as heavenly, and about points of discipline that have been formally recommended as salutary, that some solemn mutterings have been heard as to the influence of a final authoritative Convocation. On the supposition of such a dignified assembly being constituted through the Convocational immergings of York and Canterbury under Royal bidding and seal, there would arise an intense curiosity as to the issue. The members of a hundred specified denominations, as well as a multitude of generalising Evangelicals, who begin to see but little in the title of Reverend as in august harmony with Christianity, would feel a very profound interest in its every proceeding and action. That such an assembly, of so responsible a character, which should be brought together to determine upon vital controverted matters, might not be wanting in association with venerable antecedents, doubtless some analogy would be retained in its formalities and acts with those Councils that comprised universality in their representation, and which as to the first four of their number have possessed the reverence of the revered among the reformed. Now, the usage of the most early, as likewise the latest, of these Œcumenical Councils, has constantly been, with regard to teachings which were unorthodox or stood in need of explanation and confirmation, after many prescribed prayers to Heaven for guidance and enlightenment, to set forth in the most lucid and exact form the subjects they were convened minutely to deliberate upon; togather what was the belief of each bishop, and the traditions of their several dioceses, on the points under consideration, and thus chiefly through such a medium to make manifest the truth and the authority of a faith "that is one in essence, in assent, in origin, and in excellence." By a similar arrangement also, through her above national council, if it may be thus termed, is the Protestant Church in this land to manifest her identity in tenets with those of the first ages of Christendom, to prove that the faith for which she, as so avowed, is so Apostolically solicitous, is the unchangeable one "once delivered to the saints" (Jude iii.), the faith which the Justins and Irenæuses died for, which the Augustines and the Jeromes expounded, and which the Ambroses and Gregories enforced.

Never indeed was there a period when the Church as established by law in this country, was so imperatively called upon to prove herself to be possessor of this faith " once delivered to the saints," as also of their characteristic energy, fortitude, courage, promptitude, and disinterestedness, as now; for never was there a period when such extreme positions in heterodoxy, as already touched upon, were assumed with such assurance and impunity as within this Empire. Their aggregate gives some advantage to the reasoning of a wise Plato over a Protestant Christianity so befooled as it is in the liberty of making endless expositions upon what may be easily " wrested to one's destruction." The Convocation, therefore, whose providential purpose ought to be, if it has any purpose at all, to extinguish heresies, to prevent schisms, to correct and resist excesses, would find ample matter under the above details, and consequently cogent reasons for wide and marked exclusions in definitely vindicating a first faith for the Church she represented in solemn conclave, and so fearlessly and firmly affects to defend. For though the Established Church tolerates every conventicle, whether that of the Swedenborgian, the Quaker, or the Sandemanian, it must be readily granted as being both imposing and circumspect to set forth through a general gathering of her hierarchy what is condemned or maintained within her regenerated and so-styled Catholic sanctuary. Imposing in the first place, inasmuch as it would display a close imitation of the conservative zeal of early and acknowledged Christian times prudent, in the second place, as it might arrest, by the display and exercise of authority, a gradual continuation of insidious encroachments upon fundamental teachings, which ultimately tend, perhaps, to more disastrous consequences to Protestantism than a constancy of influential conversions to Catholicity. But who can bring himself to hope for such a formal and distinct setting forth of teaching to stay innovation and to affect harmony in those things that have been severally referred to by early reformers as Christian essentials, though they should be confirmed through a Convocation with the appendage of royal assent? For even in the formal assemblies of the first reformers there were almost as many divisions of opinion upon the theological points for examination, as there were divines congregated to discuss and decide. Some few confessions of faith were indeed drawn up and ventured on in their publication, to secure an Apostolical reputation; but no sooner were they put forth than they were instantly assailed with clamour as being in direct conflict with the most obvious meaning of the Inspired Word. At these epochs of Christianity, books upon books, and pamphlets upon pamphlets, rapidly passed from the press to make still clearer what was affirmed as clear in Scripture, and these, as may be readily surmised from foregoing and kindred matter, received a happy rejoinder and a ready compliment in kindly speech and sentiment. The titles of some of these writings are both quaint and amusing. One is set forth as " The brief and the necessary apology of Mark Beumlerus, in which are laid open the primary causes why the tongue and the hand of Mr. James Andrew, like unto Ismael, should be upon all." Another has for its title, " A demonstration of the frauds and impositions by which Egidius Hunnius saucily strives to corrupt the doctrine of the Orthodox Church." A profound work is headed " The Ass-Bird," addressed to the Heidelburg Sacramentarians, which presents a novel kind of metamorphose, inasmuch as Mark Beumlerus, thinking rashly to pass into the nature of a falcon, by some funny mistake is transmuted into that of an ass. During these voluminous controversies, doctors in ecclesiastical gatherings of ten reverentially met, but finally to part in mutual anathemas.

Yet those who could scarcely agree upon an article of belief, were the gifted men who ostentatiously put forward themselves as the chosen that were to bring things round to their original purity, and consequently identifying themselves with primitive authority, and with those even that were appointed to " go forth and teach all nations." If they were of such a primitive teaching and under an authoritative mission, why have not consistent, effective, and lasting results, been attendant upon their several conventions and labours? Why have there not been shown those complete and conclusive assents as to dogmas which were displayed in the Council that condemned Arius, in that which anathematised Macedonius, or in the one that cut off Nestorius? These Councils at their termination, by the harmony of their decisions, founded upon the traditions of ancient Churches, made evident what was Apostolical in doctrine, "in defiance of meddling rulers, truckling ecclesiastics, perverted statesmen, and deluded mobs." Can it be possible that these Councils were composed of any materials similar to those which constituted the Assembly of Smalkald, the Synod of Dort, or what might constitute any prospective Convocation, if there is daring enough to assemble it, for the settlement of disputed matters of creed in relation to the National Church of this country? If so it is difficult to comprehend why a vast body of Christians should have an admitted unity upon a hundred alleged "fond conceits, damnable heresies, and monstrous doctrines," whilst the so-styled godly reformers were the reverse in concord. This, however, ought not to be cause for wonderment for the confiding in the Reformation, on giving a due consideration to the present immediate matter of discussion, since private judgment vitally affects all final doctrinal decisions, as absolutely interfering with its full and sacredly claimed exercise. It follows from this that a Christianity without fixed and defined teachings becomes a mere epithet. In leaving the inspired text open to every opinion it nullifies within it all that is doctrinal, as it leaves at every one's will to pronounce this or that to be dogma. The Bible, with the Protestant public, is much in the same position as the picture that was hung up by a celebrated artist in the market-place for the free judgment of every passer-by. At the termination of two days that were exclusively given, one for censure, the other for approbation, it was found in a respective reckoning up of pencil notings expressive of disapprobation and approval, that the negatives and the affirmatives were so equalised upon all its prominent details as to make positive decision a bewilderment. On the other hand for Protestantism to reject or control private judgment would be an impossibility. It has given existence to Protestantism, and which maintains it as legitimate in seeking the true sense of Scripture, and hence such an astounding aggregate of absurdities and impieties. The very worth of Luther's mission is bound up with its entire toleration, as well as that of every other heresiarch, who, though so much opposed to each other, were in full accord in giving Apostolical patronage to what is the endless source of extreme conflictions in doctrine.

By Protestant Convocations then that may, which is not very probable, be summoned to explode that which is false and retain that which is true, unity will never be realised as it is within Catholicity, which is swayed, not by the frowardness and whims of self, but by what is ancient and universal. It is not to be denied, again to be adverted to, that disputes, as objected, have been both loud and persistent within the Catholic Church, yet this has ever occurred upon what had not been formally decreed to be dogma; this is human, but when Catholic authority spoke, it had its speedy hush among the contending, like that which fell on the clashing and foaming waters of the sea of Genesareth—in this there is what is Divine. "In connection with this authority, vainly," remarks Bossuet, "do Protestant Reformers seek to reassume what is attached to the significance of Church, and oblige individuals to succumb to the orderings of their assemblies, since when once this authority is destroyed it can never be reinstated; the same right that Reformers usurped against the Church at their quitting her will ever be wielded against themselves. Disputes must thus be interminable amongst those," proceeds the same writer, "who have deprived themselves of all power, order, and submission." Upon the above

matter it may be confidently affirmed, whatever may have been done in the past, that as to the future all attempts at Protestant national Convocations will be sedulously shunned, as it is deeply felt by the chief part of those who constitute the Protestant hierarchy that their most formal congregations would be but a parade without a reality, a show which might for the hour have an influence, yet without a lasting gain for the result. The hierarchy of this land inane in its own action has its upholding in the secular power, at whose ordering and disposal it will always remain—a power which includes a very miscellaneous Christianity, and but very little of Christian knowledge, except what it may comprise in a sparse mingling of the clerical character. With many of the British Senate it would certainly be a more than momentary difficulty in discriminating between a precept and a tenet, a mortal and a venial sin. Nevertheless it is a power with a sway "that can," says Blackstone, "change the religion of the land, and do, under Heaven, everything that is possible." In this necessary alliance here of Protestant Christianity with secular might, for vital help, most pertinently in this place may be introduced what Macaulay has so forcibly delineated forth in his review of Southey's "Colloquies on Society":
"The whole history of the Christian religion shows that she is in far greater danger of being corrupted by

the alliance of power than of being crushed by its opposition. Those who thrust temporal sovereignty upon her (which with Catholicity is an impossibility) treat her as their prototypes treated her Author. They bend the knee, and they spit upon her; they cry ' Hail!' and smite her on the cheek; they put a sceptre into her hand, but it is a fragile reed; they crown her, but it is with thorns; they cover with purple the wounds which their own hands have inflicted on her, and inscribe magnificent titles over the cross on which they have fixed her to perish in ignominy and pain." But what could induce Imperial Parliaments and Lord Chancellors not to look on prelates as mere handmaids to the State, though they do but for distinction's sake wear aprons, nor when occupying their places in the Senate House to view them almost as so many well-appointed and placid dummies in a coiffeur's shop?

Nothing but the sudden appearance in Christendom of some phenomenal bestirrer of souls and kingdoms, who in an implied mission from heaven, though failing the miracle, might obtain independent rights for mitres without trenching on those of crowns. Of this now, with an enthralled Protestant prelacy, there is scarcely, in its own reckoning on prophecy, the hope of the Jew as to a coming Saviour to free him from bondage. Yet some years ago Christian

Israel did expect in the marvellous workings of a priest named Ronge, as impressively detailed in clerical and secular journals, to be righted as to her sanctuaries in vassalage to thrones. Ronge commenced alike with Luther to manifest a sacred calling by amending that which nations and ages had identified with truth. First it was, however, as to numerous alleged abuses and superstitions that aroused the slumbering ecclesiastic; anon he passed from small things to greater, from reprobations to anathemas; and then what was once held by him as orthodox became an object of execration. Speedily the vehemence of his accumulated censures began, as at that time so averred, to alarm populations for their continued credence in the teachings of the olden belief, which imperilled, as he affirmed, the salvation of their immortal souls. Under augmented illuminations and spiritual impulses, Ronge finally commenced to fashion forth an Apostolic something for the nations of the earth. But this prayerful devising was not quite in accordance with the persuasions of hoping and expecting Churches, and Ronge commenced to fall off in estimation with the once confiding, from the worth of the "gem of purest ray serene." Nevertheless, during his toils to propagate what possessed novelty and defied elucidation, he was cheered on by a score of visionary or venal journalists, by the most enthusiastic panegyrics, and by the benedictions of multifarious tabernacles. Yet this did not decrease the thickening objections to Ronge's conscientious theology, and a succession of revised formularies was the result of his deeper consideration on an Apostolic belief in order to respond to continuous startling objections, yet without satisfying the many Munsters and Storks who in the days of this second, as in those of the first reformation, rapidly sprung up among his bosom confederates, and raised about him a perplexing din of dissent. Had Luther been living he doubtless would have complimented Ronge, inconsistent as it may be, upon a few of his revised orthodox positions, with a participation in the epithets that he so prodigally bestowed on Zuinglius; Calvin would have been possessed with a burning desire to have linked him to the stake with Servetus; and distracted Melancthon would have been more instant with his beloved mother to remain in the ancient faith, which with tremblings he had forsaken for speculative formularies and inconstant dogmas. Every subsequent liberal amendment that Ronge introduced into his repeated revisals of an Apostolic belief failed to make a closer union among the members of a pure Germanic Catholic belief. Each week had its narration of fresh causes of rupture, and of a more widened discontent. Congregations of a more orthodox and simplified creed were almost continuously forming apart from the one once especially favoured by the Most High, and others as quickly emerged from these, for a yet more Apostolic primitive teaching unto the enlightenment of mankind and the attainment of salvation. Thus did things steadily proceed, at a period of some expectation among reforming or protesting men, who had the Scripture for their guide without the Church for their commentator. And thus it was by reforming much and proving little that all was brought into depressing doubt.

Such has been, and will be invariably, the ending of those who will not receive a faith however hallowed, but must make one. The Protestant world became finally quite satisfied that if Ronge had lived with Apollos, he would not by his teaching have been equally worthy with Apollos to have watered what St. Paul had planted. Yet writers that have reflected deeply and have written largely upon people and their customs, their laws and their creeds, have in substance, with one of prominence in the above class, declared "that by such a movement as that of Ronge an important structure might be raised; it would not be a true Church, but it would have all the machinery of a true Church—namely, a congregation and a clergy, founded on just principles of social economy."[1] It was

---

[1] Notes of a Traveller, by S. Laing.

such a description of things that was fairly to meet the spiritual urgencies of the times, and to throw Rome into as great a consternation as if another Attila was again battering at her gates, for which Protestants, under a more intense consideration on the Christian truths that were yet to be discerned in Ronge's Evangelical ruminations, were to be exemplary, grateful, and benighted Catholics, to "thank the Giver of all good gifts" for the light, consolation and confidence they would yield. It was said that at the period in question some spreading infidel societies in Germany were specially buoyant that " the children of light " under the tutelage of the founder of a genuine Christianity would yet grow wiser, and ultimately become with them the "friends of light." As to the adjunction of some, bewildered by repeated contradictions among the pretenders to sound orthodoxy, and importuned by passions that ever strive for an uncontrolled indulgence, the " friends of light " were not disappointed.

The heart at first becomes corrupted, and then the faith, and this at last sometimes entirely goes, and nothing remains but the name of Christian and Voltaire's god and Liberty. But not a few, on the other hand, sought for a religious system where the advocacy of principles would not be of a fluctuating nature, and where the aggregate of things would make the wisdom as well as the authority of every decision evident.

In this all-important search, it is not long, as many from other sects besides that of the Rongeites have experienced, before the solicitous and persevering seekers behold a Church of unity and majesty disclosed to their view, and every closer approach to this Church has increased assurance in what is beheld, and when once within her, nothing has remained to keep up a distressing incertitude, from which those are never quit whilst speculatively loitering among reforming and recriminating sects. Within this Church it will be found that the most minute tendings towards heterodoxy cannot escape an unremitting surveillance, as already intimated, and that the singular and dangerous opinion will receive as prompt a censure as actual heresy, a condemnation. Of such a Church it ought to follow that unity, her claim, should be an obvious characteristic, which the learned Samuel Wix significantly terms "the very essence of Christianity." On this all-important consideration, natural enough it is that some Protestants of influence, in contemplating the reverse of unity in Protestantism, should be forced to exclaim "that Protestants are as scattered troops going a diverse way," that "the Roman Church is not divided with so many dissensions, but presents a plausible appearance of venerable antiquity, ordinary and constant agreement . . . . but with regard to our people, they are carried about by every wind of doctrine, now to this and then to that part. If you know what is their belief to-day, you cannot tell what it will be to-morrow." Such are the testimonies in favour of Catholic unity from Andrew Dudith and Sir Edwin Sandys, who very conclusively may be considered not to have expired on their beds of down with a tranquil conviction of any immediate approach of their faith to the "one faith" of St. Paul. It certainly may be unhesitatingly said that not even a plausible appearance of harmony among Protestants evinces itself in respect to those things which the most trusted in of their theologians have pronounced to be fundamental. The collective wisdom, moreover, that framed the Thirty-nine Articles is complimented with but a very scanty *bonâ fide* support, and numbers there are now who indignantly refuse to rest their hopes on the creed of a St. Athanasius, to whom an Œcumenical Council listened with admiration as to a Solomon for his wisdom, and with deference as to a St. Paul for his orthodoxy. Can it be that such as these have any association with a Church that St. Irenæus and St. Cyprian refer to in the following concise and explicit form—" That this Church is like unto a family that has but one soul, one heart, and the same voice, and preaches on every side in complete accord"?[1] "Thereisbut one God, and ono Christ, and one faith. This unity will not admit of a division, nor can this body be in any way disjointed."[2] Most assuredly not. The Catholic Church has God for her Author, and what immediately proceeds from the Deity, whose attributes in their mutual operations are ever in harmony, cannot be productive of contradictions. The Babel that is constructed by human hands may have its conflictions, but not the Church which has God for its architect, and a rock for its basement. The Church, therefore, that is pervaded by such a necessary unity, which is indicative of that unity of purpose which ought to reside in man, with the will of Him whose image he bears, cannot but easily, in a comparison, vindicate a superiority for herself over every conventicle that is declared to be of God.

A forcible illustration of what is here advanced, and already urged by an acute Catholic prelate, presents itself, if Protestantism be brought into contrast with the other great dissentient body from Catholicity—namely, the Greek Church—and a respective reference then be made of the two contrasted Churches with

---

[1] Adversus Hæreses. [2] De Unitate Ecclesiæ.

that Church which has been above pronounced to be the immediate work of God. The Protestant Church, it will be seen, in what she is, in doctrinal opposition to Catholicity (except as to the denial of the procession of the Holy Ghost from the Son as well as the Father), is also in opposition to the Greek Church. On the other hand, whilst the Greek Church denounces with Catholicity the heterodoxies of Protestantism, Protestantism, in conjunction with Catholicity, condemns the Greek Church for maintaining that the Holy Ghost proceeds from the Father alone. Thus Catholicity, like the ark that Infinite Wisdom devised, and Infinite Power preserved, conserves her integrity among the wrecks of human contrivances, and in the two great rejections from her communion receives an unequivocal assent for the entire of her dogmas. Strange indeed would it be, therefore, that Catholicity should not be entitled to a decisive preference, when possessing a suffrage which neither of the other two contrasted Churches with herself could deduce in their own respective favour, if placed in the same relative position. This reasoning ought at least to weigh with those who are fully convinced that there can be but one orthodox Church, that has its origin and its keeping in eternal truth, and that an unchanged and agreeing Church includes a proof of orthodoxy beyond the pretensions of any other, has the best right to belief and obedience. But in passing now from the mark of unity to the next mark, confirmatory of a Divine abiding, as claimed by a Church in whose regard Thorndyke, the author of the celebrated work "Just Weights and Measures," frankly concedes, "There is no dogma necessary to salvation which she does not teach, there is no dogma prescribed by her which is incompatible with salvation," what a complete testimony comes into view to prove that the inspired tongue of this Church never needed the glowing coal from Heaven's altar to free it from any contracted impurity, and that she has ever spoken in a language which seraphs might take up and mingle with the holies they give utterance to in the presence of Him "who hateth iniquity, and curseth its doers"! Is. c. v. This evidence presents itself in the detailed declarations of her Councils, and in the approved expositions of her divines. The wisdom of her discipline will also be found to be corroborative of the soundness of her morality. And yet the most gross allegations and the most revolting charges are most recklessly renewed against a Church that puts forward sanctity, as well as unity, as one of the characteristics of her being the pure spouse of Christ upon earth. It is indeed not to be contested that many of her children have not profited by her exhortations, nor attended to lessons that are capable of increasing the merits of the most forward in piety, yet the wilfulness and the perversity of many within her cannot affect with the slightest stain her sanctity. The casual imperfections of Moses could not interfere with the purity of the rays that illumined his countenance, and compelled the most contumacious to revere, nor could the failings or the guilt of some of the Apostles furnish matter for any imputation upon the holiness of their Divine Teacher.

In confirmation of the sum of these observations a celebrated polemical writer has made a few remarks as eloquent as just. "We must not confound," he says, "the weakness of the minister with the holiness of the ministry; we respect the sanctuary in which Stephen officiated and Nicholas profaned; we revere the place from which Judas fell and to which Matthias was promoted; the Scriptures respect the chair of Moses though they censure the several Pontiffs who sat in it, and no Catholic canonises the vices of Popes, though he respects their station and dignity."[1] To a reflecting honesty the injustice must be obvious of confounding (which is so common a practice among captious sects) individual perversity with the morality of Catholicity. The principles which are laid down in the Catholic catechism and expounded in the Catholic temples

---

[1] Remarks on Mr. Wesley's Letter, &c., by the Rev. A. O'Leary.

ought to make obvious to the Lutheran or the Calvinist the true nature of the Church that claims sanctity, and not the wantonness of private acts. Yet, in spite of the flagrant and calumnious tales of a "Monk Lewis" that so often succeed in the nursery to the romantic and defaming narratives of a De Foe, in spite of lengthy revelations about convent and monastery, which, in the more modern speculations of the mercenary or the malicious, comprise almost every amount of crime within the power or daring of the vicious to accomplish, a general impression exists of a superior morality prevailing in the Catholic Church. Hence it may not be extravagant to affirm that the guilt of the consecrated in Catholicity furnishes matter for greater scandal than the criminality of the teachers of a hundred faiths. Certain, however, it is that no system of human ethics ever has or could realise such perfection as that which is so edifyingly displayed in the Catholic communion, that none but a Church Divinely taught, whose language and ordinances are in keeping with the sublime mysteries which she upholds, could effect such a marvellous change in man, and bring all his words and deeds into so close a conformity with the dignity of the Divine image within him. The unction, too, which is the invariable attribute of genuine and exalted piety, that pervades the pages of so many of her devout and gifted children, must be received as an additional testimony of the worth of the principles in which they have been reared. Remove from Catholicity the numerous spiritual works which have this unction to engage the interest of the pious and to stimulate the feelings of the tepid, and to which she has an exclusive right, and Christendom at once loses upon many a vital duty the most important supplementary details, in sublime, pathetic, and ardent words to the exhortations of prophets, evangelists, and apostles. In vain would an effort be made to repair its loss from the religious treatises of any complexion of Christian penning without the domains of Catholicity. Moral instructions may indeed be met with in abundance, as they are to be met with in the works of a Socrates and a Plato, of a Seneca and an Antoninus, but they want that grandeur and appropriateness in their matter which made a presiding Felix tremble, and that fervour in their tones and teachings which elevated the mind of a sinful Onesimus to heaven.

Nor is this to be wondered at as to the spiritual writings of Protestantism when we consider the lives of its chief founders and abettors, their declarations upon a justifying faith, upon the immiscibility of justice, upon the merits of good works, upon the effects and nature of the sacraments, upon the inutility of mortifications, their retrenchment in public worship of practices the most capable of inspiring devotion and creating reverence, together with a certain independence in deciding upon affairs of conscience, conceded to all without restriction. From this there will not proceed much to stimulate piety or incite to good deeds. It will not realise certainly much identity between the works and lives of the Basils, the Austins, or the Bernards in their spiritual labours and actions.

But in continuing the present important matter of these pages, in expatiating upon holiness as manifesting the possessing Church to be the work of God, how prominently does zeal stand forth to claim for the Church termed Catholic, in combination with what has been already given in detail in her support, an exclusive right to what evinces a celestial origin! Through this virtue the perfections of Christianity make their most winning display, and Infinite Power, Wisdom, and Goodness their most sublime manifestations. She is equally fervent in promoting the truth as in advancing holiness, and during the course of her ardent missions could, like her benign Author, repose with affability and affection among sinners and among enemies. She allows of no hesitation in deciding when a good is to be done, and nothing can deter her from attempting its accomplishment. No siren voice can lull her into slumber. No bribe can induce her to compromise with duty. No danger can make a halt in her noble purposes to make, if possible, the dominion of Jesus Christ equal with His creation. In the midst of the greatest obstacles and severities, with the salvation of man and the glory of God for her sacred objects, she has exulted and toiled when heroes that have won nations for kings have wept and despaired. From her heated and suffused brow in her penible and unremitting strivings, nothing has trickled down upon the earth without yielding some return to heaven. To be convinced that Catholicity does incontestably and exceptionally retain zeal in her service, after so exalted and animated a form, let the incredulous or the prejudiced traverse the cities of the world which cling to the faith from which Luther separated and which Calvin reviled. Let them sail to territories once but little known and hardly approached, where Catholicity made her first hazardous settlements, unaided, unfriended, teaching and expounding from her then scarcely sheltered sanctuaries, and they will behold this virtue portrayed in the person of him in whose anointed hands religion has placed her interests—who has an office to fulfil towards God like unto that of the glowing cherub in heaven, to uphold the throne of His infinite sanctity on earth—who has a duty to discharge towards man upon which depends the integrity of nations, as well as the virtues of homes, the just homage of the creature to the Creator, as well as the fidelity of the citizen to the State. They will witness it in the religious institutes of either sex, of an austere profession which a penitential fervour for past sins, or a stirring solicitude for greater perfection, has founded in the daily carrying out of practices that may shock pampered nature, but which have a close analogy with the life of one "who had the Son of God to commend his actions and to praise his virtues." They will discern it in a variety of orders, congregations, and confraternities, that have been established in the Catholic Church to befriend the distressed, to succour the stricken, to convert the erring, and to reform the dissolute. They will witness it, in fine, in the performance of diversified and perilous labours, that sickness, obedience, or death can alone diminish, suspend, or terminate.

At the most marked times of fierce controversy distinguished Protestant disputants could discover the presence of a zeal under the above commanding as well as endearing forms in Catholicity, and they possessed the creditable honesty to proclaim it. Sir Edwin Sandys[1] and Stubbs[2]—the latter a celebrated polemical divine—in writing upon the anointed of the Papacy and their deeds, affirm that they were

---

[1] In his Relation, viii., sec. 48.
[2] Motives to Good Works, pp. 44, 45.

men of memorable integrity of heart—men of wonderful zeal and spirit, "who for good works were far beyond us, and we far behind them." And in making a reference here to the chief founders and reformers—the Dominics and the Francises, the Brunos and the Bernards—of religious institutions, that are made to furnish such frequent matter for lampoon, caricature, and scandal, but which at the same time can count centuries for their existence, name the most distinguished of men for their members, and enumerate primitive councils for their eulogists—in what words does not a Luther, with other Protestants, speak in substance of them, "as men of God, as pious and holy writers"! Devoutly addressing himself to that illustrious man St. Francis Xavier, who proved by his conversion of kingdoms his spiritual brotherhood with the apostle of nations, Baldæus, in his history of the Indies, cries out, "Would to God that having been so renowned by your ministry, our religion allowed us to adopt you, or that yours did not oblige you to renounce us!" It is recorded of James the First that after reading one of the most practical of the spiritual works of St. Francis de Sales, he subsequently bluntly asked his bishops, on an occasion of meeting them, why they could not write with such persuasion and feeling, and with unaffected sincerity desired to become acquainted with the saintly author. Had Divine Providence been propitious to his wishes he would have beheld a man who made it affectingly evident that a solid and courageous piety might be united with the profit of an apostle to the urbanities and the proprieties of life, that timely condescensions gave advantages sometimes beyond inflexible purposes, and that the harsh accusations of the erring might be respectfully and calmly replied to without compromising or injuring the interests or rights of truth. In the intrepid yet meek Bishop of Geneva, a king would have beheld those features and that deportment which yielded a sway that neither his crown nor sceptre could ensure.

But under whatever phases virtue may be viewed in the devout and holy within Catholicity—whether in that of a Francis, recommending himself by affabilities in the midst of courts, without the mean servilities of those who throng them; whether in a Romuald, walking like Enoch in peaceful solitudes, in an uninterrupted communication with his God; whether in a Borromeo, seeking in the midst of the ravages of pestilence to succour the expiring among the fetid bodies of the dead; whether in a Xavier, in imparting the truths of Christianity to the grossest of intellects on the most sterile and perilous of lands; whether in a Cupertino, threading his way through the most disreputable quar-

ters of a city to allure to instruction the depraved
child of either sex ; whether in a Vincent, in filling
the eyes of the obdurate with the tears of compunction
that often glided down the cheeks of the most abandoned in the galleys upon their manacles of infamy ;
whether, in fine, in an Ignatius, in the establishment of
spacious colleges where the philosopher might be
formed without prejudice to the saint, and the mis-
sionary might be perfected without the austerities of
the Trappist—all will concur to manifest the sanctity
of that Church which lays claim to such models of
diversified excellence as the children of her discipline,
and as the living providences in succession by charity
to Him who came to seek, to enlighten, to console,
and to save. The profound Leibnitz, who so disinterestedly and impartially contemplated at large the admirable dispositions in the Catholic Church for the
fostering of the most generous, active, and devoted piety,
and which furnish so obvious and exclusive a suffrage
in favour of the claim of this Church to sanctity, in the
realisation and conservation of holiness by her varied
religious institutions, thus gives utterance to his feelings
in the most ingenuous and glowing words : "I confess
that I have always ardently admired the religious
orders, the pious confraternities, and similar admirable
institutions, for they are a sort of celestial soldiery on
earth, provided that corruptions and abuses being re-

moved they are governed according to the institutes of the founders, and regulated by the Supreme Pontiff unto the use of the universal Church. For what can be more glorious than to carry the light of truth to distant nations, through seas and fires and swords, to traffic in the salvation of souls alone, to forego the allurements of pleasure, and even the enjoyment of conversation and of social intercourse, in order to pursue undisturbed the contemplation of abstruse truths and divine meditation, to dedicate one's self to the education of youth in science and virtue, to assist and console the wretched, the despairing, the lost, the captive, the condemned, the sick, in squalor, in chains, in distant lands, undeterred even by the fear of pestilence from the lavish exercise of these heavenly offices of charity? The man who knows not or who despises these things has but a vulgar and plebeian conception of virtue; he foolishly measures the obligations of men towards their God by the entire discharge of ordinary duties, and by that chill habit of life devoid of zeal and even of soul which prevails commonly among men." Leibnitz, a philosopher whose patience of investigation made his renown as much as the apprehensiveness of his genius, could never have been moved with such a warmth of conviction if the feelings which by nature ennobled his heart had not been yet more elevated by studiously contemplating in the Catholic Church the deeds of zeal that cannot look on anything with apathy, or leave undone that for which Heaven has a solicitude and a counsel. But between the several religious institutions and establishments of Catholicity in modern times, which have edified the philosopher, and won the admiration of the sceptic, by the many and fervid virtues to which they have given rise and perfected, what degree, it may be asked, of mutual relationship subsists with those of the first ages? Why, one of that near nature which a close response to the rules of first religious institutions must necessarily yield, and which have for their respective object the determination of the hours of prayer, of meditation, of study, of instruction, of labour, of watching, and of periods of fasting. All this subsists now in vigour within a Church which presents an unvarying unity in doctrine throughout so lengthened an existence, and which is ever complemented by an unfaltering discipline—a Church which is as consistent in morals as fixed in dogma, which approves through the medium of unswerving principles, of institute and rule, to beget sanctity and to conserve it. This assimilation with the past will be as ceaseless with her as her faith and her virtues. Some of her professed may even occasionally not have been in full conformity with the diversified intentions of her institutions, and the thoughtful wisdom that prevails within their rules; this, however, has commonly not failed to give birth to a zeal to amend evils whose ardour was in kindred with that of the martyr and the saint of primeval days, who had the inspired to learn from and to imitate.

To the sublime mysteries and the pure morality of the Catholic Church, which she will constantly unfold and uphold, as also to the animating and fervid character of the devout acts and spiritual works of her gifted and submissive children, may be adjoined the profound worth of her solemn ceremonies in heightening the majesty of her sanctuaries, as well as in giving a religious impulse to the listless and to the tepid. Whatever indeed reveals itself under a Divine form will eventually command its sacred edifice, and ensure an appointed amount of religious rites. Those among uncivilised lands, though they may be of a rude and fantastic description, are corroborative of the truth of the assertion in an elementary stage of things, as also in the universality of the fact. Man is as much a sensible as a rational creature, and a numerously prescribed order of things that is set forth among empires to give grandeur to thrones, as well as to maintain the sacredness of temples, furnishes lucid proofs of the soundness of the axiom. Thus, likewise, levees, inaugurations, and anniversaries have their quota of diverse forms, that not only monarchs may be approached with respect, but that the multitude may be duly impressed with the honours accorded to merit, and that distinguished national events may be solemnly and impressively perpetuated. "Ceremonies are," says Fénélon, "with regard to God, those marks of respect for a father, as exterior honours and homages are for a king. Is it not evident that men, attached as they are to the senses, and whose reason is so weak and feeble, should have need of something imposing in order to impress upon them the homage that is due to an invisible Majesty, and to awe the passions into reverence? This sentiment is so natural to men that every character of people that have adored some divinity have had their exterior worship, have had some external demonstrations termed ceremonies. . . . Protestants themselves, who have so much criticised ceremonies, have been forced to retain many of them, so true it is that to mankind they are vivifyingly necessary."[1]

Ceremonies, however, notwithstanding all that has been urged, are, it is objected, not essential to religion; be it so, yet God himself first dictated the matter of religious rites, and the subsequent minute detail of His holy will under this head was of a far more complicated and multiplied nature as to forms

---

[1] Fénélon—Du Culte Religieux.

and vestments than those now prescribed. But who will dare to cavil at His appointments as to what might best tend to elevate the thoughts of the contemplative, to fix the attention of the thoughtless, and to realise veneration even in the irreverent, " who ordereth all things sweetly "? (Wis. c. viii., v. 9.) Ceremonies are not essential to religion, as readily admitted, but religion without them would be as inanimate as faith without good works. For that which the glory of God intermingled with in the Temple of old, the Catholic Church can have no exclusion as to her sanctuaries. She has therefore instituted solemn rites for the sacrifice of her altar, on which Jesus Christ our Victim and our Propitiator is offered up, and she has appointed for the celebrant and his attendant ministers a symbolic attire, that the mind might be impressed with the faithful correspondence of these and of every accompanying ceremony with the majesty of the adorable Victim, that so ineffably accords with all foregoing figures, whilst at the same time the heart may be quickened in its movements by the display of emblems and rites which are so immediately connected with the chief circumstances and events of the sacred passion. Melancthon, in the certitude of their profitableness, earnestly recommended to the reformers the retention of rites, ceremonies, and vestments, for whose respective adoption there was a warrant of so ancient a date. Moses in the Judaic Church entered into most numerous and minute details on the above matter, in conformity with the dictates of the Almighty Himself, and what was subsequently countenanced by Jesus Christ might well be continued by the Church He founded. But those who wished to simplify things down to whitewashed walls, and to reduce dignifying robes to the scantiness of a bib, who would not tolerate as much ceremony before their communion table as they willed their obsequious beadle to enact before a bluff and substantial, staid burgess in the porch of their dreary kirk, looked upon Melancthon as a second Saul for making such a reserve upon specious and fair things which the Lord had commanded not to be spared. Yet, in the sight of Heaven, what Divine authority can there be for execration upon those practices which nature, in their deep response to the most lively emotions of the human heart, vindicates, which the unerring Disposer of all things has enjoined to be employed, and which have been sacredly recognised by Him "who did all things well." Ceremonies have seldom ceased to produce effects which have profitably seconded the earnestness of words. When prominently intervening in spectacles or set forth in paintings, they have sobered down the most volatile, and made even the dissipated momentarily thoughtful in the midst of their frivolities and their levities, their gibes and their pastimes. Why should robe and rite be excluded from sanctuaries which have realised such effect, and added dignity to the throne of the King, and in the former case given grace to the statues of the renowned? They may fail to give existence to the lively emotions which chant and music produce, yet they rarely fail to create a feeling which, as heretofore declared, testifies that man is born religious.

Others will doubtless say that denouncement falls upon excess in the ritual enjoinments of Catholicity, and not upon every admission of vestment and ceremony that have so varied, so ancient, and so holy a use. Nevertheless, before denouncements are uttered upon excesses under the foregoing considerations, as inimical to the worship of God, " in spirit and in truth," some influential Protestant prelates should determine among themselves what ought to be considered the *juste milieu*, and which, when officially announced to their clergy, would generally secure a uniform and profitable observance. A few essays have indeed been made at no very distant period to arrive at such a consummation of things, and by many among Protestants so devoutly wished. Yet, as in doctrine so in discipline, the chaste purposes of some of the

Protestant episcopacy had to encounter a host of mob vetos and maledictions upon the profaneness of the endeavour. Though the tone of the episcopal charge was devout and moderate as to the employment of rites and ceremonies as influential for good, yet still the cry of "Watch over of the primitive purity of your churches as you would over the independence of your homes!" was kept up by those who mistook their violent prejudices for religious sentiments, and their irreverent successes for providential Christian triumphs. So appalled, indeed, were those of the venerable episcopal bench who had so formally and chivalrously spoken out on the salutary introduction of an additional display of ritual matter into their denuded and abbreviated sanctuaries, that they sagaciously devised a retreat for themselves through the medium of explanations adopted in their subsequent formal pastorals. These, however, were as ambiguous as to the Apostolic purport of preceding tolerations in the use of vestments and ceremonies as that of the oracle of Apollo to Pyrrhus, King of Epirus—"Aio te Æacida Romanos vincere posse."

But in reference to Catholicity, in what portion of her ritual matter is there manifestly a pernicious excess, and consequently, under some considerations, meriting equally the displeasure of God with the unhallowed fire of the censers? It must doubtless be, if it exists anywhere, in the prescribed forms and vestments employed in the celebration of a sacrifice which itself has been pronounced idolatrous, and yet it is given in one of the best-attested records to be met with, either in profane or ecclesiastical history, that St. Dominic, on hearing of the calamitous death of the young Lord Napoleon, ordered his lifeless body to be brought into his presence, and when this was done he vested, preparatory to the offering up of the holy sacrifice, at the conclusion of which he advanced towards the lifeless body of the youthful nobleman, still being attired in that ancient instituted detail of vestment, so closely figurative of the linen cloth with which the Jews blindfolded the eyes of the Redeemer, of the white garment with which the attendants of Herod clothed Him, of the cords with which the prison officials bound Him, of the purple cloak with which a Roman soldiery deridingly invested Him, and with an unfaltering voice exclaimed, "Napoleon, I say to thee, arise, in the name of our Lord Jesus Christ!" On the instant, before a breathless and transfixed multitude of every description, the bidding of the perfect was obeyed, and life reverentially arose before the saint and the altar upon which the venerable founder had so recently elevated the consecrated elements, "This is my body, this is my blood," and so profoundly adored.[1] Could the charge of idolatry here incidentally alluded to exist in the sacrifice consummated by the man of God, or was there that vicious excess which many term superstition to be found in the ceremonies and vestments used with such a sacred reference on this solemn occasion? Assuredly not. Idolatry is an impiety that has brought down the avenging lightnings of an outraged Deity. It has been hurled from its raised pedestal by the hands of Omnipotence, and cursed in language by the Most High that must have caused even the demon to recoil that first devised the abomination. Catholicity could no more extend a patronage to such an impiety than the Author of her existence could favour its practice by the miracle of the Apostle. No, the Church of ages and ancient nations, as her missions and writings testify, has more than even the zeal of a Moses in the comminution of the golden calf for its utter extermination, and her ministers, at her solicitous instance, now, as in the past, anathematise at every risk, in every land, that which for centuries had so universally deprived the Creator of His glory, and had, in impious adorations, so utterly debased the creature.

Equally also have her ministers proceeded with regard to superstitious practices under her most

---

[1] See Theodoric of Apolda, N. 92, p. 579.

minute injunctions. Did she fail to enjoin thus with superstition, as with idolatry, the renewed wonders of inspired periods would not have been hers to narrate with such authenticity. There is nothing in her rites and in her hallowings, in amplifying a little further on the alleged matter of existing superstitions, that reason can discern to be unworthy of a religious reference, or which has not a suitable conformity with the wisdom, goodness, and majesty of God. It is not to be denied that some individuals in the Catholic Church, who have been as wanting in judgment as abounding in credulity, have looked for a success and a blessing in absurdities and follies, yet on the above it may be seasonable to observe here that many Protestants have likewise their little special providences in something akin to what they reprobate; an amulet about the neck to resist some bodily evil, or an affixed horseshoe to the door to exclude some mischievous, sportive sprite, is not even among the better informed a rarity. But the grave ordinances of Catholicity under every form are not to be confounded with the casual extravagances of some of her credulous children. Were everything that is employed under a religious consideration as accessory to a preservative, a cure, or a good among Catholics tested before its use by the universality of its practice, or by the decisions of authority, there would be little left

H

for a laugh or a censure. When superstition commences religion ceases. Catholicity, therefore, is ever on the alert, that has as much sympathy with inept expectations as absurd creeds.

Nevertheless, under the most vigilant of supervisions, it is almost impossible to be entirely quit from some entwinings of a noxious growth. Yet wherever superstition has increased into prominence and mischief, Catholicity has always been instant in disentangling and uprooting that which, however gaudy it may be in flower, can never yield the blossom's worth. Thus does she act who evinces in her unbroken unity and in her untainted sanctity that that conservative hand is with her in her hallowings which blessed the few loaves, and made them equal to the pressing need of unprovided multitudes. Thus does she act who equally manifests in the prodigies worked by the heroic in the practice of her virtues, as in the visible glory in Jerusalem's Temple, the sanction of the Deity for rites which not only give solemn moments to Catholicity in her churches, but witness, as well as history, to the antiquity of her existence and the undeviating nature of her doctrines. She has willed also, as well as the institution of rites and ceremonies, the keeping of annual solemnities and festivals, which have for their subject-matter the most august mysteries of Christianity and the memories of the most distinguished among her saints and martyrs, that by forcing at stated periods the chief objects of faith upon the attention, and representing them as it were as actually passing before the eyes, and by conjoining appointed commemorations of the most conspicuous in virtue and the most fervent in faith among the servants of God, a vivifying impulse might be given to the belief of the Catholic and to his faithful fulfilment of every obligation. In this disposition of things by a Church in whose precepts are to be found aids to the observance of the Commandments, is found also from time to time a refreshing interval for the toiling by a suspension from labour, which Protestants who have thrown off the oppressive yoke of Rome have no idea of giving, through such a religious and instructive medium, to the drooping and exhausted in their vineyard.

SECTION III.

IN the foregoing matter it has been shown that the benedictions and precepts of the Church are intimately conjoined, that the Church of God, like her Divine Founder, who tempers His justice with His mercies, never imposes an obligation without some interminglings of relief and consolation. Let us now pass on to the consideration of the ecclesiastical education of Catholic students, and ask, can it be true, as averred, that whilst it may even improve the mind it corrupts the heart? To this it may be readily rejoined that if a portion of a theological course, when entered upon, does give to the Catholic aspirant to holy orders a gross knowledge of sin, it is, as with our first parents in Eden, accompanied with the terrors of God's judgment upon guilt. At all times, but especially during a course of theology at Catholic colleges, in which mysteries have a most sedulous explanation, and immoralities a prudent exposition as to their degrees of turpitude, the voice of saint, of martyr, and of the primitive Father is continually heard in setting forth to the ecclesiastical student the momentous obligations of the priesthood, and urging their deep consideration thereupon, by all the motives that inspiration, reason, and example can furnish. The daily-assigned meditation, and the fulfilment of diversified daily religious duties, must likewise tend to increase and invigorate virtuous purposes in preparing for the suitable discharge of sacred obligations, and to fortify the heart when the subject-matter of the theological readings is occasionally, as with the Scriptures, perilous in its references. In duly considering these religious provisions and obligations of Catholicity to well befit the Christian to enter finally on a sacred charge, it must be evident that conscience has in them her best auxiliaries, and for an ecclesiastical student to resist the influence of their daily intervention to compass a lasting good, by a wilful persistence in some grievous guilt, is to realise in himself a calamity beyond that of the state of the most abandoned worldling. On those, moreover, who are admitted to holy orders the Catholic Church imposes a solemn obligation during life of reciting at certain hours apportioned parts of the Breviary, which chiefly consists of extracts from the Scriptures, writings of the Fathers, and a brief narrative of the lives of saints, martyrs, and Apostles. Thus, by this daily reading at assigned hours, which requires the most weighty reasons for its dispensation, it is sought that the clergy may be maintained in the true spirit of the Catholic Church, that memory may not fail in her history, teachings and observances, and that prayer, under the most sublime, affecting, and practical of forms, may obtain through observance of this precept of the Church the force of a salutary custom. In the Divine office, next in importance to Holy Writ, the ordained of Catholicity, though centuries have passed away since its primitive institution, find nothing in it that has become antiquated or changed as to doctrines or morals. The reformers pronounced the Breviary to be of a superstitious character, through which term they designedly got quit, not only of the Breviary, but of a large amount of enjoined pious usages and practices. If it is here objected, as it has been often objected, that incredible things are introduced into the Breviary, as also in other accredited books of Catholicity appertaining to saintly lives, it may be readily replied, without giving any direct support for what has therein been advanced and so derisively referred to, that the statements termed outrageous and preposterous are able to assume for themselves at least a negative position. In the early periods of Catholicity, when Christians were comparatively scarce, and their virtues otherwise, the Church, confiding then, had not adopted so rigid and protracted a scrutiny upon some of the alleged extraordinary events in connection with her heroic children. Hence what in regard to some introductions was ecclesiastically countenanced at first days would probably, in a present searching and extended inquiry, not be admitted. In further respect to this subject, an able canonist, in alluding to the Breviary, writes that many things were there retained which had a certain amount of probability, and had the authority of certain grave vouchers, though, perhaps, the opposite sentiment had more patrons. It is not contrary to the Catholic faith to challenge the worth of what is recorded in her Divine offices; there is mischief, however, in discarding entries that are attested by testimonies which men have usefully determined among themselves as well calculated to yield a moral certitude.

Moreover, in the matter of canonising, the Catholic Church is neither multiplying nor precipitate. The severity of her now-instituted proceedings on what has preceded, to arrive at facts, has astonished the most biassed of Protestants—attestations which, as to their entire amount, have in their minds almost approached to demonstration, being set aside as not having sufficient weight to satisfy those who were deputed for their learning, their ability, and their piety to carry out so responsible and onerous an undertaking, and were called upon in this investigation, before coming to a decision, to consult their reason as well as their conscience, and certainly, as impressively remarked, they had a solemn motive to do so by all that was awful in religion, sacred in an oath, and fearful in a censure. Thus does she proceed that does not succumb to interest or to passion in testing a right to a title that kings cannot confer or riches purchase, and when the deeds of time are summed up may have a halo which the archangel, in his highest heaven, may not surpass in its glow. But let those who would condescend to learn more in detail, and satisfy themselves upon what has gone before, or in close connection therewith, peruse the lives of the saints, prepared and commented on by a man who was as great by his piety as by his erudition, whose judgment best disclosed the character of " the wise unto salvation," and whose prudence omitted from the marvellous of their lives what might tend to make the devout despond or the criminal despair. In these pages, whose style is as simple as clear to the most ordinary capacity or education, is also evinced what are the excellencies of Catholicity in her varied institutions to which the charity of her fervour has given existence and preserved in vigour, and which history proves to have been the chief providences of the nations where they have been founded and propagated.

It will likewise be equally evident in these writings that the Catholic Church, under every violent persecution and imminent peril, has condemned corruption in morals alike with perversity in doctrines, as when deserts were peopled with saints, and general councils anathematised the first impious avowals of heresiarchs. Nothing will be discovered here to be wanting as to rules in reply to every spiritual difficulty, nor as to motives to make everything subsidiary to the interests of sanctity. It will be found that with saints, as well as philosophers, science and learning at large received the closest cultivation, and that the holy were as assiduous in their schools in developing their various branches as in expounding the sacred Word and stimulating the youthful to piety. "God is wonderful in His saints," and this has been best verified in the writings of Alban Butler, in what is secular as also in what is religious. And what a contrast do those present in conduct to the records of Catholic sanctity who rose up and raised their voices in contradicting the expositions of General Councils on tenet and precept, and who, upon being challenged, assigned at random periods for the corruption and consequent abandonment of a Church by its Divine Founder to which they had solemnly pledged their faith as to her perpetual infallibility! These persistent and sweeping reformers, at least as to the chief part of them, upon the doctrines of Catholicity, and who affected a suitable revolt at her so vaunted obligations and observances, confessed to imperfections and vices that would scarcely have fitted them at these immediate times for an admission among the Shakers or Jumpers, much less for an introduction into a staid family of Christian love. Zuinglius averred that he was consumed by an unholy fire which had drawn upon him the reproach of the Churches.[1] "I burn," exclaims Luther, "with a thousand fires. . . . . I, who ought to be fervent in spirit, am fervent in impurity."[2] Calvin, whose death was of a most horrible nature, that of despair, "was a bad man, a rabid dog," as Bucer declares.[3] History has the above words for her entries of those who announced themselves, under the impulse of the Most High, to be sacredly authorised to enlighten, to reform, and to save— "those," says Erasmus, "who so zealously set fire to the house to get rid of the cobwebs," but who were not very scrupulous in refraining from what inspiration excludes in the classification of guilt from the kingdom of heaven.

Yet it is not intended here to be inferred that criminal excesses always accompany heterodoxy. Tertullian, in quitting the Church, did not depart from that rigidness of self-denial which the solitaries of

---

[1] In Parenes. ad Helvet., fol. 44. [2] Luther's Table Talk.
[3] See the German Wolmar, from whom Calvin learnt both his Greek and Hebrew, and derived his love for freethinking.

Egypt scarcely surpassed. Whilst he was adding to monstrous doctrinal conceits, he did not fall off from severity of morals. Melancthon, notwithstanding his close fellowship with Luther, did not appear to be swayed by his gross doings, if he was so by his indulgent theology. Discreet in private society, and far from being arrogant in public dispute, he ever presented an edifying and modest comportment to that of his violent and voluptuous chieftain. But whatever other exceptions may be gathered to the above of a strict life remaining when orthodoxy has been widely receded from, they will be, as to their number, in the paucity of white blackbirds and black swans. To this Protestants may pertinently reply that their creed is as independent as the Catholic of human frailty or human excellence—that they have a firm conviction of its soundness, notwithstanding the merits or demerits of its heralds, that Luther or Zuinglius, or any other prominent reformer, though licentious in teachings and carnally infirm, could impart a truth as well as Balaam could give a blessing. Yet, when a few start up in the midst of millions to set forth what is to be the future belief and practice of Christian kings and a Christian people, that possess a tranquillity of conviction upon a distinct amount of teachings whose entire orthodoxy successive Councils from early Christendom had confirmed as a respective heresy, might have made it imperative thus to proceed and loudly to proclaim, as the envoys of God, that much of this teaching was false—that the Church which upholds the contrary, even under anathema, had become thoroughly depraved in her character, and that it was their high and responsible calling to point out and to manifest succinctly and clearly what had and what had not a Divine paternity—to separate the wheat from the chaff, and to furnish those counsels to men which might enable them "to walk before God and be perfect." In all this, as a celebrated writer observes in substance, there is naturally looked for in the self-styled reformers an outward display of sanctity, as being the necessary concomitant of " a sensitive conscience and an illumined understanding."[1] For with the office of an apostle Christians have ever been taught to expect its due accompaniments, if not miracles, the most decisive proofs of a Divine intervention upon occasions which have raised up the prophets of old, at least, as the same writer remarks, "to behold it seconded by a holiness and by a purity inaccessible to human passions." " Upright people, when they see on every side justice," he further observes, "do not find it to be so difficult to be convinced of the truth, but

[1] Rousseau.

they cannot very well hear the voice of God except from the mouth of virtue."

But how conspicuously and persistently in the reverse of this do not the first proclaimers of reform evince themselves to be, in the midst of their wanton and wayward proceedings, as to a saintly character, so absolutely required to support words uttered with such lofty empire! What a contrast do they not yield in regard to the Fathers they so sedulously maligned, who had strengthened the chief posts of Catholicity with the piety and learning of their disciples, and for whom many Protestants that are in a certain degree influenced by tradition yet retain a veneration. The Fathers, as history attests, maintained a corresponding conformity in their lives with the demands of the sanctuary that they always held in such a holy and vigilant keeping. In them the controlled passions did not debase man, but dignified him by their prompt obedience, and their animated action in forwarding what engrossed the thoughts of the inspired. They had the impulse of the spirits of Ezechiel for their ardent and instant movements. In the fervent virtues of the venerable of Christianity was to be found more persuasion than in the apologies of Tertullian, in defending the faith of its members. Their sanctity gave them a mastery over the enthroned which was never exercised with their domination. The merits of their souls appeared in their attenuated and benign countenances, and the energy of their proceedings never partook of turbulence and impetuosity. If these erudite and unflinching champions of the Catholic creed, as also the most engaging examples of holiness, failed to correct the perversities and the errors of the insubordinate and the contumacious by their exhortations or their censures, they strove in the stillness of the desert, in the privacy of their abodes, or at the foot of the altar, by their austerities, their tears, and their prayers, to propitiate the Most High and to soften the hearts of the obdurate. Never did these uncompromising antagonists of heresiarchs forfeit their worth in the Book of Life by elevating themselves in audacious rebellion against a Church which is to speak in the place of Him who established her unto the end of time. "He that heareth you heareth me, and he that despiseth you despiseth me." (Luke, c. xx.) If a Cyprian, as especially here to be selected, who taught that God is one, and Christ is one, and the Chair is one, founded by the Lord's Word upon a rock, and that it is an impiety to abandon their mother, was erroneously positive in a matter of ' moment, his final heroic death by martyrdom, which was to be expected from his exalted virtue, furnishes every assurance that his conduct did not include that obstinate defence of error which makes the formal heretic.

Such then as above is the broad difference between Fathers and reformers, between those who were an ornament to the Church " which is without spot" and those who were separated from that which vivifies. Yet the Luthers, the Calvins, and the Zuingliuses, who present so striking a contrast to the Fathers under so many momentous aspects, were the men set apart, as confidently asserted by the myriad, to bring things round to their original purity as to truth and holiness, as they existed at a period, it may be presumed, when the Antonies prayed, the Athanasiuses expounded, and the Gregories preached—men who condemned the practices of the monastery and the desert in which saints were reared, or sought for greater perfection, who censured the decisions and defamed the memories of those whose judgments were received as laws for the well-government of Churches, and impugned observances that had had their dictation in the experience and wisdom of immediate primitive ages. If such as these had the manifest will of Heaven in their favour, with an approaching evidence to that of Gideon in the old and Barnabas in the new law, then the prodigies of the desert, the sanctity of monasteries, the oracles of Councils, and the ordinances of ancient patriarchates, made the delusion of Christendom.

However, since it is by their fruits, as the Gospel lays down, that certitude as to worth is to be obtained, Catholics are assured from foregoing facts that the reformers were not in Apostolic commission. What they have produced is not what thrives, blooms, and arrives at wholesome maturity, upon the soil the great Householder ordained to be assiduously cultivated. Their descendants may continue to toil indeed upon some spots of their own choosing, but the sweat of their brow will never supply for the dew of that sky which certified to Gideon whence came his appointment in the guidance of Israel.

But here, in reference again to religious institutes which primitive reformers endeavour as much to bring into odium, and abolish, as primitive Christianity sought to establish and to propagate, it may be asked what can fairly be fixed upon these, which include so many varied, laudable and sublime purposes, so as to make obvious their vicious and pernicious character. The reformers in order to give some colouring to their vehement denunciations against both monasteries and convents have alleged revolting crimes and gross superstitions. The Catholic Church, in successively establishing diverse religious orders, did not expect that frailty and perversity would not have an occasional presence among the accumulated thousands of her religious throughout the universe, when a few among the twelve, with Infinite Wisdom for their counsel, and Infinite Sanctity for their model, by their failings preeminently added to the afflictions of the Man of Sorrows. But it is a very different thing to pronounce that the greater part of those who are living in a state of perfection, as so termed, were given up to iniquity or immersed in mummeries. The varied constitutions of respective religious institutes, some more, others less austere, yet all calculated to advance in an assured degree the novice or the professed in piety, scarcely could be carried out, even by the fervent, with every days' uniformity in merit, without some waywardness of will, but persistent vice could hardly in a religious house be daily defiant upon discipline without impeding and embarrassing the action of authority, the result of which is confusion, which in the general dispositions and surveillance of Catholicity does not admit of a very lengthened existence. Yet even the extreme laxity of a religious institute, with its consequent serious evils, upon which early reformers have dilated with such affected warmth and bitter invective, has occasionally awakened a zeal which, in its unabated activity in bringing about a first devotedness in an order, has equalled that of the pious founder of the order itself. Purity and fervour have again presented themselves, to obey with alacrity, and to persevere without a murmur. When, however, it has appeared hopeless to vivify, the hand that has sanctioned and blessed has promptly removed that which, like the barren fig-tree, unprofitably encumbered the Householder's soil. As to the grievous and many charges against the religious houses at the period of the Reformation in this empire, they came from those who felt about the same solicitude for the perfection of communities as the wolf for the innocence of the lamb. Their ultimate suppression, for the enrichment and luxurious indulgence of the few, left poverty without its refuge, the school to the conscience of the hireling, and the right to teach and minister in sanctuaries to the caprices of the obsequious to the shifting acts of a then time-serving British Senate.

On foregoing matter there is, nevertheless, a curious circumstance to be noticed as to the hostility to religious institutes, that the travelling writers of modern days, at least as to some of their number, that have been, like the first reformers, most virulent in words and most prolific in inventions, have seldom terminated the details of their numerous and devious peregrinations, so replete, as they complacently conclude, with national enlightenment as well as national amusement, without discovering much in various religious orders for edification and even for enthusiasm. On a visit to one or other religious establishment the strong emotions of Sterne, which arose within him during his brief interview with the lowly Franciscan monk, seem gradually to have come upon them; they have finally been rapt into admiration whilst contemplating the devoutness of a countenance that was so expressive of the goodness of the heart. But of late there has been something more than incidental fervid admiration of those who were once inveterately biassed against both cowl and veil. A spirit of emulation has now sprung up among many pious and influential Protestants of vieing even with the practices both of convent and monastery. They have even apparently a hope through the rigour of rule and unctuousness of prayer to arrive at the sanctity of the heroic of the desert. Alas! it is the rash attempt of the son of Apollo, whose untrained hands deepened the calamity of his course. Where there is not strict and lengthened Catholic tutoring there will be but little of careful and permanent observance as to what is of Catholic institution. In an unanimous belief and its discipline alone are to be found the essentials towards effective and permanent results. There may be a hush in dispute upon dogma, yet still the claim to private judgment subsists, and a strong tendency to exercise it, which early education has implanted, will ever exist. It is impossible to have also that uniform and ready obedience which best evinces the vocation of the religious subject, and to which conscience, not caprice, yields permanence. Without indeed, the boundaries of Catholicity there can be no expectation that Brother Nicholas or Sister Anne will do continuous honour to either of their so-called institutions, and present an unreserved submission, without which neither ancient nor modern monk or nun will have much to show beyond a grave parade of vesture and demureness of feature. As well might it be expected to find abiding throughout Magdalen Court the purity that makes the fervent Christian as sensitive to sin as to a grievous hurt, or within Creed Lane to meet with on every side concordance in belief, that does not at this period dwell within the consecrated precincts of York or Canterbury.

In alluding to writers in general, that have pronounced so contradictorily on the subject of religious establishments, now condemning, now lauding, few, it may be remarked, include more confliction in language in respect to the above than the late Lord Macaulay, and conspicuously so in his observations on the Jesuits. "Before this order," he says, "had existed a hundred years it had filled the whole world with memorials of great things done and suffered for the faith. No religious community could produce a list of men so numerously distinguished, none had extended its operations over so vast a space, and yet in none had there ever been such perfect unity of feeling and action." This is somewhat close upon what Catholic writers have in the main uttered in reference to the achievements and merits of the disciples of Loyola at the period in question—" men whose intrepidity knew no faltering in perils or in trials when a Christian was to be made, who joined the ardour of their zeal to that of profound science, who carried the light of the Gospel from one hemisphere to the other, and who animated each other to courage and patience in resisting iniquity and error at home." And yet the deeds of the Jesuit, that stimulated the waning zeal of Catholic Europe, and did more to forward the triumphs of that belief than the armies of Charles, were, according to the same influential historian, intermingled with the most grievous failings. Iniquity had its lenient interpretations and even tolerations among those, Macaulay alleges in substance, " who hazarded their lives in the midst of the plague-stricken, and among men of the most ferocious character, to impart succour and enlightenment, that by this nefarious and accommodating truckling, that by this making themselves all things to all men, their confessionals chiefly might obtain a celebrity beyond all others, and become predominant to every eye by their attendant crowds." Deceit also, as the same writer anxiously gave the British public to understand, had a very subtle defence and a very diversified employment among the subjects of St. Ignatius, though often, as record affirms, the slightest prevarication upon their Christian belief amid barbarians, "where life was more insecure than that of the wolf," would have rescued them from chains, mutilation, and death. But is it possible to common sense that such an intermixture of good and evil with so responsible a class of men should have had a being, and yet an admitted marvellous bettering of life in empires should be the result of their sudden and expanded mission? The assiduously collected opinions of some benignant divines belonging to the Society have, it is true, been construed into startling concessions, that have left little apparently to disturb the peace of the dishonest or the dissolute. However, sweeping constructions are not always to be assumed as decisive facts, though they may procure fame for wit and give countenance for the assertions of party. "An endeavour has been made in the 'Provincial Letters' to prove," says Voltaire, "that the Jesuits had a design of corrupting mankind, a design," affirms the same writer, "that has never existed in any society, nor is it possible to exist." The alleged license which goes to neutralise the enjoinments of the Decalogue would have received its adequate censure from a Church that watches over with equal vigilance the integrity of morals as that of belief.

Under no qualification could Catholicity compound with iniquity to attain an end, though empires were to be the august gain. It is impossible to hope for success whilst kicking against the goads. Catholicity may allow her missionaries to assume the attire of either Turk or Brahmin, but she could no more permit them for a spiritual advantage to do reverence to the Koran, or to prostrate before the idol of twisted body and distorted feature, than she could allow the trader for a temporal profit to be false in his scales, or a merchant to be unfaithful in his contracts.

It may not be difficult indeed to cite a few examples of individuals, somewhat ceding, at home or on foreign soil, to what religion could no more countenance, though done in her name for a good, than a theft or a lie. Deception is the reverse of truth; it brought about the fall in Paradise, and could not possibly be admitted to serve a Church that was established to repair the primeval calamity. But thus it is that the imputations of Protestants upon Catholic practices, considering Catholic expositions upon Christian obligations, ever beget a difficulty that is more tasking for the assailing to master than for the assailed to prevail over. The weapon, also, which is brought down on the armour that is tempered by Heaven almost invariably glides off to the hurt of the striker. The Catholic Church is symbolised as a rock which resists the wave that would eventually undermine the loftiest of the pyramids. Here there can be no frail mingling with what admits of a speedy loosening, then a gap, and finally a ruin. Impossible it is for deceit to consort with truth, which vivifies this Church, and which under another figure is termed by a spiritual writer "the light of heaven," which can alone enlighten the mind and regulate the heart, which alone is the source of a good conscience and the terror of a bad one, which alone can inspire magnanimous thoughts and form heroic souls; it suffices to secure our love if she but manifests herself to us, and in doing so she cannot but make us known to ourselves. "Where deceit abides truth cannot dwell," and were Catholicity such a huddle of incompatibilities as she is represented to be by Protestants, her unswerving features and her unchanging voice, that are so strongly in contrast with the ever-varying tones and lineaments of her adversaries, would comprise something of the prolonged wonderment of the miracle.

Yet, after all, what is the amount of bitter animadversion upon Catholicity's upholding of deceit, and her declared confederacy with many other unholy helps, to compass some spiritual or secular purpose, in comparison with the vehement maledictions on the confessional, by otherwise almost continuously apathetic

Protestants in spiritual things? Moderate indeed. A simple-minded man now passed away, deep in Paul, deemed that as to the confessional, "confessors merited a murderer's rope on a public scaffold." This would if effectively carried out have made martyrs of confessors in the estimation of those who lived in his own admitted and unexceptionable teaching periods of uncorrupted Christianity. May he rest in peace! Nevertheless, notwithstanding the recent augmented glow in Evangelical ire upon the confessional and its unconstitutional supporters, for the information of the Apostolical yearners after Sion's unsullied purity, in the Book of Common Prayer, as to the visitation of the sick, it is thus laid down: " Here shall the sick man be moved to make a special confession of his sins if he feels his conscience troubled by any weighty matter, after which confession the priest shall absolve him (if he heartily desires it), after this sort : Our Lord Jesus Christ, who hath left power to His Church to absolve all sinners who truly repent and believe in Him, of His great mercy forgives thee thine offences, and by His authority committed to me I absolve thee in the name of the Father, the Son, and the Holy Ghost." Behold then confession with a sacred entry among the spiritual aids of Protestantism, with a direct reference to the Most High for its practice, and in the wording of this entry is implied, in order to ensure the efficiency of a confession, the necessity there is of the declaration of those sins at least, with distinctness and clearness, which according to St. Paul, as to their several and kindred natures, exclude from the kingdom of heaven. Surely in all this there ought not to be any conscientious motive for vehement dissent on the part of the consistent Protestant, who looks for something authoritative in the constitution of the Christian creed, and values the high warrant of the Sovereign that goes to determine Protestant orthodoxy and discipline in these wide realms. At the most busy time of the lopping mania of pristine reformers, confession was spared, as having an indisputable ancient record for the productiveness as well as the soundness of its fruit. Luther was at one here with ancient doctors and General Councils, as being convinced that the confessional yielded a good of something more in value than the apple of the lake that droops over the most accursed and sterile of soils. Yet what is confession with Protestants, that has only honour for its secrecy, and no power to enforce its usage, as even recently admitted in the debatings of Convocation? A term only! Just as might be expected as to a Church of adoptions that go to make up a show of Christianity, which here are "verba et præterea nihil." It is within the fertile boundaries of the Catholic Church alone that what is of Heaven's planting is not to be uprooted, and has a continuous fostering which casualty cannot frustrate or make worthless.

It is within, then, this Church that confession so amply develops the magnitude of its utility, and the sanctity of its origin, by best replying to the cry of an embarrassed and afflicted conscience, as well as a troubled and depressed mind. It has had an uninterrupted hold upon the confidence of Christendom from the earliest times, notwithstanding every misrepresentation of passion to mar its influence, or motive of interest to infringe upon its inviolability. Whose devising could this be except that of Him who preserved the silence in heaven, like unto confession's hush on earth, during the mighty conflict of His archangel with the chief opponent of His will and mercies? He has not allowed even a muttered word essentially to affect, since its institution, the holiness of its object. Several of the prominent reformers, besides inconsistent Luther, beheld with thoughtful foreboding the final dire consequences of its disuse in the lasciviousness and excesses of insubordinate multitudes. And with what force did not a prelate whose premature death made the deep affliction of an Apostolic nation, and the lively regret of Catholicity at large, describe the baneful results in the countries where its practice had been suppressed or abandoned! In referring to France on this subject, this gifted man is particularly impressive. "The fall of the chair of mercy in that country," he says, "was followed by a moral earthquake. The bridle on the heart of man was broken, and once freed from restraint it furiously rushed headlong into atrocities which no imagination could conceive nor a pen of steel describe . . . The confessional was restored to France, and on its restoration the reign of morality recommenced."[1] This providence of morals will always give a conspicuousness to the sanctity of the Catholic Church among empires, and will always prove the greatest check upon what is productive of their greatest woe—vice. Hence it has its most bitter reprobation from those who are most hardy in iniquity.

As to the requirements for confession, they are the same for the supreme Pontiff as for the child at the age when commences responsibility. When these are deliberately and wilfully failed in, as to vital matter, then mercy is forfeited, and the offending become more involved in guilt. In one of those books which at intervals are so sedulously and cheaply published to arouse the Evangelicals of this empire into increased vigilance and hatred in regard

---

[1] Dr. Maginn's Letter to Lord Stanley.

to the broad-spreading children of a Church that is characterised by unity and holiness—in which charges are revived in all their original malignity, grossness, and vindictiveness, and in which the hypocrite, the villain, and the voluptuary are clothed in the robes of the nun, the monk, and the priest—it is asserted that in the Catholic Church, the Church of the Alfreds and the Edwards, of the Wykehams and the Wainfleets, absolution from sin has its scale of prices, varying as crime may differ in a respective flagrancy. This, of course, as customary, is averred to rest upon a most detailed and unimpeachable testimony. Nevertheless, the teaching of the Catholic Church is that there can be in respect to confession no reconciliation with Infinite Justice except there be contrition for grievous sins, as also, if practicable, their plain disclosure in the confessional. "I have sinned," exclaimed David, but the contrite heart was equally required for a renewal of that friendship which adultery and murder had severed, and this could not have been realised except through the intervention of grace, which is necessary for the accomplishment of every spiritual good, and which may be obtained by the prayer that makes some approach in fervour to that of Elias in bringing down fire from heaven, but cannot be purchased by any of the glistening pieces of silver that completed the perdition of an obdurate Judas. But this unmitigated severity among Protestants generally in condemning confession, which Paganism had a consecration for in the most solemn of her rites, which Judaism had its warrant for in the inspired page, and which nature even has its sanction for in the alleviations of remorse by the disburthening of crime, may possibly have its principal source in the detailed impurity of the matter introduced into Catholic prayer and devotional books, in order to aid the memory and quicken the conscience in an examination on sin. Should this be so, it may be promptly said that if the language of the Prayer-book is open and plain, so is the Scripture, in the setting forth of criminal acts to be abhorred. The general enumeration of sins, however, in the Catholic manuals of devotion, in the enlightenment and order that it yields, at least, substantially tends to lessen the labours and solicitudes of the priest, and to give a greater security, as well as quietude, to the penitent on what is confessed.

But let the wrathful, who so unreservedly denounce any portion of the Protestant community that may somewhat favour confession, bring their chaste minds to consider the practice of examining counsel in the divorce Courts of Great Britain, and they will be speedily convinced that there is little abashment as to the questioning of either sex, as nakedly as words can well compass, that a due knowledge of the guilt or innocence of the accused may be elicited. Is there reprobation here? No, there is approbation. It is done that the ends of justice may not be frustrated, but attained. Let attention be also turned upon, as so heralded forth, the truly Christian journals of this empire and it will be felt that they are not very suppressive in their police reports as to felonious attempts or lascivious proceedings, nor is there indeed much of a startle for those otherwise susceptible readers in the perusal of indelicate details, as reported in those most circumspect journals, that are scarcely without a daily paraded malediction upon Catholic teachings and practices, especially confession, that tends in its impartings and instructions to such a restraint on passion, and to tranquillity of conscience, for a chief abomination. But Catholicity is a ceaseless foe, and must be incessantly attacked, in whatever she strenuously upholds and enforces. Hence among numbers, though having a State recognition, an aversion to days of devotion and saints' days, the rejection of fast days and days of abstinence, together with such a revolt generally as to confession. This animosity in respect to Catholic discipline is evinced also under a political consideration, for should a Catholic ruler be conspired against, seldom can the ruling imprison the rebellious without the dungeons being of black-hole dimensions and the sentinels of Janizary commiseration, whilst there is an unctuous recognition of the equity of a sentence that scatters from the cannon's mouth the body of the traitorous Sepoy over the arid plains of British India, for vultures to raven and gorge upon.

Yet, notwithstanding all that has been urged in respect to the confessional, which aids both the sinner and the saint, and has the countenance of a sovereign supremacy for its use in Protestantism, it is still exultantly and buoyantly advanced that some of the priesthood of the Catholic Church have, at comparatively recent periods, given a revolting prominence among their enumerations of the sources of Romish demoralisation to the tribunal of penance, and who finally sought to improve their perilled souls' condition "in a worship pure and undefiled"—that is, in the reformed, the revised faith. Can it, then, be sincerely credited that among the motives which determined the above to take such a step as that of entering within the assuring precincts of Protestant spirituals, the iniquity of the confessional was the predominant impulse? Considering the testifications of history, it may perhaps, without rashness, be affirmed that as to the greater part of sacerdotal recedings from Rome, what was carnal, rather than what was spiritual, obtained a mastery over the heart—in other words, that the joys of Martin Luther were more affected than the raptures of St. Paul. Dean Swift had in general a very strong suspicion in regard to the transfer of clerical allegiance from Rome to Canterbury, that virtue had ceased in the ordained of Catholicity when credence in Protestantism commenced. At least, St. Patrick's renowned Dean did not wish his garden to be encumbered and disfigured with unsightly mounds, by the occasional weedy flingings of His Holiness over his wall. An enlightened and a sanguine lord,[1] with the solicitude of Churches upon him, must once have deeply felt the poignancy of the foregoing words, proceeding, too, from so shrewd a commentator upon men and manners, when a calamitous blight came upon his hopes as to a wide harvest of souls in fair yet, as considered, perverted Italy, through the mission there of some denounced foreign priests, who very speedily evinced, under forms as criminal as reckless, that they did not preserve chastity or righteousness with the rigorous conviction of a St. Antony or a St. Benedict.

But if the confessional has had its ignominious brandings, through those even who formerly sat therein to dispense its infinite mercies to the sincere and the contrite, it so happens that at this period it has its

---

[1] Lord Shaftesbury.

fervid sanctions and its wide employment with those that afford some substance and weight to Protestantism. They have, however, for so conscientiously acting, the censures and the frowns upon them of the many among Protestants, and especially of those through whose high administrative spiritual offices the Book of Common Prayer can, with any certainty, carry out some of its principal injunctions. What confidence can there be then in the religion of the lofty in episcopal titles, who for the most part scowl upon and condemn an educated and Conservative class of Protestants for putting into practice what is formally detailed forth as of an imperative Christian obligation, in pages where the consciences of the reformed belief are, it may be presumed, to be impressed with what most surely tends to their Christian improvement and to their Christian safety—who, indeed, morally repudiate teachings and duties backed by sovereign authority, and prescribed as essential, in thwarting their influence and their exercise? Let those reply who read well, who think well, and who pray well. They must, at least, conceive that all is at hazard where the earnest and the observing are opprobriously discountenanced, even by the Legislature, in what the first reformers registered as orthodox, and as a preservative of and an incentive to devotion. What a fiction of a Church is here disclosed, and what fearful conclusions there ought to be with the reflecting on the "one faith and the one baptism," with the years of eternity in their minds! However, it is just here to observe that the Church which entitles herself Catholic as well as Christian can have no more recognition for a sanctuary that upholds so largely her teachings and adopts her rites, yet rejects her authority, than sympathy for the one where the contending lion and the unicorn figurative of dogmatical strife are more conspicuous than crucifix or apostle, and where the habiliments of the officiating retain, as with doctrine, a mere vestige of ancient vestments. This Catholic as well as Christian Church, it is to be added, is not Romanism, a term which comprises in its Protestant purport an assimilation to the mingle within the witches' cauldron of the foul and the deadly to compass very ungodly ends. Her discipline lies not at a guess or a will, its dogma is not with the shifting opinions of a people, or the construction put on it by a Government to suit a more illumined period. She is identified with what never alters, and heaven and earth will one day testify to her ever-consistent united mission.

Yet it is not intended here to represent Protestantism with any set purpose of bringing about that wide doctrinal indifference and general tepidity in religious works to which divisions in a Christianity without authority so inevitably lead. Among Protestants in Great Britain the observance of the Sunday is conspicuously edifying, and under this head Christian decorum could hardly be surpassed. The quiet in the streets on this sacred day, the demeanour of the people, and the reverential bearing of assembled congregations, must impress upon the minds of foreigners that whatever difference there may be in doctrinal professions, at least under a common religious aspect there is uniformity. Many however amongst such a concentration of varied sects are far from thinking that the Sunday here has yet its due and holy keeping. But reproach on the part of these is sustained by little good sense, as with them it is desecration of the Lord's Day to run up an accidental rent, or to rinse out a tea-cup. This is to task the service of the Most High with all the mischievous extremes of a scrupulous and an infatuated Israelite. Yet these excesses are not to be wondered at, since private judgment has such an indefinite and unrestricted freedom in these domains. It would be truly surprising that there should be so much absurdity in doctrines and not considerable excess in observances, as the million can speak with the right of the mitre upon the latter as well as the former. In reference to this subject of devoutly honouring the Sunday, should one Catholic country be especially referred to, where that day is little distinguished from an ordinary day, through an unchecked liberty of trading, employment, and theatrical amusements, an answer is to be found in the difficulties existing with the authorities in the enforcement of a salutary restriction. The lengthened rule of infidelity of the past in France, that made it patriotism to oppose every dictate of Christianity, has rendered it almost impossible within this occasionally most fickle and often disturbed of countries when under well-disposed Christian rulers, or through Christian prelates, either by edict or pastoral to repair or withstand the consequences of revolutionary doings and Deistical enactings. Not even for a few hours can a pause be effected in the din of labour along the broadways of commerce on the sacredly appointed term of rest, and it would be futile to think to close the theatres against a spectacle-seeking and for the many a volatile people on the day that Christianity is emphatically called upon " to keep holy." To connect, however, profaneness with every species of recreation on the Sunday has never been contemplated by the Catholic Church. She who is as considerate in rule as definite in precept has not exposed her administration to unnecessary difficulty by forbidding what may be beneficial and innocent according to the discreetness or purpose of the Christian. On this subject our Redeemer did not escape censure, and in the reply of nfinite Wisdom the Catholic Church has learnt how to qualify her sacred ordinances, and to temper them to circumstances. In prudence virtue has always had her safest guide, and avoided many a path of peril and embarrassment.

To what has been said on the keeping of the Sunday here might be added the strict religious education that is given in many Protestant homes in this land, and to this may be readily joined a steady munificence in the substantial support of institutions which check the progress of calamity among thousands, and yield a prompt and an effective succour and help to the unfortunate, the needy, and the afflicted. Benevolence in this empire may be said to be as extensive in its consequences as it is varied in its objects. But in admitting the preceding, which is strictly due to Protestantism, heroism in Christian works will he rarely hers to record. Her education, though commonly it begets reverence for what is sacred, and religious staidness, is not at all calculated to stimulate to the practices of the saints. It is, indeed, of a very brief character as to references in her historic books, as also those of instruction, in regard to what appertains to exalted virtues and heroic deeds. So largely has she prescinded from readings of this nature, which conferred on them at early times among the Catholic faithful an interest next to that of the perusal of the inspired Word, that churches and also streets named after saints and martyrs, the renowned of early ages, that edified and died for Christianity, would be as little known to thousands as now is the reverse. And whence did the custom emanate of thus designating church and street by the names of those who gave their lives for their faith, or in dying to themselves gave to it life? It came from the exercise of Catholic wisdom and piety, whence alone they could come to perpetuate the memory of those who fought unto death the good fight with the ardour of an apostle, and of those who, if they did not die for the faith, edified Christendom in the perfect practice of its virtues. In this designation of streets especially the busy and the indulgent world was to be reminded of " the one thing necessary," and of the necessity of self-control, whilst traversing the thronged highways in pursuit of gain or pleasure. But, in fact, what is there, without any intention to detract from that which has been just conceded, in Protestantism of original and independent excellence for the sure furtherance of a spiritual good? Little. Almost entirely what there is of sufficiency as to wisdom in a canon to promote discipline, or unction in a prayer to elevate devotion, may be traced, even as the most efficient of charitable institutions in Great Britain now exclusively under Protestant administration to that Church which comprises in her ordinances the experience of ages, and in her petitions to the Most High the words of those who enlightened Christendom by their instructions and edified it by their works. But as to the above fact, without a fixity of creed, which conserves reverence for the subject-matter of an ancient collect, and extends vitality to the acts of an ecclesiastical ruling, Protestantism, in this retention of some venerable things, cannot derive from their use the solid and continuous effectiveness of Catholicity. This must ever be otherwise with the Church which will be discovered to be as uniform in ceremonies and rites as unfailing in precepts and perfections. It is for her alone also to preserve and continue the record in history of the sedulously proven miracle that evinces the heroism of the sanctity which proceeds from her faith, as well as what she canonises on earth is crowned in heaven.

The miracle! This, at the present time, is held in derision by the greater part of erudite and scientific Protestants. There may be, indeed, a respect for piety, and some deference for Gospel teaching, but that at the bidding of any Christian, however distinguished by fervent faith and heroic virtue, the dead arose and the blind saw, though supported in its possibility by the attesting of inspiration, the cry is with the petulance and obstinacy of St. Thomas,

"I will not believe!" Their creed is that the established laws of nature are superior to every evidence, though it may even be physically conclusive, in regard to their particular suspension; thus with them a well-authenticated miracle is something of a dexterous and successful juggle. This rejection of the supernatural, with whatever testimony it may be confirmed, goes to bring entire distrust upon every averment. It interferes with every test to decide the value of what is affirmed, and affects what is asserted in the natural as well as in the supernatural order. You are unwisely incredulous with the contemners of the supernatural if you do not assent to what, in their estimation, ought to carry conviction, and you are foolishly credulous if, under the same testimonies, though under other relationships, you yield a credence. It is, indeed, the old story on their part, the shifting of a difficulty without obviating it. " Miracles," observes Pascal, " must have had a being, or false ones could not have an existence, as there could not have been false religions without a true one." [1]

But whilst admitting this reasoning, it might be urged that this gives rise to a difficulty to be overcome, inasmuch as one supernatural wonder might command

---

[1] Pensées de Pascal.

such an amount of evidence on the side of perversity and error as to defeat the purpose of another in favour of orthodoxy and morality. The Egyptian magicians matched in the marvellous the miracle of Moses. But there is wherewith here to obviate the difficulty, for in the contention in prodigies the mastery remained with the hand that penned the belief and the duties of the Jewish people. The Almighty, to whom it is as easy to interfere with the laws of nature as it is impossible for Him to countenance falsehood by what is supernatural, is sure to have a final and obvious triumph over the instantaneous magic of man, or rather the permitted malicious efforts of the demons, as in the final contest in the heavens, and thus to make victory more evident and supreme for Omnipotence. Profane as well as sacred history testifies that all eventually cedes to the visible sovereignty of His will, in succeeding conflicts with truth, who in His dealings with the children of Israel, while conducting them into the promised land, employed the waters of the earth in opening a way for the march of His providence, as also empires, in employing them as instruments to forward His holy ends. When circumstances have apparently demanded it as strongly as in the days of the Apostles, the dead have arisen in primeval vigour, the blind have been enraptured by immediate sight, and the crippled have at once bounded into exulting activity. These have had a place in the pagan lands that St. Francis Xavier and others have traversed in the propagation of Christianity, and are formally witnessed to by the executive of governments, as likewise by the voices of populations. In the publication of the old law, says Fléchier very pertinently, God desired to control by wonders a race given to idolatry, and to induce them to recognise their Creator. In establishing His Gospel, He sought through the same medium to bring about a credence in His mysteries, that are so much above the powers of nature and the practice of what was so strongly opposed to natural inclinations, whilst manifesting that He was not less the Sovereign Legislator of men than the Master of nature herself. In the exercise of all this He continues to make known, in the confusion of pretensions, His One Holy Catholic and Apostolic Church, and under the most valid of testimonies that can ensure the convictions of mankind.

And here it may be appropriately observed, in respect to those who admit only the miracles set forth in the inspired records, that at this early period, when the Ottoman banner in a sacred temple has had its honour equally with that of the Christian knight, it would require but little of the bold and adroit logic of those who reject miracles altogether to induce them to confound the Revelations of St. John in worth with the visions of Mahomet. How often has this been lamentably evinced in those who have read with enthusiasm the writings of the infidel, without much fear for the consequences to their exceedingly qualified belief! The resolve has been by many taken at last to abide by the infidel writers. Intellect now with them is everything, and religion is scarcely secondary in influence. Nature now imparts rectitude to the passions, and makes of virtue a chimera. The profoundly intelligent and the robust of heart have finally few startles at an eternity, and few fears of an omniscient eye. They are at peace with themselves, and have no misgivings about their sublime indefinables, that are to better humanity far beyond the dictates of religion. When they come to their last moments, the calm of their convictions is not to be disturbed. They will eventually, such is their consoling credence, lie in their graves with the same future as the cattle that crop untroubled the grass above their perishing remains.

Yet, here might it not be asked, do not the stern and uncompromising mental restrictions of the Catholic Church tend to bring about the great calamity of man freethinking that affects so seriously both moral and doctrinal matters? Certainly not. Catholicity has no injudicious narrowings upon the mind to limit her expansions, as the straitened and pent-up course of a river for a purpose, and thus in this constraining of her powers to put herself to the hazard of some final outburst of overwhelming ruin. She has her restrictions, but they are not impediments. She excepts from such an unbounded liberty of way as would lead into interminable disasters. The mind, in some respects, is to be dealt with as the body, should what is sought be pernicious in its nature. If man is created little inferior to the angels, according to the Royal Prophet, it is reason which gives him the near and sublime approach to beings whose refulgence is in the reflected glory of their Creator, and whose felicity is in the contemplation of His ineffable attributes. Never did the Catholic Church, by her decrees, interfere with this provident, protective, and ennobling faculty in its rightful exercise. She must have a profound interest in the salutary action of reason, which makes man the fitting subject of her sacred dispensations, and which is worthy to brighten in the rays of Divine grace. It is not, therefore, with Catholicity, a despotism, again to be repeated, that will not permit reason to widen her information in science and art, in order, as affirmed, that every fond and enthusiastic averment as to extravagant teachings, extraordinary deeds, and supernatural events may have an unhesitating and unreserved assent. She is a religion that has her constitution in sound principles, and the assiduous attainments of man upon their comprised details are next to the revealments of Heaven, the effective medium through which she obtains for herself dominion and submission, reverence and affection. If the Catholic Church does most imperatively exercise a Divinely conferred prerogative of prohibiting, it is when especially an attempt is made to discuss what she has decided through her guaranteed Divine illuminations, from which reason emanates, to be a truth, or when reason is forced on an inquiry in the world of inspiration, which, considering the vastness of the subject, she is totally inadequate to compass, and the usurped liberty of doing so for the purpose of arriving at the complete knowledge of what is beyond mere human comprehension has almost invariably terminated, whatever may have been the speciousness of first essays, in bewilderment, bereavement, or infidelity. Were the assent to her religious truths exclusively dependent upon the entire comprehension of them through reason the infinity involved in them would make conviction an impossibility.

From all this, in other words, it may be readily deduced that Catholicity never insists upon a halt in the paths of life. She has her forbiddings on the entering upon those devious ways that have their fitful tracing in the gleaming Will-o'-the-Wisp, whose followings finish in almost sure calamity. She is always ready to excite emulation, yet not without a salutary caution. Practical knowledge judiciously selected, and solidly attained, vivifies the man, and the good which has God for its end in the expansion of truth always has its sublime and enduring profits. But let the plain question be put, what was history before the Reformation as to her entries of science, art, and general learning, under their several aspects? Was it comparatively a blank? No, the reverse. And he who will not believe it without enumerations, details, and references, may not have read history yet if otherwise, like a child just out of spelling, unable to comprehend a single narrated fact. Record as to the above subject-matter of immediate consideration will be found to have had her best furnishing from Catholicity, that has ever been learning's chief refuge in peril, as it has been her chief promoter in first advances. She is the patroness of science and art, as well as truth and holiness. In regard to the former, her missionaries, in the midst of savage hordes and idolatrous multitudes, have found in their diversified and interesting details an eventual attention for teachings of which the philosopher would never have heard if Heaven had not spoken. All was light to him who prayed for wisdom, and whose head was wreathed with the glory of the God of Israel, at the dedication of His holy temple. Catholicity under any circumstances will not falter in that intrepidity which she displayed during the edicts of a Julian, when her schools were in equal danger with her Churches, nor in that munificence that has founded the most renowned colleges in Christendom. In the lecture-halls, and in the almost priceless stocked emporiums of the world, Catholicity, in her informations and contributions, will be discovered to be most happy and numerous. In the former science will be ascertained to have a most developed and conclusive teaching from those who firmly believe with Leo XIII., the present Pontiff, whilst as to the latter there will not be presented to the eye anything that Catholicity does not match in wonder and utility.

Enter the vast crystal construction, itself a marvel, which encloses the copies and models of the most prized labours and works of man, both as to modern and ancient times—of man, who is to be seen here in his most savage state, in his first scanty covering, with his uncouth spear and his fetid hut, inferior in its framing to the housing of the instinctive beaver. Let Protestants who ever lustily proclaim Catholicity to be an enslaver of the human intellect consider well what they behold here, which, in the studied disposition of things according to the gradual advancing excellence of man in time, so sublimely witnesses to the grandeur of his nature unto the present evolutions of his genius and felicity of his immediate condition; let the most enthusiastic among their number for the dignity and the welfare of humanity be at last satisfied with what he here beholds, even under a cursory view; supposing on a sudden, if it were possible, everything vanished of Catholic creation, and nought remained but what was of pure Protestant origin, all then would comparatively appear as a blank to the eye, like in the language of Addison, " upon the finishing of some secret spell, a fantastic scene breaks up, and a disconsolate knight finds himself on a barren heath." Little indeed would remain for the admiration of the gifted, or the information of the learned. In all this it must be deeply felt by those who are open to conviction that the Catholic faith includes no hindrance to the completion of a good, and has no interdict upon reason within her own legitimate realms, nor is there a fear with Catholicity that as reason makes her acquisitions there will be a diminishing in credence as to her doctrines. No intellectual advancement that has been made or may be made will necessarily as declared shake conviction in her tenets. Her teachings are not subordinate to the elucidations of schools. A widening knowledge may continuously add to undisputed principles, but Catholicity will not thereby be

L

constrained to alter her formal definitions, since the latter will be discovered to be not less true than the former. Nor do her approved divines talk vaguely, that they may have a refuge in perplexity. In support of what has just preceded a distinguished writer may here be aptly quoted: " What axioms are to science, dogma is to theology. As there can be no science without fixed principles and primary certainties, so there can be no knowledge of God nor of His revelations without fixed and primary truths. Such are the doctrines of faith delivered to us by the perpetual and the Divine office of the Church. The intellect of man is feeble and vacillating until it has certain scientific principles to start from. These once given it acquires firmness and power of advance. One truth scientifically proved becomes the basis of many. The physical sciences, each in their kind, are proofs of this. The same is true in the science of God. The truths of the natural order are confirmed and perfected by revelation. On the basis of natural truths rests, by the disposition, the order of revealed truths, such as the Holy Trinity, the Incarnation, the Church and its supernatural endowments. The horizon of the human reason is therefore expanded by revelation, and reason elevated above its natural powers, and in this both its freedom and perfection are secured."[1]

---

[1] Cardinal Manning.

Yet reason, under doctrinal considerations, must be determined, as to be inferred from what has preceded, by a proven Divinely instituted authority, that can alone free from all difficulty upon the truths which she sets forth. Reason, in her full sway and matured excellence, as so deemed at an Augustine period, came to very sorry conclusions on the belief as well as the duty of man. In these free Christian days of the many, the judgment of unconstrained self has been equally productive of what is immoral as of what is impious in matters appertaining to creed and sanctity, consequent upon that authority being prescinded from that is identified with Him, under the most supreme of evidences, who said, "Without Me you can do nothing." Reason can never discern distinctly, in contemplating the supernatural, without that light from above which exceeds in vividness and worth what flashed into existence at the bidding of the Creator. St. Paul, with all his genius and learning, could never have attained to that knowledge in which his raptures were constituted, except through what came down upon the Apostles, and illumined the soul as well as inflamed the heart. If we could bring all things within the compass of reason, "then our religion," declares Pascal, "would have nothing in it mysterious or supernatural, and at the same time, if we violate the principles of reason, our religion would be absurd and ridiculous."

But it is almost useless thus to urge in defence of Catholicity, which Protestantism stoutly affirms to be in conflict with reason, and to be a Christianity that has passed from truth into falsehood. Her members, nurtured for the most part in misrepresentation and enmity, cannot bring themselves to become better acquainted with the merits of Catholicity, by listening to the statements of the traduced and the vilified, in the place of the allegements and fictions of their passions and prejudices. "*Audi alteram partem*" (hear the other side), is a widely-known saying, and in no courts of law among civilised nations is it so well responded to as in those of this land. Within this empire, in acting up to the above maxim with patience and fidelity, in despite of every influence and position, in all justiciary matters, protection is extended to the character of the most lowly as well as the most exalted, and the consequences of precipitancy, bias, hatred, malice, dishonesty, and mob delusions are in a great measure defeated. Did Protestantism, instead of musing and fuming over its own party averments, thus, as in the halls of judicature in this land, act towards Catholicity, it would be found that there was nothing of a defective or of a preposterous nature in her formal proceedings; they would learn that her principles are varied phases of truth which furnish in the legitimate deductions therefrom a warranty for all her decisions and ordinances; whether they might refer to dogma or science, they would ascertain that she has no benedictions for what is despicable, nor adorations for what is not Divine; they would discover that the sign of the Cross, the ready indication to sects of the presence of the Catholic faith at this immediate hour, as also of the primitive martyr's Apostolic Creed when speechless on the strained rack, was never employed in anything unworthy of Him who hallowed it by His death; they would know that indulgences are not the priced mercies of heaven which obdurate criminal opulence could alone well purchase, and so loll out life with the serenity of a Dives, without a fear for the future, but only a considerate remission in the temporal punishment remaining due to Infinite Justice, after the pardon of sin through a sincere confession and a due contrition in the sacrament of penance; they would, in fine, come to understand that she who is recorded in the Scripture as the mother of God, and yet whose praise makes commonly instant controversy with Protestants, is revered, not adored, in the Church that was founded in the blood of Jesus Christ, which had its source in the immaculate heart of her that inspiration terms blessed, and whose name is to constitute the reverential eulogy of future generations. And let the intelligent and inquiring Protestant, after a close and unbiassed investigation into the alleged superstitions, usages, and corruptions of Catholicity, direct an impartial and searching eye towards the numerous sects of the day, who father upon Infinite Wisdom their vagaries and their follies as the sound import of His holy word, and how quickly will he behold conspicuous matter for a sigh or for a lament! How speedily will he behold many stepping out from among these myriads with the importance of self-assurance, who recognise " a Christian ministry," not as a priesthood but as a pastorate, whose office is not to offer sacrifice, or to perform sacramentarian miracles, but to teach—what? To deny " old truths and to teach new ones." " To sap a solemn creed with solemn sneer." Finally, the language of abomination is the issue of all this audacity, and thus does its appalling utterance ascend to the heavens, " The God who would only rescue from sin at the price of another's suffering is the worst of all false gods, inasmuch as this is the lowest abasement below the common level of human goodness yet reached." Yet it is in the mystery of the Redemption, so prominent in love, that the Almighty, says St. Paul, in His Divine wisdom, contrived to reconcile the excess of His goodness with the interests of His justice. However, no dire consequences are to be apprehended from what is so lauded when boldly outspoken by the so-styled well-informed, and occasionally cheered by a miscellaneous assembly. But certainly, at these immediate times, in reference to freedom of opinion at large, it must be felt that the direst of results must be consequent upon the wide diffusion of those captious, anti-religious works published by men who would indeed be, for a purpose, rather hailed as Christian than infidel, yet, however, have small credence in a dogma, and about the same measure of obedience for a precept, who take more interest in the star that twinkles in the tail of the Great Bear than what gleamed upon the stable of Bethlehem, and who would much prefer to place a philosopher on a pedestal than add a saint to the calendar. It is this sacredly prized liberty of self-thinking and of self-judging, that has eventually brought about such tepidity and so great a dwindle in belief with many, as also such a scantiness of consideration for the decalogue, that though Christianity is sometimes decorously affected, it might be very well doubted whether the strict Mahometan, with his beads and Alcoran, with his prophet and God, would be superseded in earnestness and devotional works and sincerity of credence.

Nevertheless there is not a startle at all this, but

only at the progress of Catholicity, which is not only pronounced to be an enslaver of the intellect, as just in detail disproved, but also heralded forth as despotic in her principles among kingdoms and nations. The historians who have best succeeded in manifesting her to be worse than the first foes of Christianity, in stripes, racks, fires, torments, and fetid dungeons, are most known among Protestants as being most trusted and thus most read. Tyranny, in its wide acceptation, is a flagrant interference with the natural or common rights of humanity, and which employs what is best at her disposal to force those within her control into submission to her will and decrees, that are as oppressive as degrading. But this cannot be made to fit in with the rulings, provisions, and practices of the Catholic Church. She has, as already amply detailed, a demonstrated charity for her chief virtue which must secure for her some countenance, some assurance in the uttering of a direct contradiction to the imputed charge of tyranny in her regard. Actuated as she is by a fervid zeal, and so indisputably displayed in her varied beneficent institutions and her considerate discipline, it is no less impossible for her to condemn without compassion than to decree without reflection. Her disposition of things in daily administrations could not well be made to consort with deeds of injustice or oppression. To be opposed in act to what realises a confiding influence would be continually to raise or aggravate a difficulty in her ruling. As to the headings of her testamentary instruments, they are pervaded by a tone that is not in dissonance with the voice of Him who chided when supplicated to destroy. Her strenuous action must comprise the compassing of some broad and solid good, or humanity would have had its revolt. With salutary authority, as history abundantly confirms, she has withstood both princes and people, and admonished and censured when either side was grievously in the wrong or oppressively aggressive. Her sacred ministers are the medium of communication between the two great divisions of society, and one of the principal inculcations in their ecclesiastical forming is, that mercy should ever be prominent in all their sacerdotal ministrations, as it is among the attributes of that God who deputed them to win, to reform, to aid, and to save. Indeed, within the Catholic Church there are express exceptions made to those, as to their entering into the sacerdotal state without a dispensation, who from the circumstances of their own or their parents' calling are likely to be callous upon what quickens the sympathies of life, or repulsively rugged in ordinary intercourse with their fellow-men. But notwithstanding all that may be advanced, how eager are Protestants to renew their several charges in proof of tyranny, and prominently among the number the establishment of the Inquisition as a contradiction to the affirmed paternal character of Catholicity! As to the above it may be promptly granted that the patronage of high spiritual authority was extended to its use, but not to its abuse. The chief object of establishing the Inquisition was to check the progress of heresy and infidelity, that were productive of sad calamities in the State as well as the Church. If there was a suspicious secrecy in its proceedings it had its close counterpart under this consideration in the judicial arrangements of several of the reformed States, and perhaps in this country the orderings and the doings of the members of the Star Chamber, that were not much abashed by Magna Charta definitions, furnished a somewhat near resemblance to the revolting proceedings of the alleged tyranny of the Inquisition.

However, with regard to many of the averred deeds that have a most studied prominence in the horrors of history, secretly perpetrated within deep, damp, foul, and gloomy dungeons, upon the enlightened, the philanthropic, the patriotic, and the maligned, they are, for the most part, inventions to suit a purpose, somewhat analogous to those outward, grim embellishments of a few of the gaols of this land, that have not a very close correspondence with the actual appointments within their monotonous and sturdily spiked walls. At periods, it is not to be denied, of an unquiet and audacious character, when increasing and frenzied sects, in the early times of the Reformation, were continually plotting and striving to decree from thrones as well as to dictate from pulpits, when protracted wars had made a dissimilar mingle among populations, and endless conspiracies were to be thwarted only by the most stern and prompt measures, the Inquisition, which was introduced into several kingdoms at the instance of their respective rulers, occasionally did strike a blow which excited indignation as well as spread consternation. But it was never inflicted at the signal from the anointed; on the contrary, for the most part, it will be found that their words were tempered with mercy on delivering up to the secular power the convicted to be punished for their crimes, their treasons, or their blasphemies. The Inquisition was not set up like a French revolutionary tribunal, for slaughters and seizures, but for safety and correction. However, even the ghastly recitals of a Limborch, in his history of the Inquisition, have not gone beyond, in agonising and deadly inflictions, the collected records of the martyred missionaries in England by the abours of a Challoner. Thus, if in some lands in which the Inquisition was established, the turn of the wheel upon the doomed, at the bidding of the executive, has given instant birth to a pang that has at once overspread the features of the writhing with the livid hue of death, it has been equalled by the up-ripping knife at Tyburn, and probably the disembowelling of men, whilst nearly in the full pulse of life, was seldom if ever practised at the most wanton of human sacrifices among the encircling and prancing savages of Owhyhee or Atooi.

If the constitution of things which exists among religious orders be examined into, as well as the general discipline of the Catholic Church, it will be readily seen that provisions are made to prevent tyranny, as also to ensure obedience; and not unfrequently it occurs that a superior obtains his position through the unfettered suffrage of the community which he edified by his prudence and charity before he was elected to govern and to instruct. The canon laws too of Catholicity are thoughtfully founded in the sedulous adjustments of the administrative experience of ages for the permanent well-being of her ecclesiastical government. They give as carefully a defined right as intricate matter will permit of, and cautiously provide against its vicious abuse. The chief severity of their action falls upon what is criminal in conduct or contumacious in discipline.

Nor is this, when it has a place under the most

stern form, to be deemed oppressive, since the laws of the Church, as the laws of a State, in which the latter owes so much to the former in the wisdom of their framing, would have but little efficiency if there was not included in them, to arrest disorders and correct the perverse, some adequate penalty and punishment. These ecclesiastical laws, that are held in such revered estimation for their extended existence, and the prudent matter they comprise to sustain faith and protect morals, not only provide against the exercise of arbitrary rule, but baffle in a great measure the embarrassings of caprice and the efforts of clique, that are almost as mischievous in their results as the acts of despotism and vindictiveness. And what is the privilege of Catholic Synods? The right to speak out, and to speak out boldly, upon the subject-matter under discussion, either to correct a grievance or promote a good. In a legitimate yet in a respectful freedom of expression the wise even have often learnt their best lessons, and the devout have preserved themselves from many indiscretions. Under this heading the saint as well as the historian have spoken without disguise upon the proceedings of prelates and princes, yet this did not prevent the canonisation of the former, nor lead to an entry in the Roman Index of the writings of the latter. So much for the asserted illiberal and tyrannical character of Catholicity. Yet it must be acknowledged that he who is very expert in coupling cross-readings together may adroitly clip out from decrees, pastorals, and encyclical letters some passages which, when prescinded from subsequent or foregoing words, would present the front of arbitrary dealing. But are these warrants for triumph? Can any subtle and unfavourable construction put upon them maintain a general imputation? Could this patchwork be Catholic system? Tyranny could never conserve any protracted existence within the nicely attempered enactments of Catholic ecclesiastical polity without giving rise to protestations which would satisfactorily prove that the presence of tyranny has not made or upheld a despotic spiritual ruler. To act as a tyrant and to counsel as a father must necessarily be of short duration.

With the usual hasty asperity of unread or perverse prejudice it is also declared that she is unceasingly conspiring to dominate over nations, and to bring them into subserviency to her pretentious claims, and in the existing temper of many at these immediate moments, especially those of Protestant Germany, such a charge is strenuously insisted on, and preeminently so by those in power, who little trouble themselves about the consciences of others, since they are little scared by their own. Yet it is well to meet it in a first reply as to the alleged absolute, despotic, and monopolising character of Catholicity by adverting to the conduct of Pius the Ninth in 1848. At this period ominous forebodings were rife on every side, and furnished serious matter for the solicitous reflections of the Ministerial advisers of the chief rulers of Europe. Cities of the most influential character had their placards and their meetings in order to defeat enactments that went by revising and suppressing, as vehemently set forth by men that headed meandering and shouting mobs, to reduce millions into a condition that was little superior in advantages to the lot of a negro. The sovereign who should be most expeditious and ample in his concessions was to be the idol of his people and the model for all within his anointed rank. His name was at once to become pre-eminently illustrious among the most renowned benefactors of his kingdom and of humanity. The monument that was to be elevated to his memory, like the most sublime of the Pyramids, was to defy the earthquake's shock and to resist the undermining of time. Pius the Ninth, to the astonishment of deeply misconceiving Protestantism, so replied in the ministrations of his territories to the representations of the many as to stimulate the most Conservative of princes, as well as to induce the most conciliatory, to respond in some signal respects to the loud cry of the hour. But assassinations, pillages, and widening demands, as likewise desperate onslaughts upon the reasonable and the peaceable, readily evinced the patriotic character of the greater part of the vociferous and the wrecking in the furtherance of the cause of mankind, and marred the benevolent intent of what was conceded, which, if co-operated with sincerely and persistently, might have been a country's blessing. Liberty is not an unbounded licence, which, in its extremes, becomes the worst of calamities. It is for the subject and the sovereign to possess such a share of independent action that right may be confidently defended or maintained on either side. Acting on this view of things, the benevolence of Pius the Ninth did not clash with his conscience. But just weights and measures did not satisfy all within his domains, and thickening demands, with increasing outrages on any delay in concession, demonstrated to common sense that further compliances would not induce the reckless and the depraved to roll up their flaunting, gaudy banners and disperse in peace to their homes. Soon had Pius the Ninth to flee from the Eternal City which he had so often paternally blessed, warned to do so by the murder of his chief minister, and by rattling shot within his own palace walls. A man remained in his place for the salvation of Rome, who had ready epithets for Christianity in " cheat," " swindle," and "imposture." In arms finally against his subsequently proclaimed King of Italy, being struck by a bullet, he was nearly taken off in the midst of his blasphemies. However, much to the deep affliction of his then anointed master, he survived the injury. He still lives, yet not to turn the Tiber, and spread fertility over pestilential wastes, but revile those who have any conspicuous reverence for religion, without being himself valued by any one of influential position in a present Sardinian administration for a single stable good.

In further reference to what has gone before in the recorded judgment of many that senates have listened to for guidance, it is better that a Government should exist with grievances that might be termed even oppressive than that facile reform should give rise to unstaid and levelling factions, which are much worse than arbitrary and oppressive rulings. Those who thus think and weigh things well ere they designate with opprobrious terms old administrations will doubtless readily admit the justness of the following observations: "People," says a writer quoted by Feller,[1] "cannot well conceive what danger there arises to a State in suffering men without authority, and often with little capacity, to declaim right or

---

[1] Dictionnaire Historique.

wrong against received usages and ancient institutions, to cry down what has every claim to respect, and to trample upon every principle under the specious pretext of doing away with excessive abuses and senseless prejudices. The public at large, ever greedy for novelties, ever disposed to confound temerity and audacity with genius and experience, ever the dupe of emphatic words and charlatan promises, easily persuades itself that men who judge and condemn with so much assurance have superior views, and that their ancestors were not possessed of common sense. By these proceedings of political regenerators is the public often carried away, and they are the more dangerous as they are generally of a novel character, and what calamity does there not result from them to a nation?" Nothing could be more directly to the point upon the foregoing subject, and it may be unhesitatingly affirmed that here Catholic sentiment readily blends with what comprises such sound sense, and is confirmed by such lengthened experience. Nevertheless, sound sense, with the additional testification of lengthened experience, argues and urges in vain, as, when an opportune occasion presents itself, the wild and turbulent enthusiasm of visionaries will be continually incited by those who, generally speaking, are far more sentient upon private gains than public interests. It is with these that Catholicity, the unvarying providence of kingdoms and nations, cannot, with any confidence, make any association, and therefore she is unceasingly in many unquiet States maligned and execrated. She is not able to ally herself with tumult, which compliance can never tranquillise whilst man is under the counselling of passion. She can have no federalism with secret societies under oath, which might, in certain circumstances, prefer their respective politics and decisions to the statutes and ordinations of States, undismayed by the array of troops and Christian denouncings. Nevertheless she, who in her belief and her hierarchy gave birth to Magna Charta, could not have much aversion to rational amendments which are not sweeping reforms. She can countenance also and respect, what the celebrated Dr. Doyle sets forth in his able letter to the Marquis of Wellesley, "every established institution that is not opposed to the laws of nature." "In Poland," continues the same writer, "Catholicity supported an elective monarch; in France, an hereditary sovereign; in Spain, an absolute or a constitutional king indifferently. In England, when the Houses of York and Lancaster contended, she could lend her authority to the declaration that he who was King *de facto* was entitled to the confidence and submission of the people. Under the above several varied forms of government people were to give ready obedience, both as to their laws and their rulings complete and undivided." The oath that was pronounced loyal in this empire, and had to be taken before entering the Senate House by the emancipated Catholics, made no scruple for them at the communion-rail, nor did the thoughts of it cause a shudder in the closing moments of life. In being loyal on earth they did not forfeit their fidelity to Heaven. But often nothing will silence the sophistry of delusion, prejudice, and hatred, though what is adduced may be as potent as the sayings of Solomon. Catholicity has an inspired mission to fulfil, and it is from her imparted truths, and the duties and obligations, again in substance to be repeated, arising therefrom, that all sound legislation has derived its principal information, and the most efficacious means of enforcing its enactments. In this no trenching upon righteous claims to secure wealth, and no monopolising of power to oppress, will be detected to upbraid her with, from whose hand the scales of justice have their best poise, and which weighs with the certitude of the One that inscribed on the walls of the palace of the sacrilegious and blaspheming Balthazar his deficiency and his doom.

SECTION IV.

It may now be fitting to advert to an ancient title that has hitherto been assumed for a Church in these pages which exclusively appropriates it to herself, as being best able to make out her claim during ages to unity and sanctity. It was by the term Catholic that the primitive martyrs of Christianity, who had the disciples of the Apostles for their masters, designated their spiritual mother, and no other term could be better adapted to make abortive the endeavour of heresy to identify herself with orthodoxy under the wide denomination of Christian. The Fathers subsequent to these early periods have ever demonstrated the providence comprised within this designation of orthodoxy, by its effectually defeating the pretensions of the heretical to a right of membership through the common appellation of Christian with the Church of Christ, whether as to asserting Ebonites or Marcionites, that were ever met with these explicit words: "Christian is my name, Catholic is my surname. By the former I am called, by the latter I am distinguished." No subtle advancement has hitherto effectually interfered with the just assumption of the above definitive distinction by the Church of ages and nations, and laid open sacred ground to be trodden on at will by the devious and adventurous feet of those who in multitudes indignantly insist that there ought to be nothing exclusive in Christianity which it does not admit of, as being founded by Him who rejected no one by dying for all. But the epithet of Catholic, that discriminates between orthodoxy and heterodoxy, has a consecration in the most remote and venerable of traditions, and therefore it is hardly possible to pronounce it, with its centuries of included distinction, comprising also unity and sanctity, to be an innovation in Christianity. This ancient term, although implying universal, cannot, most assuredly, be employed to grace Congregational Churches, so recently established —Churches that so readily as members admit all to adoration and prayer—Churches that cry out, with Christian philanthropic zeal, "Come in, Jew, to do homage—you believe in God, but take off your hat; enter, Mahometan—you believe in God, but don't take off your slippers"—Churches that affect to make a truce between truth and error, and to find in the sincerity of respective convictions, though hugely differing in tenets, what would without one faith content both Apostle and Evangelist. "Protestants," says Gilpin, though somewhat favouring the above doctrinal latitude, "cannot take up the title of Catholic, since it implies infallibility, which is not congenial with Protestantism, which, in propounding definitively something for doctrinal assent, attributes, as affirms the preceding writer, infallibility to no Church on earth. The most obvious sense, therefore, in which the term Catholic can be considered as a Protestant article of our belief, is this, that we call no particular society of Christians a holy Catholic Church, but believe that all true and sincere Christians, of whatever communion or particular opinion, shall be the objects of God's mercy."

Another Protestant divine, now deceased, is in absolute confliction with the foregoing exposition, as is to be inferred from his language in a sermon entitled " an attempt to demonstrate the Catholicism of the Church of England ; " herein he declares that Catholic, a name so dear to all who are imbued with the love of primitive Christianity, is used, to speak logically, as a word of second intention to distinguish the one true and Apostolic Church." Further on he continues : "Now, if, in the profession of belief in the existence of the Catholic Church, the primitive Christians had intended nothing more than the acknowledgment of large masses of believers in the name of Jesus Christ scattered over the face of the earth, no one in his senses would have objected to that which was self-evident.

To have denied it would have involved an absurdity too gross for the most weak and illiterate of mankind to have been guilty of, and to have inserted the article in the Creed would in consequence have been a work of supererogation. But if, on the other hand, they intended, as we maintain, to distinguish by that title the true and Apostolic Church from the different sects of schismatics and heretics, then they asserted a fact against which those sects would vigorously contend, and then also we can readily account for its adoption in the various symbols or creeds of the Church." Thus oppositely to a reverend brother does a reverend divine speak who doubtless considered himself as a member of the Church which as he would intimate is truly and strictly Catholic, by her teaching the entire of the doctrines which the Apostles taught, and consequently according to his own expression marks the distinction between the Church of Christ and the legion of reforming and perfecting sects, that nevertheless assume severally to themselves a special and genuine Christianity. Upon this exposition also as a prominent one confidently rests the right of those to the term Catholic in whose favour unity and holiness have been so repeatedly claimed. Yet strange it is that a minister in connection with the reformed Church should insist upon such an orthodox and exclusive position. However, suffice it to say that the late

Dr. Hook, who has been selected, in conjunction with Gilpin, to evince the extreme antagonistical views of Protestants upon a title that has a hallowing in the most venerable of symbols for a most definite purpose, could no more demonstrate, by the concurrent testimonies of the several members of his community, that uniformity of belief existed between himself and them upon a body of dogma as orthodox and Apostolic, than Gilpin could prove that his broad interpretation, as giving a just right to the term Catholic, was logically proved, whatever may be the conflictions in tenets among sects, through their having a common credence in a Divine Redeemer.

Moreover, it is here suitable to observe, besides the most general and obvious meaning of Catholic, implying an harmonious universality of belief amid a vast body of Christians, numbering above two hundred millions, acknowledging the see of Rome as the centre of their unity, there is a resolution of its meaning to be met with in the diffusion of Catholicity throughout all parts of the world, and lastly Catholicity has an explication under the head of time, as yielding from its earliest use down to immediate periods an unswerving response to its set forth vital orthodox import. Whosoever therefore would make good his pretensions to the appellation just discussed, that has subsisted beyond the sites of empires, and which rulers, in its annexation

to the title of sovereignty, have equally prized with the
cross that makes the most prominent ornament of their
diadems, must prove that he has not separated from a
teaching which upholds unity and sanctity as well as
Catholicity as essential characteristics of the true
Church. The endeavours of the heterodox to usurp
the title of Catholic have not only been frequent, but
are also of very ancient date. In the venerable days
of the great St. Augustine, the Donatists, within
their very circumscribed spot of existence on this earth,
without sanctity and without orthodoxy, imperiously
asserted their exclusive claim to the denomination of
Catholic, and they persecuted those with unmitigated
ferocity who styled themselves Catholic if not witnessing to their spurious Christianity. But, said their
inflexible yet meek opponent, and in his words is included wherewith to match the effrontery of every
fresh pretentious sect unto the completion of the
Divine promise, "if a stranger in these streets (of
Hippo) were to inquire for the Catholic Church, it
would not be to the Church of the Donatists, but to
ours (styled Catholic), that he would be directed to
proceed." Certainly in present times the postman with
Catholic Church in the address would first seek the
Catholic and not the Protestant Church for a right
delivery. Centuries, as just shown, have not interfered
with the surety of this test, and if a stranger ages

hence were to inquire for the Catholic Church in the streets of London instead of those of Hippo, it would not be to any one conventicle of the Baptist, the Calvinist, or the Lutheran that he would be directed to wend his way, but to that place of worship which possesses an altar on which is offered up a Divine victim that St. Augustine knelt before and adored. Catholic is a title that must exclusively remain with those with whom it originated. Luther, on separating from the creed of his forefathers, could never retain the distinction of Catholic for his indefinite Christianity, nor could, nor will, his confiding and endlessly designated descendants ever secure what their patriarch failed to preserve.

It is repeatedly advanced that a legitimate assumption of the term Catholic may be secured in the fulfilment of one, at least, of its acceptations, which Protestantism, as complacently put forward, realises in its universal spread; a solid foundation, however, for this alleged claim to rest upon must necessarily be comprised in uniformity of belief. The dispersion in all parts of the world of numerous classes of Christians affecting one common denomination, although as diversified in creed as in language, cannot be that universality of propagation commenced by the Apostles in their several inspired missions, and whose voices, as from the commencement, were to be heard finally in complete accord to the uttermost ends of the earth. Catholic implies, "I believe in a Church that is registered in the most ancient of creeds"—not, as Bossuet profoundly remarks, "as merely existing, but in the entire of her tenets." It is through such an integrity in creed, by its undivided belief, that those who have Rome for their common centre, in their utmost spread, establish a right to what they claim—namely, the distinction of Catholic, which is synonymous with orthodoxy. But not so the term Christian. The reception of baptism makes the latter, the profession of doctrine determines the former. Whittaker himself seems to have been fully sensible of the total inutility of renewed contention on this point, since, in his reply to Reynolds, he says, "We are forced to employ the name of Protestant," and forced, also, he might have added, to admit the respective names of Lutheran, Calvinist, Socinian, or of some other illumined sect-founder, even under the most preposterous view of a Christian creed. The title of Catholic can alone be maintained as absolutely and exclusively her own by that Church which can trace up the possession of it to the earliest times, and no separation from her communion, however large in number, can invalidate this right to a name by which so many millions are distinguished who are identified in creed. "Here we stand upon our rights," as Cardinal Wiseman forcibly puts it, "as the successor to a dynasty claims the crown of his ancestors, or as any member of the aristocracy in this country holds the lands of his ancestors, legally given to them from whom he inherits them; whatever branches of the family may have separated from it, or accepted other claims or prospects, that cannot shake the right line of succession of which he is the representative."[1] This language, in a contending upon the claim to the distinction of Catholic, can only, it may be confidently declared, as resting upon what has preceded, be fearlessly responded to by those who are able to count centuries for its consecutive possession, and who can, with equal assurance, defy those who deny their legitimate pretension to the title to prove at what period they lost their right to it, when the designation of Protestant was unknown. To make this evident at any period in the past is an impossibility; and united millions will retain the term Catholic in the future when the designations of a thousand sects shall have disappeared, and even when those of the Primitives and the Gospelites shall have been changed into the pure chalcedonites and chrysolites which give splendour to the celestial Jerusalem. The distinction of Catholic, in which it is lawful for a saint to glory,

---

[1] Cardinal Wiseman. Ninth Lecture.

and which exalts more the lowest of the faithful by its spiritual import than the most ennobling of temporal distinctions, needs no adjunct to complete its signification of orthodoxy, as having an entry in that belief to which tradition extends a worth next to inspiration. Its most obvious sense excludes sectarianism, of which Protestantism is composed from its adoption; for Catholic Lutheranism, Catholic Arminianism, Catholic Calvinism, must sound as incongruously on the ear of the reflecting Christian who seeks for unity, which best indicates truth, as Catholic Arianism, Catholic Jovinianism, and Catholic Pelagianism.

Not less has the unchangeable and authoritative Church of Ages an exclusive right to the distinction of Apostolic than to that of unity, sanctity, and Catholic. The term Apostolic, according to a celebrated writer just quoted, signifies "a continued and unaltered succession from the time of the Apostles. This unbroken genealogy it will be for the above-designated Church alone to show which has her sovereignty, though so trenched upon, yet in that city which once decreed for the world."[1] In this Apostolicity, for which heresy hardly dares to compete, history will have no eventual startle for the faithful.

---

[1] Cardinal Wiseman. Ninth Lecture.

No final confusion will prevail here, as with Israel, when every prediction as to Israel's offices had been accomplished. Of this Apostolicity the Church in which is fully realised the figures and promises of the old law will always be able to manifest herself to be the possessor. She has hitherto done so, notwithstanding every temporary embarrassment and disturbance that insidious and influential factions gave rise to, and why should she not be able to do so beyond that period "when some traveller from New Zealand shall, in the midst of a vast solitude, take his stand on a broken arch of London Bridge to sketch the ruins of St. Paul's"?[1] Yes, why not unto those last convulsions of nature when empires shall commence simultaneously to totter into one common and final ruin—in other words, when probation shall have ceased, and virtue be raised to God? In this descent from a first spiritual supremacy to a present ruling, within this Apostolicity, wherein the orthodox find their joyful certitude and the heterodox their insuperable difficulty, the various Churches spread over the face of the earth in communion with the see of Rome can best prove the validity of their orders, their missions, and their jurisdiction. In this Apostolicity then they discern a supreme spiritual rule, and to it

---

[1] Lord Macaulay's Review of Ranke's History of the Popes.

they yield their profound and unswerving obedience. St. Cyprian says that the Primacy was given to St. Peter to show the necessity of unity. All without its domain is most assuredly disunity.

Those who think that a Church may be Apostolic without any reference to an uninterrupted descent from a first spiritual authority, make little account of any character of successionship to orders, doctrine, mission, or jurisdiction, and with happy complacency say we are told to "search the Scriptures," and have therefore, as must be obvious to common sense (a very common form of their insistence), no need to seek elsewhere, either in writings or in any so-styled spiritual supremacy in teachings, for interpretation or security. "The Holy Scriptures, comprising, as they do, the dictates of Infinite Wisdom for the enlightenment of mankind, are clear as to their meaning and object, and consequently the most humble of intellect may come to peaceful and Evangelical convictions if stimulated in the truly Christian search by uprightness and singleness of mind." Such, under a condensed form, is the substance of arguments which the myriad diversified progeny of Luther, Calvin, Zuinglius, and Socinius severally employ who deem themselves to be heavenly-favoured, yet are almost as opposite in their doggedly affirmed tenets as Carpocrates the Alexandrian and Photius the patriarch, to obtain a suffrage for their fondled and hugged convictions. Many there are, however, whose reading, perception, and earnestness will not allow them to be quite at ease in a close adhesion with any one of the foregoing great divisions in Protestantism, who conjoin with their respective whims upon the Gospel the certitude of "entering into the joy of their Lord." These have a considerable misgiving as to a present religious persuasion to which they have not been able to impart even plausibility by subtilising on certain generalities, and who cannot quite discard as immaterial the united voices of those who swayed the past by their erudition and their sanctity, in proclaiming an Apostolic lineage, that were once themselves bewildered in the interminable wanderings of the human intellect, and held under the thraldom of the ever-craving passions.

Amongst these ancient and venerable witnesses to the vital importance of Apostolicity St. Augustine is one of the most prominent. This renowned Father thus emphatically sets forth, in evidence of what was conclusive with him, that the Church to which finally he devoted heart, intellect, and learning after so many doubts and seekings was Apostolic in her holding, and manifested the Divineness of the promise in the sustained harmonious detail of her teachings: "The agreement of peoples and nations keeps me in the

Catholic Church—an authority begun by miracles, nourished by hope, increased by charity, and strengthened by antiquity, keeps me; the succession of Bishops from the chair of the Apostle Peter, to whom the Lord after His resurrection committed His sheep to be fed, down even to the present Bishop, keeps me."[1]

"The blessed Apostles," says St. Irenæus, "having founded and built up that Church, committed the sacred office of the Episcopacy to Linus, of whom St. Paul makes mention in his Epistle to Timothy. To him succeeded Anaclitus, and after him the third from the Apostles who obtained that Episcopacy was Clement, who had seen and conferred with the blessed Apostles, and had before his eyes the familiar preaching and tradition of the Apostles, and not only he, for many were still alive who had been instructed by the Apostles. But to Clement succeeded Evaristus, and to Evaristus Alexander. Next to him, thus the sixth from the Apostles, Sixtus was appointed, and after him Telesphorus, who underwent a glorious martyrdom. Next Hyginus, then Pius, after him was Anicetus. To Anicetus succeeded Soter, and to him, the twelfth in succession from the Apostles, succeeded Eleutherius, who holds the Episcopate. By this order, and by this succession, both the tradition which is in the

---

[1] St. Aug. Contra Epist. Fundam.

Church of the Apostles, and the preaching of the truth, have come down to us, and this is a complete demonstration that the vivifying faith is one and the same, which, from the Apostles even till now, has been preserved in the Church, and transmitted with truthfulness."[1]

Through this venerable system of things, which Tertullian challenges "the heretic to feign," that is manifested in its integrity which had its foundation in the Apostles. It leaves nothing for human wisdom to suggest as to arriving through a series of deductions to firmer conclusions upon a Christianity, which as to religion was from the origin of things. Luther, affirms Dr. Klee, must have acknowledged an Apostolical succession, by his acceptance of the Council of Nice.[2] And Fulke, in his answer to a so-called counterfeit Catholic, says, " You can name the notable persons in all ages in their government and their ministry, and especially the succession of Popes, you can rehearse upon your fingers."[3] Equally unable to do this as to prove the validity of its ordinations, "Protestantism," as Dr. Milner[4] conclusively remarks, in respect to its preaching and ministry, " under

---

[1] St. Irenæus Adv. Hæres.   [2] Præscript.
[3] P. 27, and in his rejoinder to Bristow's reply.
[4] End of Controversy.

its several degrees is performed by mere human authority." To this may be appropriately added what Philip Mornay[1] remarks as to reformers who, having no Apostolic commission, "yet should notwithstanding first constitute Churches, and then afterwards those Churches should be made to confer a calling on the preachers." This is wholly preposterous, and directly contrary to the course set down by the Apostles, where it is said: " How shall they invocate in whom they have not believed? How shall they believe whom they have not heard? How shall they hear without a preacher? And how shall they preach except they be sent?" Rom. x. 14. As to this necessity that is imposed upon those who assume a mission for the reformation of Christianity, of demonstrating, though little heeding any direct descent, that this mission is one in sacredness under Heaven with that of the Apostles, it is forcibly dealt with, whatever may be his motive for so reasoning, by the infidel Rousseau in his "Lettres ecrites de la Montagne." "When," says this writer, "the first reformers commenced to make themselves heard, the universal Church was in peace, all were unanimous in sentiment, there was not one essential dogma debated among Christians; whilst in this state of tranquillity

---

[1] Tréatise of the Church, c. XI.

suddenly two or three men raise their voices, and cry out to all Europe: 'Christians, be on your guard; you are deceived; you are wandering from the right way; you are on the road that leads to hell; the Pope is Antichrist, the agent of Satan, and his Church is the school of deception. You are lost if you do not attend to our warning.' At this unexpected outbreak, astonished Europe remained for some moments in silence, marvelling what would be the result. At length the clergy, having recovered from their first astonishment, and seeing that these new comers were gathering followers around them, as it is usual for every lusty dogmatiser to succeed in doing, considered it to be time to come to some explanation with them upon the matter. Accordingly they commenced by demanding of the reformers what was their motive for attacking them with such clamour." The reformers are represented as haughtily replying, "that they were the apostles of truth (but without an Apostolical genealogy), called to reform the Church, and to lead the people from the paths of perdition into which the priesthood had conducted them." "But," as asked again by their interrogators, "from whom do you derive this high commission to disturb the peace of the Church and public tranquillity?" "Our conscience," they answer, "reason and an interior light, the law of God, which it is impossible to resist without a crime, it is these which have called us to this holy ministry, and we follow our vocation." "You are then the envoys of God?" the Catholics are made to reply. "In this case we agree that you ought to preach, reform, instruct, and that people ought to hear you. But to confirm this sacred right you must commence by a display of your credentials; prophesy, cure, illuminate, do miracles." The same writer concludes from foregoing and similar subsequent arguments that those who had no more right to interpret the Scriptures as they pleased than those they anathematised, must cease their babble or realise the miracle to witness to their Divine legation. This they could no more do than, as Erasmus quaintly observes, "set all things right again with a lame horse."

Yet the reformers certainly manifested a little more prudence in not making an attempt at a miracle than the self-styled prophets that essayed to bring down fire from heaven to hallow their pretensions, and to enlighten the crowd upon the imperturbable profaneness of the disbelieving and deriding Elias. It is in vain to struggle against a Church for spiritual superiority that is to be recognised each moment, as from the first that witnessed her birth, by characters as unchangeable as the Divine Being that endowed her with infallibility. With whatever splendour succeeding heresies have, at their several epochs, glared out upon gaping multitudes, it has gradually died away like mimicking meteors beneath the celestial system. That which is the creation of Omnipotence will always remain as conspicuous and unaltered in character as the constellations above, and prophecy in connection with it will even outlive the eventual disordered skies in the completion of the last of her foretellings. In the midst of the confusion of sects, "God," remarks Bossuet, "was never wanting to His Church. He knew how to continue to her signs of empire which heresy could never assume. She was Catholic and Universal—that is, she included within herself all times, and was spread on every side. She was Apostolic; continuity, succession, the chair of unity, and primitive authority were possessed by her. All those who separated from her had first recognised the proofs of her Divine mission, whilst, on the other hand, they could never disguise what made known the novelty of both their own teaching and their rebellion." [1] Thus spoke a prelate who added eloquence to the doctrinal expositions of the Fathers, and whose arguments are ever as forcible as were his convictions. And thus also speaks a saint often quoted, who was wise as he was charitable:

---

[1] Discours sur l'Histoire Univer.

"To a society holding the faith there needs in this faith an authority at once sovereign and infallible; if there be a God, if there be a Providence, there must be also an authority." [1] Never, indeed, in respect to foregoing matter, will anything be discovered wanting in the Catholic Church to indicate a final authority as to tenets and morals. She will ever face the rebellious clamours and the defiant bearing of those that make divisions within, or attack her from without, undismayed. She who is impressed with the lineaments of rule, which that hand alone can impress, for the salvation of all men, that deeply marked a scowling and an obdurate brow for the temporal safety of one man, is gifted beyond Ezechiel's favouring. Her several characters, though distinct in themselves, have each a strict and an immediate bearing one with another, as making but one common indication of orthodox teaching, and as deriving their respective being from one common source. This will be discovered to be on the part of Apostolicity, in a respective reference to Unity, Sanctity, and Catholicity, even as these three latter have severally among themselves, and the reason for the close and ever-enduring relationship may promptly be deduced from what has been previously laid down.

---

[1] St. Augustine.

By these characters or marks, the evidences of a Church that is without spot or wrinkle may be speedily discerned, and which have always enabled the orthodox to make their appeals, their challenges, and their battles with promptitude, with assurance, and with triumph. So obvious are they in their indications that even fools may discover where truth has her dwelling, not less than the wise under the steady lustre of the star which so faithfully made known where abided the Saviour of the world. These marks are nevertheless of so sublime a nature as to defy the most ingenious efforts of the gifted to counterfeit, and as well might it be contemplated to impart comeliness and interest to the sunken and shrivelled features of the mummy that had an existence before the Christian era as faithfully to realise their august counterpart. Without them, though through men is manifested their Divine nature, as the brightness of the Deity in the person of Moses, there would remain nothing but man. Without their controlling majesty the unawed imagination would be as wanton in these days as in the past. The perplexed judgment would be without that evincing orthodoxy that is sure to yield conviction to patient investigation. All, indeed, would be as it is now with the heretical, ceaseless uncertitude amid endless pretensions to certainty. A supreme spiritual authority could not be defined or supported, nor could any creed be heralded forth, that would not have its eventual moulder equally with the hand that drew it up. The aggregate of this argues that these four marks, Unity, Holiness, Catholicity, and Apostolicity, in indicating a Divine Church, ought entirely to remove all distressing doubts upon doctrines and morals. Heresy or self-opinion must necessarily be, and ever will be, in strongly contrasted opposition to Catholicity. She has nothing within her of that construction that is mutually auxiliary in advancing the inquiring towards definite conclusions upon her numerously propounded creeds. It is in the province of Catholicity alone to attain the peace of surety as to the existence of truth in every formally pronounced matter of faith and morals, by perspicuous and continuous proofs, which ignorance or perversity could alone summon up audacity enough to question or to deny. The inspired volume has also, in these above-discussed marks, so conclusive upon the Divineness of the Church of the Fathers and of ages, the best reply to what is set forth in her sacred pages for the recognition of an infallible teacher, and there needs but little reading with sincerity of purpose to substantiate the assertion. Let then private interpretation strive to make out, for any description of her almost countless tabernacles, a like orthodox character, in an obvious response of similitude to the delineations of Holy

Writ, as to what is never to fail, and success would be here as great a wonderment as that a religious persuasion declared to be false, and which is so, should be invariably unique in her teachings, whilst that which is pronounced to be orthodox, and is so, should be perpetually in division on doctrine. This would be to have the testifications of truth without her presence, or the reverse, to have her presence with the significations of falsehood.

But can it be put forward by some that whatever significations Catholicity may display of possessing truth it is merely fortuitous? If it is so advanced, it is the extreme of effrontery, yet it is not surprising that such an advancement should be made among the shifting and manifold comments on Catholicity by Heresy to frustrate every attempt at a semblance to a Divine institution, since she ventures on maintaining the Godliness of her own preposterous fiction, and thus leaving open even infinite Wisdom to an imputation of countenancing the extravagances and absurdities of spinning Christian dervishes, and howling competitors for a first hearing with Heaven.

However, it is only necessary to say that the proceeds of chance can never have permanence. They cannot have anything in common with that Being with whom Catholicity alone makes good her blending, " who was yesterday, to-day, and is the same for ever." (Heb., c. xiii.) In contrast to Catholicity when one form of heretical creed passes away it will be followed by another equally characterised, equally fated, because equally of human construction. And it may be readily assumed that this unstaid state of creeds and of interminable bewilderings will never be bettered by a Church which, as Cardinal Manning lays down, "contains within herself the principle both of her creation and her dissolution—private judgment." Yet it is curious to consider, in regard to a multitude of dogmatising instances, and the distinctions thereupon, the necessary consequences of Luther's blessed disenthralment of Christianity from every spiritual interference with self-enlightenment in determining orthodox credences, with what sensitive and subtle apostolical discriminations those seek to have their several religious persuasions adequately responded to through the medium of public advertisements. In respect to those who do so, it is imperative to observe that they are, however, in common honesty, absolutely to be distinguished from Canon Smith's "consecrated nest of cobblers," and also from those that are legally qualified, at one shilling a head, to made known the Gospel and to determine its sacred purport. These several and somewhat opposite significations of sound Christianity, as to the advertising, are adroitly selected for the public information or amusement by the author of "The Developments of Protestantism." But thus does he proceed, "As to Anglican rectors and curates, in their communications to the *Ecclesiastical Gazette*, to obtain congenial believing labourers in the cultivation of the vineyard of their Divine Master, they refer to a great variety of standards." One class appeal to the "Church" as the type of their sentiments. "So that we have," continues the same writer, "gentlemen of High Church views, of High Church principles, of sober Church views, of what are commonly called High Church but not extreme views, of old Church of England principles, of moderately High Church though not Tractarian, of Anglo-Catholic principles, of sound Anglo-Catholic views." "With many the phrase Evangelical is the sole test. Some are simply of Evangelical sentiments, or decidedly Evangelical principles, or strictly of Evangelical views or sentiments Evangelical, not Calvinistic." Such are the diverse, perspicuous intimations to the several truly Christian faithful, sought for by the most looked-up-to of the constituents of Protestantism in this liberal and fostering land of reformations, that are well calculated to confound even the most penetrating and painstaking of Attorney-Generals, and to render it not a very surprising circumstance that the Thirty-nine Articles should be so frequently signed "with a sigh, if not with a smile." In all this the distinguished author of a treatise on "Church and State,"[1] who declared unity to be essential to the witnessing of the presence of truth, would find very little, among so great a variety of decidedly Evangelical superiorities, in confirmation of doctrinal agreement within his Church, of such a deemed staid Apostolical succession. On the other hand, a late illustrious critic in the *Edinburgh Review* declared "that the Church of England was, in fact, but a bundle of religious systems without number." Then, on the instant, he chivalrously asks: "Do we make this diversity a topic of reproach to the Church of England? Far from it. We would oppose with all our power every attempt to narrow her basis. Would to God that a hundred and fifty years ago a good king and a good primate had possessed the power as well as the will to widen it! It was a noble enterprise worthy of William and of Tillotson."[2]

But what basis does Protestantism possess, since private interpretation confounds her with sheer opinion? If the late Lord, whose writings the preceding gifted century has hardly surpassed in ability, had deeply and dispassionately considered the nature

---

[1] Mr. Gladstone.   [2] Lord Macaulay.

of Protestantism with the solicitude of final moments, he could not have arrived, notwithstanding what he has so fervidly advanced, at much that was either conclusive or consoling. He could scarcely have been assured with the Apostle on the point of quitting this world that he had kept the faith, "the one faith," amid a multitude of tolerated and latitudinarian beliefs. On the other hand, he would have arrived at something definite for his intellect and consolatory for his conscience had he, before an everlasting adieu to genius, learning, title, and fortune, too often the exclusively prized possessions of a present, but not in themselves of much consideration in a future world, reasoned with Athanasius and Augustine, instead of being absorbed in the planning of a William and a Tillotson, to perfect the devisings of a fitful Luther or a confused Melancthon. Nevertheless, this eloquent historian, who was so insultingly exceptional to one of the chief dogmas of Catholicity, and ostentatiously favourable to the convenient generalities of the immediate day ("broad bases"), with praiseworthy candour said: "We often hear it declared that the world is steadily becoming more and more enlightened, and that this enlightenment must be favourable to Protestantism and unfavourable to Catholicism. But we see great reason to doubt whether this be a well-founded expectation. We see that during the last two hundred and fifty years the human mind has been in the highest degree active; that it has made great advances in every branch of natural philosophy; that it has produced innumerable inventions tending to promote the convenience of life; that medicine, surgery, chemistry, policy, engineering, have been very greatly advanced; that government, policy, and law have been improved, though not to so great an extent as the physical sciences. Yet we see during these two hundred and fifty years Protestantism has made no conquests worth speaking of. Nay, we believe that as far as there has been a change, that change has been, on the whole, in favour of the Church of Rome. We cannot, therefore, feel confident that the progress of knowledge will necessarily be fatal to a system which has, at the least, stood its ground, in spite of the immense progress made by the human race in knowledge since the days of Queen Elizabeth."

Stood her ground! Catholicity has, as already shown, evinced this in the Empire of Great Britain, so signally to be selected for a proof of the continuous action of a Divine Providence for her preservation and ultimate influence. She has spread herself far and wide, notwithstanding the accusations and the maledictions of a host of inimical sects. She has progressed among those most distinguished for their zeal, their learning, their genius, and their position—among those who were most hardy in clothing her with what might best beget contempt and ridicule, but who at last recognised her Divine origin, as did the centurion, amid the ignominies and woes of shrouded Calvary, the Divinity of a Redeemer, that the mob had reviled, mocked, belied, and execrated at the instance of Pharisees, Sadducees, priests, and rulers. "Magna est veritas, et prævalebit," "Great is truth, and she will prevail," whether heresy shall marshal the kings and the chief powers of the earth in fight against her, or employ every infatuating influence to control her destinies and to frustrate her action. Christianity, at her first establishment like unto the sowing of insignificance, each day almost imperceptibly grew, until time, as in nature, made her a wonder for contemplation. Though frequently hemmed about by the most stubborn obstacles, these could check only, yet could not prevent her from making her profitable expansions; she survived storms which proved fatal to kingdoms, and throve above their ruins. That Providence was always with her, of as certain as wise purposes, which is not less in the whirlwind that purifies than in the breeze which attempers the glowing atmosphere into steady ripening warmth. She has as provident and beneficent a sky over her as the chosen who, in their every disposition

o

and arrangement of things on their journey to the promised land, filled the hostile prophet with transports —from whatever point he viewed them—and forced him to exclaim, "How beautiful are thy tabernacles, O Jacob, and thy tents, O Israel!"—Num. c. xxii.

Protestantism, with her uncontrolled strifes and endless conflicts, cannot put in here with Catholicity for a comparison as to the above. History gives her no period of authority, the source of order, and time will not supply for the vital deficit. This religion could give no satisfactory reply through its Archbishop and Primate to the Christian fundamental inquiries of Mr. Maskell, at a juncture when a calamitous dispute had finally set in, though quite consequent upon the nature of Protestantism, that seriously interfered with the prompt administration, and even with the vital necessity of giving baptism itself. "Whether," answered the Archbishop, "the doctrines concerning which you inquire are contained in the Word of God, and can be proved thereby, you have had the same means of discovering as myself, and I have no special authority to declare." Such was the straightforward reply of His Grace, and such as follows was the exclamation thereupon of the astounded interrogator: "Can there be any religious system devised on earth so destructive of spiritual life, and so opposed to the reality of spiritual practice, as one which, under the guise of purity and moderation, throws open all doctrines except one (and what is that?) to the decision of each man's private judgment, and suffers us to believe (as we will) either this or that, or, if we dare to do so, nothing at all? Nor do I see how such a system once openly avowed can fail to lead thousands into infidelity." So have many thought likewise, and many highly gifted and educated men, yet self-sufficient thinkers, have likewise proved the correctness of the above declaration by ultimately discarding all rites, festivals, and creeds, and yielding, as so expressed by the strong-minded of the day, "to the intuitions of their own souls, and to the instinct of truth," have rejected an historic theology, as they are pleased to designate it, and taken up "with a rational faith, a personal religion deeply rooted in the heart." However, there is nothing in all this incomprehensible and impious avowing to be amazed at, since, when it is insisted upon that religion ought to be totally subordinate to reason, the consequence will be, as observes Pascal, "to prescind from all mysteries and what is supernatural, and which is as hurtful as entirely to exclude the application of the principles of reason from what is connected with religion."[1] The calamity is aggravated considering that there is

---

[1] Pensées de Pascal.

absolutely no authority in Protestantism to correct or recall those who have receded into wise Socrates and sublime Platos, that cease not to praise Aristides the Just and leave unnoticed Jesus the Perfect—a description of men who have not the courage to discard openly the name of Christian, but who for the most part know very little indeed of religion, its foundation, or its origin, and hence in a great measure the daring of their blasphemies and the precipitancy of their judgments. In respect to this it would be as desperate an affair to get up an enterprise against Magna Charta, as for Protestant spiritual rulers who so devoutly exclaim, "O providential Luther, Christendom's timely rescue!" to struggle against the continuous, certain and sad results of free opinion.

But if it were summarily asked, in the words of Pilate, "What is the truth?" in Protestantism, and what is it in her heterodox to deny, and which would exclude from an enthronisation in a cathedral, or from a chair in a university, it would be under such a direct questioning almost impossible to return decisive replies, so as to comprise authoritatively what would orthodoxly qualify for State positions, whether as to secular or spiritual, since within Protestantism, upon Christian fundamentals, belief is as miscellaneous as the shelves of an image-vendor, a mingling of the Divine with the monstrous, of the ridiculous with the solemn. In the reformed religion, then, that includes such ample liberty for denials and affirmatives, within which every fresh folly and impiety has little need to apprehend much firmness of opposition, where there is no union, nor much want of patronage, where novelty in doctrine has its genuine Christianity, with ancient teachings, nothing can be expected to disclose itself under any influential determinate form to the thoughtful, in the nature of creed, to secure conviction, to inflame zeal, to animate virtue, and to stimulate hope. Certain it is that St. Paul, even by the light of the third heaven into which he was elevated, would not have been able to discern anything among such conflicting matter beyond "hay, straw, and stubble," not very solidly calculated to constitute the faith which the same Apostle terms "the foundation of things." All this clearly indicates the timely opportunity of a broadly spreading scepticism. Writings are now countenanced, and the authors are recommended by public acclamation, notwithstanding some high clerical remonstrances, on account of their open Deistical favourings, to offices that yield a powerful determinate influence as to the diversified affairs of this empire. The perusal of their works, and the significance of their speeches, induce very many to look on the atoning Victim of the Cross with the incredulity of the deriding Jew, and not with the enraptured eyes of the Roman centurion, who needed not the effulgence of Thabor to discern what was Divine on Calvary's darkened mount. They are prodigal enough of incense to idol self, but have not one grain to spare for Him whom both angels and men are commanded to adore.

However, to meet grave Protestant difficulties at this self-sufficient and lax period, when orthodoxy is barely a name with thousands, and rite a horror with as many, a revising of things is to be one of the momentous occupations of some future Senate. Thus by amendments and erasures belief will be qualified into something barely savouring of Christianity, and by rigid curtailments few ceremonies will be left to give expression or dignity to a sanctuary's creed. This salutary fashioning for heaven, through the votes of the congregated representatives of a kingdom, will certainly yield to Socinians and their Christian kindred a well-founded hope that the Athanasian Creed, with its denunciations, will be excluded from Protestant temples, though its sacred use on every side was recommended by primitive Councils, as including what was absolutely fundamental in Christianity. It is not improbable, in the subsequent proceedings of a State providence, that the common symbol of Christian ages, the Apostles' Creed, will finally have a place only in private devotions—at least, that it will become merely discretionary by law as to its public recital in the national churches, as having only tradition for its warrant.

For those, nevertheless, who shrink from the prospective pruning of Christianity down to an unsightly and unproductive stump, who retain some impression that in the most accepted times of the Church rigid symbols of belief were employed as the best means of preserving the integrity of teaching, both as to dogma and morality, and of defeating the sophistry and the equivocations of heresy, there are some gleanings of comfort to be gathered from the fact that prayers at both Senate Houses continue to be offered up before the affairs of the Government are entered upon, to obtain enlightenment and guidance. Here things are somewhat in analogy with primitive Councils at the opening of their sittings. But, however, little heed and little confidence is given to these pious forms, before entering upon Parliamentary matters, by those who virtually wield the sword of empire, that speedily gets through perplexities of a very varied character, that would baffle the logic of an Aristotle to unravel. Private judgment is as much at its ease within Senates as without, and more effective in ecclesiastical affairs for mischief, when biassed by political circumstances, which often beget more unity than inspiration, by the finality and coercion which it comprises. Dr. Johnson appeared to be strongly impressed with the chief part of the foregoing in substance, by the remarks that he made on his own times, which had their source in the then supreme impunity for private opinion. "The prevailing spirit of the present age," says this learned and experienced writer, "is the spirit of scepticism and captiousness, of suspicion and distrust, a contempt for all authority, and a presumptuous confidence in private judgment." Yet, whilst maintaining the exercise of private judgment, so baneful and wide in its effects, to be a rightful privilege, he goes on to say, "But this privilege ill-understood"—and who will make it salutary by elucidation?—"has been, and always may be, the occasion of very many pernicious and dangerous mistakes; it may be exercised without knowledge or discretion, till error be entangled with error, till divisions be multiplied with endless divisions, till the bond of peace be entirely severed, and the Church become a scene of confusion—a chaos of discordant forms of worship and inconsistent systems of faith."

And at this immediate period the above ruinous and certain result of private judgment is deepened in its consequences by individuals who are pronounced for the most part to be benevolent and well-meaning men, who have spoken in the full conviction of their reasoning minds, intimating by this, as Dr. Johnson further observes, "the innocence of error accompanied by sincerity."[1] The upshot of such honest judgments coming from kind hearts and acute intellects is to leave very little among thousands of that vital belief in Christianity that stimulated the once incredulous Apostle fervently to exclaim, "My Lord and my God!" Well might Archdeacon Denison in one of his charges frankly affirm what doubtless surprised many "that the inner life and character of the Church are being eaten out bit by bit, while the framework remains as before." A worse termination of Christian things could not well be conceived, as within such a skeleton of a Church there could be but a small amount of vitality, and the venerable as well as the candid Archdeacon may be assured that the Church which has been reduced to such a pitiable state of ruin through which every shifting wind of doctrine may wildly career to effect further destruction will meet with no stay in its mischievous and fitful progress, and that all this ought to convince men who do not compress their eyelids, or vehemently resist the intimations of common sense, that the above pitiable construction was under the build of those who raised Babel, and not under that of One whose work does not allow of any deterioration. Yet Edmund Burke, in

---

[1] Sermons.

the ecstasies of his Christian convictions, thus in his time refers to the durability of the Protestant Church, not quite in consonance with the deep lament of the Archdeacon as to the utter want of a lasting solidity in her build. "Her walls, bulwarks, and bastions," declares the greatest orator of his age, "are constructed of other materials than stubble and straw; they are built up with the strong and stable matter of the Gospel of liberty, and founded on a true constitutional legal establishment. She has other securities; she has the security of her own doctrines, she has the security of the piety, the sanctity, of her own professors; their learning is a bulwark to defend her; she has the securities of her universities—of the two universities—not shaken in any single battlement, in any single pinnacle." Had Edmund Burke existed unto this period of varied and wild dissent, of many modifications and rejections, he would not have been able to discern much faithfulness preserved in his figurative details as to massive resistances and unfailing securities within his own Church; but he would find the Catholic Church to be intact, the same in unity, the same in challenges, in references, as to the admitted centuries of orthodoxy. He might discern ruin around her, yet not a particle of her indestructible build would therein be discovered to have a mingle. She is a Church which again with advantage may be quoted in these pages that is all Divine, and therefore all within her is united, so that as each part is Divine, that which keeps each part together must be equally Divine. The entire then of this Apostolic Church is such that each part acts with the force of all. All this ought to convince those who do not close their eyes, or resist the intimations of common sense, that Protestantism was under the construction of those who raised Babel, and not under that of One in whose work, as above said, there can be no crumble or moulder.

With regard to the foregoing, it is to be marvelled at that Burke, with so acute a judgment, and of such profound reading, could reason so conclusively upon the unjustifiableness of the laws against Catholicity in Ireland, and yet speak with all the vividness of possessed truth upon the firmness and durability of Protestantism. But thus argues an enlarged mind which was conjoined with a capacious heart, that abhorred as much the oppressions visited upon the people of Ireland, chiefly in view of their faith, as deeply feeling for their accumulated woes: "It is proper to recollect that this religion, which is so persecuted in its members, is the old religion of the country, and the once established religion of the State, the very same which had for centuries received the countenance and sanction of the laws." But elsewhere he continues: "Religion is not believed because the laws have established it; it is established because the leading part of the community have previously believed it to be true. As no water can rise higher than its spring, no establishment can have more authority than it derives from its principle. You confess that you have been wrong, and yet you would pretend to dictate by your sole authority, whereas you disengage the mind by embarrassing it. For why should I prefer your opinion of to-day to your opinion of yesterday, if we must resort to prepossessions for the ground of opinion? It is in the nature of man rather to defer to the wisdom of times past, whose weakness is not before his eyes, than to the present, of whose imbecility he has daily experience. Veneration for antiquity is congenial to the human mind. When, therefore, an establishment would persecute an opinion in possession, it sets against it all the powerful prejudices of human nature, it opposes the stable prejudices of time by a new opinion founded in mutability. But when an ancient establishment begins early to persecute an innovation, it stands upon other grounds; it has all the prejudices and presumptions on its side. . . But an opinion at once new and persecuting is a monster, because in the very instant it takes a liberty of change, it does not leave to you a liberty of perseverance." Certainly in all this in the main there is to be met with more logic in favour of the old than the new religion—the old, which is not made up of ventured generalities that chime in so well with Evangelical freedom. She has no minute crevice in her for infidelity to insinuate the finest of edged tools to prise into a gap; she is as absolute in condemning infidelity as infidelity is so pronounced in condemning the entire of her fixed teachings—infidelity, which is always congenial with opinion, the basis on which Protestantism has her build, not calculated with the rock to ensure a very firm foundation. Thus Protestantism, again to be insisted on, in its progress, by her increasing divisions adds to the opportunity of infidelity, and infidelity does not fail to profit by the circumstance. Every attractive lure that can best arrest the public eye is employed to excite curiosity, and increase the sale of her writings, within which, ordinarily speaking, the readers will collect as little to advance themselves in any sound practical information as to bring themselves into any familiar acquaintance with the useful facts of daily life. Most assuredly they will not forward themselves much in duly appreciating what is moral or what is doctrinal. Of the doctrinal there can be but very little doubt, for this comprises the creed of the duped; and as to the moral of Christianity there cannot be a very large amount of appreciation, since not a few of Christian duties and Christian practices are classed by infidelity under the fantasies of the feeble of intellect. Most surely the writings of the ceaseless foe to what best gives grandeur to reason, and best benefits humanity, proclaimed to the world with all a showman's parade, in the midst of sounding brass and tinkling cymbals, will not contribute much to "make a man virtuous in the dark and honest without a witness."

However, Catholics can discourse on Christianity without making nonsense of what comprises a greater wisdom than that of Israel's King, and includes truths that no axioms can lessen in their value, or affect in their obviousness. But in contrast to this, the ambiguities and follies included in an infidel's belief almost amount in response to the following facetious piece of extravagance: "I believe there is no God, but that matter is God. I believe also that the world was not made, but that the world made itself, and that it will last for ever, world without end. I believe that man is a beast, that the soul is the body, and the body is the soul, and that after death there is neither body nor soul. I believe there is no religion, and that natural religion is the only religion. I believe not in Moses; I believe in the first philosophy. I believe not in Evangelists; I believe in Chubb, Collins, Toland, Tyndal, Morgan, Mandeville, Woolstone, Hobbs, Shaftesbury. I believe in Lord Bolingbroke; I believe not in St. Paul. I believe in revelation, I believe in tradition, I believe in the Alcoran, I believe not in the Bible. I believe in Socrates; I believe in Confucius; I believe Sanconiathan; I believe not in Christ. I believe in Mahomet. Lastly, I believe in all unbelief." Such, then, as humorously given, are the outrageous absurdities into which those may equivalently fall who bring themselves virtually to take a farewell of all that which, in the conviction of the nations of the earth, for centuries made the principal value of existence, and to adopt what, after death, leaves the hero, the philosopher, or the founder of a kingdom without an advantage over the bloated and noisome carcass that may be corrupting in the wayside ditch. All this, in a great measure, arises from, as just alluded to, a loose belief among many who declaim at the present day to gain followers, not to vindicate dogmas or to enforce precepts, and who are continually widening concessions to suit what is termed a rational Christianity, and at the same time are vigilantly obstructive as to the progress of the ancient faith. It is not surprising, then, that at last incredulity and voluptuousness should present themselves among the many, and induce them to fearlessly jeer at the teachings of inspiration which exact a strict belief, and make a mockery of its solemn injunctions that include self-denial.

Bitterly convinced of this, numbers here have from time to time cried out, "When and where is a national council to assemble to confront these thickening perils, to enlighten by its expositions, and to tranquillise by its decisions?" At some "Cumming" period, is the unhesitating answer, and to assemble in the chief hall of a *Château en Espagne* wherein to illumine and calm the minds of the perplexed and disturbed. Well may it be said here, "Oh, slow of heart, to believe in a Church whose government is not tyranny, whose sanctity is not unnatural asceticism, whose martyrdom is not obstinacy, whose perfection is not enthusiasm, whose gentleness is not laxity, whose strictness is not arrogance, and whose punishment is not an assault upon the rights of men!"[1] Oh, slow of heart, to believe in a Church which has ever abiding within her that Divine Spirit which is to teach her all truth, sent down by Him who opened the eyes of His disciples to whom He manifested Himself on their journey to Emmaus! Oh, slow of heart, to believe in a Church that does not exist in the midst of disputes that embarrass and confound—a Church of authority, whose hierarchy

---

[1] Father Faber.

has been so recently congregated together by a late Supreme Pontiff, the centre of unity, in a General Council as unto first ages, and its decisions are those of the belief of first ages! The efforts of the powerful and the contumacious will not be able in this to frustrate, nor will the advancements of the erudite and the devisings of the subtle be able to disquiet, the consciences of the faithful in their infallibility. Their record will never pass into oblivion, or be erased by the hand of reform. It is the Church of Councils alone that defines as well as decrees, that has now in this land her duly appointed synods, which evince her relationship with what is most ancient by their unanimity in doctrine and the enforcement of discipline. She will always provide for the preservation of that from the exterminating hand of the disobedient which was created to yield life to the obedient by the efficiency of her dispositions, and it would be as difficult to defeat the wisdom of their fitting as it would have been to have surprised the luminously armed cherubim on their ward and watch over Eden. Numerous Protestants, as well as infidel writers, are yet continually urging that there have been divisions on doctrinal subjects within the Catholic Church, which claims immutable perfection from the commencement, as being Divinely established and Divinely directed. But to this it may

P

be once more finally replied, as answered of old that division was upon that which had not been authoritatively settled to be the belief of the Catholic Church; moreover, opinions as to open questions are not the declarations of Councils, any more than that new terms must imply new tenets, or that a difference in the habits of the several religious orders are indicative of a diversity in creed. Yet when Catholic authority has formally declared the ever existing and unvarying truth in respect to moral or doctrinal points, as it has been always done, when circumstances required it, with clearness and precision, then differences have quickly disappeared from among doctors, or the contumacious from among their number. It is not so with Protestantism, as already pretty amply dilated upon, and acknowledged to in grief by numbers. They must tolerate contrary judgments upon the most vital matter whilst free interpretation has Heaven's license, as so averred by her founders, or battle without the chance of a victory.

But this unsettling privilege is not to be impeached except at the risk of the worth of Luther's evangelical veracity, and the sacredness of his mission. However, this, though it should carry a conviction fatal to the Reformation, would be useless, considering the lengthened and jubilant exercise of private interpretation, which has conducted now to what menaces the very being of a Protestant Christianity, and which so solicitously induced some years ago a few thoughtful and foreseeing men to take up with the testimony of the past upon the all-engrossing subjects of this short life, belief and salvation, rather than to chance the latter by an obstinate adherence to that which to-day is not exactly what it was yesterday. Soon sanctuaries became more animated and imposing by increased rites, for it is well-nigh impossible to take up largely with Catholic tenets and to remain without an increase in corresponding and congenial ceremonies. Hence what was into some churches introduced, a gorgeous and solemn rite, set the frigid and scanty Christianity of many marvelling, and those that inherited a profound reverence for evangelical simplicity yelling. But if the Tractarians of the period enlarged in compliment towards Catholicity, by introducing into their Creed a number of the most known and prominent of her doctrines, they had a considerate care for their Protestant position, which contradictorily enough they strove to maintain by an additional virulence in their censures upon what they had not as yet pronounced as Apostolical for Great Britain, though orthodox at Rome. Their conduct could not be justified either by reason or conscience, whilst they continued at intervals to add to the value of their faith by drawing on the treasury of Catholic truths. Many, however, through the opportunities of research which university duties furnished, combined with the aids of conference, were brought nearer and nearer in profession and conviction to the ancient belief, and finally, through a special grace, those ceased to denounce who had once been most pertinacious and acrimonious as to their remaining exceptions in respect to the teachings of Catholicity—thus, like the converted one on the Cross, though at first reviling, at last resolutely and fervently turned to adore the truth, unheeding the turbulent cries around them of "Imposture and deceit!" of "Impiety and blasphemy!"

These eventual converts to a Creed that misrepresentation has made most fitting for execration were not gained over to Catholicity, it is almost needless to say, by any earthly motives, or through a due want of close and patient examination. As to the former there was little for them beyond the scrip and staff of the Apostle; as to the latter, no philosopher of olden date and fame, when Christianity began to make her final universality from the attendants of the temples of multitudinous deities, and the schools of differing masters, could have been more on the alert to detect, if possible, and to make obvious, the falsities of the teachings of Rome, than were the then so-termed Tractarians. But it was in thus acting to give a greater expansion, consistency, and influence to their Protestant faith through the medium of antiquity, the decrees of ancient Councils, and the exposition of the Fathers, they were brought to discern more clearly and minutely the grandeur and dignity of a Church which, in common with Evangelicals, Presbyterians, Baptists, Unitarians, and Rationalists, they had formerly so coarsely and unsparingly reprobated. A contributor to the *Rambler*, which has long ceased to exist, well acquainted with the foregoing remarkable religious movement in all its details, thus refers to its position at the conclusion of its first epoch: "It stood face to face with the Catholic Church, attracted, confounded, terrified. No suspicion had as yet touched its conscience that after all the Anglican Church might be no better than a mob of Wesleyans or Calvinists. The Anglican body had not as yet pronounced against the agitators. It still deemed it possible to show that the Church of England was Catholic, and the idea of un-Protestantising it was still in the womb of time. Rome was yet to be combated, far less obeyed. The British monarch was still 'Defender of the Faith,' and girding themselves up with new energies for the conflict, the gathering hosts of Tractarians prepared new weapons for the discomfiture of their foes." And what has been the success of the yet heterodox from the whirl of their gleaming weapons, in preserving their fool's Paradise from an unceasing desertion to a Church whose invincibility is perpetuated by repelling every attack, and whose heroism is always equal, as has already been shown, to every occasion. Besides the distinguished many that were once in such violent hostility against Catholicity, numbers also of note, from every religious persuasion, that plotted and fought against her with Saul's fanatical resolves, have finally been convinced of the holiness of her mission, by the indubitable intervention of what must have been Divine, and have ultimately in her ranks rendered the services of an Apostle. With these, on uniting with the Church of Ages, "that has ever been triumphant over every assault without, as well as every division within," [1] all doubt, all perplexity, all misgiving, passed finally away, and with each one the cry became, not, as ere now, "I take Luther, Calvin, Knox, Baxter, or Wesley, for my guide and the surety of my soul "—

> "But her alone for my director take
> Whom Thou hast promised never to forsake;
> My thoughtless youth was wing'd with vain desires
> My manhood long misled by wand'ring fires
> Follow'd false lights, and when their glimpse was gone
> My pride struck out new sparkles of her own,

---

[1] Bossuet.

> Such was I, such by nature still I am;
> Be Thine the glory, and be mine the shame;
> Good life be now my task, my doubts are done. [2]

Deeply to feel the necessity of a faith, and yet gravely to distrust his own creed, must make a profound and a daily misery. In respect to such a Christian, hours of tranquillity are for sleep alone. In his search after certitude, among a host of asseverations from a multitude of wrangling sects, he may become better versed in Scriptural texts, but he will not become more enlightened upon their import. "It will with him ever be the shifting of a difficulty without obviating it." One Church which stands out as definitely, as prominently, distinct from all other pretensions, and alone is known by the name of Catholic, he beholds, but it is with feelings by which he hopes to propitiate Heaven in his search for the peace of conviction. He never dreams of misrepresentation in regard to a Church that he identifies with abomination, until brought into some misgiving by incontestable statements, by an accidental reading, a close dispute, or a remarkable conversion. If even then he begins to view the Catholic Church with additional feelings of interest and favour, it is not without an occasional shrinking or startle at his progressing sympathies,

---

[2] Dryden.

through the fitful intrusion of old notions and prejudices.

But where there is resolute and sincere persistence in inquiry, it is scarcely possible that Protestantism should become the settled conviction of the inquirer, as the belief which made the glow and the teaching of the inspired. Thickening discrepancies forbid this, together with utter helplessness to remedy the evils that existed even at the commencement of Protestantism, either through the broadest convocations or the highest spiritual dignities. Authority does not abide in one or the other of these latter; it resides such as it may be considered with the secular ruling, which has the so-called reformed Christianity for its suffragan in national affairs. In this accomplished fact of things Protestantism cannot be of Heaven's providence, as Catholicity. "By me kings reign." "Lo! I am with you all days." Under the enlightenment of Damaris there is to be discovered in this what is to be reverenced and what is to be adored. Deputed majesty that holds dominion over temporal things is to be revered; the presence of the Divinity for the fixity and surety of the ministrations of truth is for adoration. The servant here cannot take precedency of the Master. In other words, truth is one with God, and cannot be in subservience to man. It is independent of time and its casualties, and the best witnessing to this is Catholicity, which was before Protestantism, that appeared with a boast and a challenge to contend for the cause of self-judgment and self-indulgence.

But in regard to those who have finally sided with what may be battled with, nevertheless cannot be overcome, it may be suitable here to impress upon Protestant minds that before entering into the Catholic Church a detailed profession of creed is rigorously exacted. Here Catholicity stands alone. Sects could scarcely insist upon it before any formal admission would be allowed of into their number. It is for that Church only thus to act which is as consistently cautious as her tenets are orthodox. In this lucid and precise profession of faith, which she insists on, there is that which readily enables the faithful to discover, and boldly to denounce, what is contrary to her sedulously defined and venerable creed. A proof of this is best given from the writings of Gother. This distinguished polemic, who lived in the most heated and heartless times of Protestant delusions and antipathies, and which he once so largely participated in and so strenuously proceeded on, thus, in the following emphatic and solemn words, anathematises those who are guilty of believing in that which even at this immediate hour Catholics are charged with in the most express and coarse terms: "Cursed is he who commits idolatry, who prays to images or to relics, or worships them. R. Amen. Cursed is every goddess-worshipper, who believes the Blessed Virgin Mary to be any more than a creature, who worships her, or who puts his trust in her more than in God—who believes her above her Son, or that she can in anything command Him. R. Amen. Cursed is he who believes the saints in heaven to be his redeemers, who prays to them as such, who gives God's honour to them, or to any creature whatsoever. R. Amen. Cursed is he who worships any bread, or makes gods of the empty elements of bread and wine. R. Amen. Cursed is he who believes that there is any power on earth or in heaven that can forgive sins without a hearty repentance and a serious purpose of amendment. R. Amen. Cursed is he who believes that there is authority in the Pope, or in any other person, that can give leave to commit sin, or that for a certain sum of money can forgive him his sins. R. Amen. Cursed is he who believes that, independent of the merits and passion of Christ, he can obtain salvation by his own good works, or make condign satisfaction for the guilt of his sins, or the pains eternally due to them. R. Amen. Cursed is he who undervalues the word of God, or that, forsaking Scripture, chooses rather to follow human tradition than it. R. Amen. Cursed is he who leaves the commandments of God to observe the constitutions of men. R. Amen. Cursed is he who omits any of the Ten Commandments, or keeps the people from the knowledge of any of them, to the end that they may not have the occasion of finding the truth. R. Amen. Cursed is he who preaches to the people in unknown tongues such as they understand not, or uses any other means to keep them in ignorance. R. Amen. Cursed is he that believes that the Pope can give to any person, upon any occasion whatever, dispensations to lie or to swear falsely, or that it is lawful at the last hour to protest himself innocent in case he should be guilty. R. Amen.

"Cursed is he who encourages sin, or teaches men to defer the amendment of their lives on the presumption of a death-bed repentance. R. Amen.

"Cursed is he who places his religion in nothing but pompous shows, consisting only of ceremonials, and which teach the people not to serve God in spirit and in truth. R. Amen. Cursed is he who loves and promotes cruelty, that teaches to be bloody-minded, and to lay aside the meekness of Jesus Christ. R. Amen. Cursed is he who teaches that it is lawful to do any wicked thing should it be for the interest or good of Mother Church, or that any evil action may be done that good may ensue from it. R. Amen.

Cursed are we if, among all these wicked principles, we hold any one to be the truth of our Church, and cursed are we if we do not heartily detest these hellish practices, as they do who so vehemently urge them against us. R. Amen.

"Cursed are we if, in answering or in saying Amen to any of these curses, we use any equivocations or mental reservations, or do not assent to them in the common and obvious sense of the word. R. Amen."

Could pen indite or could tongue utter more explicit words than the above? The anathemas have the warrant of their orthodoxy in the teaching of an uninterrupted tradition, and in the decisions of unerring Councils, and therefore must have the prompt subscription of the Catholic world. In the foregoing language, that comprises so solemn and definite a denial of old charges still brought against the Catholic religion, combined with that of the Bible being a sealed book with the Romanists, is manifested the grievous wrong that is done to a Church "which is detached from every other cause, and holds to Him alone who fills all times and all places, and which on every side evinces the impression of an almighty Hand." Within her holy precincts people cannot invent, revive, or compound between ancient and modern errors, as may be easily effected within the domain of Protestantism, without, under Heaven's provision, meeting with, as consecutive centuries undeviatingly testify, a direct anathema. Nor will Protestantism through such a venerable medium ever be able to protect herself, since it is not for her mission to define and confront opposition in vital matters, considering the fundamental differences within her own communion, and every unnatural attempt on her part to do so has always heightened defiance, provoked ridicule, and multiplied the impediments to her Apostolical action in the midst of her insubordinate and many-phased Christianity. To broaden in philanthropy then at this rational period, with its widening heterodoxies, and ever to be boldly instant in repulsively setting forth, under every imaginable superstitious, tyrannic, and iniquitous form, the nature of Catholicity, must be the wisdom of the Protestant hierarchy which "the children of light" have yet to be acquainted with.

Indeed, in all strategies employed by Protestantism to secure an advantage over an uncompromising foe, misrepresentation, by which truth was first opposed in Eden, must be her chief hope, since it made her primitive profit in her gatherings against orthodoxy. It is also less tasking, whilst being more effective, as it is commonly more easy to object with assurance than to prove with obviousness—to stimulate aversion than to convince reason. Paganism, and then heresy, at early periods adopted misrepresentation as the most effective plan to thwart a faith that has had as much to suffer from the fabrications and devisings of one as the other. On this subject the great St. Augustine, once immersed in heresy, as well as in sin, added to his virtue by his candour. "When I came to discover," says this most solid and instructive of the Fathers, "the truth, my joys and my blushes were mingled together. I was ashamed that I had for so many years been barking and railing, not against the Catholic faith, but only against the fictions of my carnal conceits. For so rash and impious was I that those things which I ought to have learned from them" (the Catholics) "by inquiry I charged upon them by accusations, being more ready to impose than to be informed of the truth; and thus did I so blindly accuse the Catholic Church, which I so fiercely persecuted, that taught not the opinions, as is now made sufficiently clear to me." Such, indeed, was the conduct of the first reformers towards a Church that God had promised should never fail, which had taught them their Christianity, and upon which, after recklessly vilifying, they largely and manifoldly made their amendments, without bringing about unanimity among their widely-dissenting disciples for a single symbol of their Godly framing. Something of a conclusive character was still wanting among them, and ever will be wanting, to bring them into any entitlement to Apostolicity. This, however, did not much disconcert the first reformers in their self-imposed mission, their sacred and predominating solicitude, and avowedly so, being rather to collect matter to upbraid the Catholics with than to put forth tenets sustained by cogent arguments to complete and justify what had been so confidently asserted. Luther, who has the distinguished credit of having first wrenched off the padlock from the inspired volume, as so stirringly given both in picture and story, and in the eager reading of which his mind gradually expanded in enlightenment, and at last burst asunder the straitenings so impiously riveted upon Evangelical liberty by a despotic Church, proclaimed, "I could have wished to have denied the presence of Christ in the Eucharist, in order to injure the Papist; but so strong were the words of Scripture which establish it that in spite of my inclinations, and although I strained every nerve to do so, yet never could I persuade myself to enter upon this expedient." This, nevertheless, fully evinces the animus of his Christian purposes.

But others were not restrained by reasonings as strong as those that baffled Luther in the fullest of his intent to vilify the Church of ages through one of her most august sacraments, the Body and Blood of our Lord—His Soul and His Divinity—under the appearances of bread and wine. Michael Cerularius, following in the footsteps of the calumniating and heretical Photius, declared that if the charges which he had brought against the Church were defeated by incontestable proofs of their falsity, he would, without delay, start others to supply for their insufficiency. Now, with prejudice or perversity truth will find it hard to contend, since from prejudice she will command but little attention for her declarations, and from perversity she will secure but little sincerity in their discussion; and it scarcely can be disputed that with thousands the unhesitating renewal of an accusation is as strong a testification of its probability as the magnitude of an imputation is with many, though obviously preposterous, some indication, at least, of what well merits censure. The Scribes and the Pharisees, failing to elicit from the Son of God something that would strongly favour their malicious designs, betook themselves to attribute His miracles to the agency of demons, and to proclaim His teaching as hostile to the religion of Israel, and thus hoping to subvert His authority among the people. Their sanctimonious speech, and their nefarious insinuations, at length attained their execrable ends, and finally scoffs succeeded to hosannas. "Quodcumque volumus sanctum est"—"What we will or wish is sure to be good "—says St. Augustine, and it follows what is otherwise here must be the reverse.

Thus, an authoritative Church, which includes in her mysteries what reason is not equal to in their entire comprehension, issues her salutary warnings to the presumptuous, and speedily condemns those that uphold error, is denounced by men who have in spiritual things their will as sacred as tyrannic in her action. She is a Church, in their well-poised conclusions, of outrages upon the righteous prerogatives and inherent principles of humanity—a Church that is not much incommoded with scruples when a purpose is to be attained—that her authority tends to paralyse conscience, and to destroy good citizenship; in fact, what has there not been at random objected against Catholicity in the heated vehemence of hostility? Taking up on rumour, without much examination, says a sensible writer, what is supported by sophistry, sanctified by hypocrisy, applauded by ignorance, adopted by simplicity, and eagerly accepted by pride and voluptuousness, their ardency in defence of calumny makes ultimately the fever of their minds, and hence the interminable delusions and misconceptions in respect to Catholicity, as well as the never-ending rhapsodies and incongruities among themselves. Catholicity, which is so misrepresented and maligned, has her spiritual health in the sound integrity of her belief and in the steady

Q

warmth of her virtue. In proportion as this integrity and warmth may be severally wanting, it will always be manifested that men in their waxing infirmities see less clearly, talk more profanely, act more audaciously, and conceive more preposterously. They have turned their Christianity into the problematical; with them Opinion has her queenship, and the most momentous of religious truths are left at the entire disposition of her deceptive and visionary majesty. Probity in temporal affairs and devotion in a place of worship, rectitude at home and propriety abroad, may impart dignity to her mien, but she will never have any dominion in a Church (though at this immediate hour might and victory think otherwise) which has hitherto remained unchanged and unimpaired, either by time or storm.

This indissoluble and infallible Church, that has its being in God not less than the creation, and has equally a Divine watching over it as that wherein is reckoned the fall of a sparrow, has been established to meet, through her sacred dispensations, the dire exigences of our corrupt nature, not to oppress it—exigences which she alone so fully knows and so fully has made known. "Man," says Pascal, "without this spiritual aid would be unceasingly subjected to deadly errors. Nothing shows him the truth; everything misleads him. The two criterions of truth, reason and the senses, besides being often unfaithful, impose naturally on each other. Our senses mislead our reason by false appearances, and reason plays it off on them in return, and thus avenges herself on them. The passions of the mind affect the senses, and leave upon them bad impressions. They deceive and impose on each other." In necessarily admitting the verity of the above words, and their appropriate bearing on present matter, it is likewise incumbent to admit the necessity there is, therefore, of the intervention of a Church which, by her authority, her teachings, her sacraments, and her discipline, can alone prove herself to be an adequate rescue from the blindness, feebleness, perverseness, and waywardness arising from man's first disobedience. A gradual abandonment of the defined teachings of this Church of love, mercy, and wisdom has been a series of errors, with, as already shown, for a closing consequence, the most obstinate and calamitous of spiritual woes, infidelity. On the other hand, a successive reassumption, as with the Puseyites, of those tenets that have been severally rejected, has never realised, independently of Catholicity, that authority which conserves the integrity of dogma and the vigour of discipline. As with the figures within a celebrated exhibition, many look like life, faithfully vested in all the details of Catholic grandeur, but the Spirit of God is wanting, that gave instant existence to the dead of the arid plain. Here the adherence of multitudes may also be secured on earth, but this will not carry the suffrage of Heaven. "Symmetry, not bulk," says Cardinal Newman; "order, not vastness; principle, not sham, are the tests of truth. These alone can be completely responded to within a Church which, for so many ages, notwithstanding every supervening difficulty, continues its sequence without alteration and without interruption."

SECTION V.

The Catholic Church, unchanged and unchangeable, is, as has been shown, alone able to satisfy the craving of the human mind for a stable and firm basis of belief. She need not fear that time, which changes all else, will avail to shake the foundation on which her edifice rests, or fret away a single stone forming a concomitant part of her ancient and venerable fabric. But on the point of her antiquity more yet remains to be said, for the Church does not date her origin from the first founding of Christianity; she did, if is true, receive her present form from St. Peter and his successors, but she can boast a more remote ancestry, since the Christian religion has immediate tracing up to a religion professed by a people the descendants of Abraham, Isaac, and Jacob, so wonderful in their conservation, so unique in their character, so conspicuous in rites, and so distinguished by miracles. At length the prophesied moment of complete fulfilment arrived; the Messiah was born into this world, and Judea, in reply to those who came from afar to adore, added to the testimony of the heavens, whose effulgent star shed its emblazoning lustre upon the rude shelter where reposed the Divine Infant and Saviour of mankind. When He commenced His mission, after years of privacy, His words, works, actions, and demeanour were without an equal in wisdom, wonder, propriety, and benignity. His sanctity haloed His miracles, which persistent and active enmity attributed to the intervention of demons. In carrying out His ineffable mission He conjoined to Himself neither the wealthy, the learned, the titled, nor the powerful, that their co-operation might not be adduced as a reason for the success of His labours. He selected the rough, the lowly, the artless, and the untutored, in carrying out the great objects of His love and mercy, who was Himself born in wretchedness, lived in poverty, and died in ignominy. After the descent of the Holy Ghost the destitute, the illiterate, and the comparatively unknown went forth, with the spirit of wisdom, counsel, and fortitude for their auxiliaries, to execute the mission of their Divine Master—to proclaim the future creed of nations, kingdoms, and empires—to propagate doctrines amongst them, and to exact their submission to laws that the mind had never yet conceived, nor had passion ever yet felt the restraint. They denounced in their teachings what philosophers had paraded forth as the dictates of truth, and contradicted what the ancients had revered as the choicest maxims of the wise. With them, in the reverse of centuries of conviction to the contrary, poverty, humility and self-denial had a respective merit, and the titled, the rich, the renowned, and the voluptuous, in the names of their philosophers and their approving deities, strove by scourge and prison, by rack and fire, to silence or exterminate the irreverent, the superstitious, the impious, and the seditious. All was in vain, in Rome as in Jerusalem, and finally the legions of Nero and Domitian marched to victory at a Christian's bidding. As Christianity prevailed and diffused her truths, men became proportionably freed from the cheats and delusions of ages. They progressed in a knowledge profound for angels, and ultimately blushed for outrages on their own sacred persons. With new duties, that had the elevation and the salvation of the soul for their all-engrossing importance, humanity in its most miserable and abject state became now an object of attention, and was solaced. Power became the faithful ally of the weak; wealth, the steady friend of the needy; learning, the assiduous instructor of the ignorant; and the leper, though recoiled from, was not forsaken. The legislative tribunals of nations and kingdoms, as well as their rulers and monarchs, now in the enlightenments of a Divine teaching, better discerned in their decisions and decrees what would best forward the welfare and order of society, and the sword of justice was more frequently stayed or sheathed at the whisperings of a religion of tenderness and compassion. By her intimations, blessed beyond the impartings of philosophy, reason became emancipated from a multitude of demoralising rites and harassing superstitions, from ferocious usages and debasing customs. In the midst of the most unbounded licence, conscience, which once had its terrors for crimes, was again heard to advantage, and in the practice of virtues long unknown to the world, a paradise was realised not inferior to that which unsullied innocence tenanted, and where Nature in her most trivial detail rendered joy. This Church, which has effected what must include Heaven's aid, immortal in the pledge of the Most High, has come out of every deadly conflict as unruffled as unchanged in feature.

But though this in its proofs makes the most conspicuous fact of history, yet there are many men at this sceptical period who do not believe in anything, however sacredly it may be termed or forcibly proved, that comprises the immortal and unchanged. In somewhat kindred with these a man has stepped forth in close confederacy with all that is powerful and triumphant to confrout Catholicity, and contemn her conservative providence of centuries, with all the

serenity of an unquestionable certitude of success—
"one who," in adopting the words of a great writer,
"is equally astute in concealing his plans as in carrying them out, who is alike indefatigable in peace and in war, who leaves nothing to fortune that he can accomplish by foresight or tact, who is discouraged by no obstacle, and never loses an opportunity to effect his purpose—in fine, one of those restless spirits that seem to have come into this world to alter everything."[1] This man, in an imperial tone, deeming all things to be ready for carrying out his heartless and irreligious projects, called upon millions of the children of Catholicity to give up to a Protestant ruling what they prize in importance with their salvation, their spiritual allegiance due to the supreme head of their faith. It was virtually responded to by millions with the cry of "Never!"—a cry which was often heard from the heavily manacled in the gloomy Mamertine prison, and also from the parched lips of the lacerated martyr in the crowded amphitheatre. This conscientious proceeding, which has so close a resemblance to the heroic days of Christianity, will no more, however, alienate Catholics from fatherland than it will make them false to Heaven. Nevertheless, a Prince of hard features and rigid gait insists, with

[1] Bossuet.

all the assurance of one that appears hitherto to have "had fortune in his pay," that those of the olden belief have forfeited all right to the possession of their ancient sanctuaries unless they fully comply with the tyrannic enactments of a Lutheran Empire, which go to confound the Catholic priest with the Protestant cleric.

The Catholic school shares also in the extreme despotism that is exercised over the sanctuary, which has become heterodox in the theology of the reformed, by the continuance of a sacrifice designated holy in the first days of Christianity. All must come to Julian's feet. Suppression and spoliation are also upon monastery and convent. Numbers from religious orders of either sex, that have done honour to their diversified professions in imparting knowledge, or in aiding at every discomfort and risk an untutored or suffering humanity, are now seeking in penury and privation for other fatherlands in the place of the one to which for ages they have been a Providence. In all this suppression, scattering, and desolation that deeply afflicts thousands upon thousands within the Germanic Empire, does Bismarck think to freshen his laurels, to freshen them in the tears of those in whose blood, shed in triumphant fight, they had their first speedy growth. The gains of diplomacy here will not be his to add to his notoriety. But should it be deemed otherwise with him, in a buoyant, hardened persistence, that evil spirit cannot partake largely of his dogged confidence who marshalled his legions in heaven against Infinite Power, and had Cæsar for his confederate on earth against Christianity, being thoroughly acquainted with the difficulty of mastering consciences imbued with a faith which is one with victory. "This is the victory, our faith" (1 St. John v. 4.) Saul, in the height of his presumption, and in the midst of his glittering cohorts, was on a sudden smitten to the earth, and the voice that said, "Lo, I am with you" (St. Matt.), declared that it was difficult to kick against the goads (Acts c. ix.) Puissant Prince, then, it may be deferentially said, with all your august and influential accessories, a facile Emperor, an obsequious Ministry, and for the major part a servile Senate, that moves under your dexterous handling with the promptitude of the flexible puppets of Junius, that were worked upon by the chief juggler, who held the strings behind the curtain, final success will not be yours, the success you expect will not always be yours, and in utter failure you may witness with the contrition of Antiochus to the impiety of your purposes.

It would well befit Germany, whose interests are not forwarded by persecution, to remember, at this threatening and uneasy period among empires, that she owes all that is within her of Christianity to Catholicity. With her conversion came civilisation, united with a religious fealty, which gave the fixity of principle to patriotism. Before this supreme, felicitous event had an entry in history, the country that is now Empire by triumphs and acquisitions was a wild and uncultivated land, in which a most insubordinate race, conjoined with a very considerable portion of the surplus of neighbouring nations, loitered for plunder or hid their priced heads. Almost every lengthened journey within its not very exactly defined boundaries was deepened danger, from prowling beasts or lurking men. It was not, indeed, without its altar, which was sometimes smeared with the blood of human victims, as best propitiating the benign deities, in the midst of discordant sounds and fierce howlings. When darkness was upon this wild country, the jungle of the East surpassed it in safety. Boniface beheld with the eye of the prophet, and with his lament, this desolation in its full spread. He advanced, and crossed confines within which every step was one of hazard. He progressed undauntedly, and cast the good seed in the midst of want and affliction, menaces and deadly conspiracies. He finally established Christianity where paganism prevailed, environed with all that could dishearten except the Apostle, and the title of "martyr" eventually became his due, by giving up his life here, that those might have life hereafter that he sought to save so fearlessly and so disinterestedly.

The Catholic descendants of this man of God, whose name ought to be preferred to Frederic the Infidel, though termed Great, are indeed at this hour sorely oppressed. To bring their Christianity into vassalage to the State, which centuries have left free in the exercise of her vital discipline, the most exclusive and exacting measures continue to be enforced, which lands not Catholic have pronounced tyrannical, and including an ill requital to those who are prominent in the national records for patriotism and heroism; those who love fatherland still, yet love the will of their Heavenly Father better; those who are determined not to be swayed by temporal profit at the risk of eternal loss; those who will not place the rights of the mitre at the disposal of the Crown; those who will not prove themselves unworthy of the virtue and blood of a Boniface, that bequeathed to them a faith framed by God, not shapen by man, nor make secondary what has been held sacred for ages by saint and martyr to the monopolising schemes of a waning Emperor, to the gains of a courtly Ministry, or to the manifest objects of the most ambitious and callous of devisers in the German realm, computed at fifteen millions as to their number; those who are now so heartlessly harassed by legislative enactments, and are gradually losing their firm and edifying pastors, to be supplied by those, if they can well be found, who have a price, like Judas that is execrated, may not lessen in their fidelity and their loyalty to the throne, and will doubtless be as ready to battle for the Empire as before for the Kingdom, but they will not very readily stand at the portals of their venerable temples as sentinels to allow only those to pass into their sanctuaries sacrilegiously to officiate who had first to set at naught the direst of censures before they became duly qualified to partake of the mess of statute pottage.

Tyranny, however, as above referred to, is not without her studied representations to justify her proceedings, and often beguiles those over to her party into whose souls the iron of persecution has not yet entered. It is commonly put forth by her as a chief motive, under the heading of daring and deeply concerted conspiracies against the welfare and stability of the State, by some large, influential bodies of Catholics, that are in this instance characterised as being of the most ambitious and aggressive purposes. The most shallow and hasty of surmises are acted on as facts, and this often realises a greater mischief to a dominion than what might arise even from successful and wide plottings. But history here is to be read in her many prominent exemplifications and details in support of this, and in which also tyranny generally will be found to have had her sure overthrow. In connection with the foregoing, to leave well alone is certainly the supreme wisdom of a Government. It was what Frederic the Great acted upon, as the records of his life inform us, in regard to his Catholic people, and we do not read that disaster was the sequel. In a letter to D'Alembert, he says, "I respect each one's right, upon which society is founded." Joseph the Second, in adopting, though fitfully, a reverse conduct, troubled his own repose as well as that of his subjects, and felt so deeply the unique results of his despotism and misrule, in ecclesiastical as also in secular affairs, that he had for his epitaph over his grave, "Here lies Joseph the Second, who was unfortunate in all his enterprises." "To prevent evil," as solidly remarked, "is the great end of government, the end for which vigilance and severity are properly employed." But what evil started into gigantic being among the Catholics in the German Fatherland, to transfix Protestantism with terror, who so recently and so readily gave their money and their blood in aiding and fighting for their country against assailing France? Mere conjecture, for an honourable and grateful Empire to act upon, will not be a satisfactory reply to the world for a conduct that involves suppression of religious houses, the exiling of priests, and the sorrowings of hundreds of families for the loss of their pastors, with no spiritual refuge left for them but anointed and venal apostates.

However, from all this it may be readily concluded that the cherished hope of a crowned head, animated by the assurances of an infatuated adviser, that has very presumedly mysteries for pleasantries, is totally to suspend within German realms the action of an hierarchy that is modelled on one of a celestial order, and to silence the voice of its spiritual head, which is heard and obeyed, as with that of the Apostles, at the utmost ends of the earth. Yet here it is to be well considered that what is to be made subordinate to secular, and hitherto seemingly successful, wills, under political reckonings, goes in the aggregate to constitute a Church within which all is Divine, and upon which no breach can be effected, and no flag will flutter indicative of triumphant possession. Napoleon, with complacent confidence, came to a similar conclusion, as some other sanguine and distinguished personages, as to forcing the Church into a complete subserviency to the forwarding of their broad aggressions and political schemes. Nevertheless, the more than hero of his day, who had bestowed sceptres wrested from hands enfeebled by useless struggles to retain them, was met in his broad and impious requirements with absolute refusal and ultimate censure. He heeded not the latter. An almost undeviating success had made all things appear possible to him. "Priestly denouncing," he exclaimed, "will not cause the muskets of my men to fall from their hands." He gathered about him his martial strength, that had hitherto astonished the world by the suddenness of victory over leagued empires. He marched against the most imperial and potent of his foes. He never feared the Heaven above until, overcast with clouds, the storm commenced in piercing winds and whirling snows. The benumbing cold quickly brought arms and standards to the earth, and then those who bore them heavily fell upon them, never more, like the prostrate warriors of Sennacherib, to rise again. A steady sequel of disastrous defeats was in proximate attendance upon a calamity whose details can scarcely at this period be read in history without a shudder. But thus does Macaulay speak of one whose fortune once equalled his continuous and vast purposes, when in captivity at St. Helena: "He dragged out his existence as a prisoner in an unhealthy climate, under an ungenerous gaoler, raging with an impotent desire of vengeance, and brooding over visions of departed glory. Napoleon died without a throne, and Pius reascended the exalted one from which Napoleon had rudely ejected him, and then conducted him in ignominious state into a land where now he is not forgotten, if not remembered with a former enthusiasm." In one of the most magnificent castles of Europe, and of the world, that succeeding monarchs have contributed to enlarge and beautify, Pius's memory is conserved in his venerable and faithful portrait. It has its conspicuous place among the portraits of some of the most renowned rulers, ministers, and warriors of his all-eventful time. Whatever the artist could do to impart majesty to the features of royalty, sagacity to the lineaments of statesmen, and hardihood to the brows of the warrior, is done. But, in viewing the countenances of the illustrious, the eye of the spectator must be principally arrested by the looks of one on whom faith and virtue have so deeply impressed the indications of confidence and resignation that they cannot but yield in their contemplation, to a religious mind, that more was to be obtained from the God of armies by the prayers of the saintly Pontiff than could be gained by the forces of sovereigns, the counsels of statesmen, and the exploits of the valiant. At the period when nations were in deadly conflict, the voice of Pius, at the head of his hierarchy, the staff of truth, was heard with its ancient and wide influence, and unless it had been elevated no other would have been listened to in the name of Christianity. This voice excommunicated those, whether principals or associates, without faltering, whatever may have been their influence through position or renown, who strove to usurp what was sacred, and to make it subservient to their own profane ends. Thus has the departed Pius the Ninth acted, with no less edification and courage than his holy and firm predecessor, in the midst of assailments that may shake the Pontifical throne, yet, whatever mischief may be done to it, the Hand will repair which built it up.

But after this form has the intrepid and eloquent Dr. Windthorst, in the German Reichstag, addressed those who have, in their descriptive reference, termed the colossal bestriding of the Pope on earth a sworn ruin: "There is no doubt that the primacy of the Holy See is an integral part of the constitution of the Catholic Church. The Catholic Church has become part of the fabric of the German Commonwealth, with a title that has the priority of all German States. By violating her rights a precedent is created for the violation of all other titles to property, whether as to public or private. If you believe by recalling your minister from the Papal Court you will wean the German Catholics from their spiritual allegiance to the Holy See you are greatly mistaken. The war waged upon our Church by the Chancellor of the Empire has thus far the un-

doubted effect to recall the most lukewarm of Catholics to a religious life. You may be quite sure that this minister is not wanted to attach the hearts of the Catholics more firmly to the Holy See. Let the difficulties be ever so great, we Catholics will always find the means of manifesting our warm and heartfelt sympathy towards the venerable man who is seated in the Vatican. It is most characteristic that the new German Empire should commence its existence with a war against the Church, and with breaking off, or at least trying to break off, from all relations with the Holy See. The political leaders of Germany fancy that they are able to demolish the Catholic Church, and especially the primacy of the Holy Father; this has very much the presumption of the Titans of old as to their narrated attack on heaven, finishing in most humiliating discomfiture. Let our modern Titans be even more powerful than those of antiquity, their struggle will not end in triumph. His Holiness is sure to remain in possession of the battlefield."
"The sovereignty which best maintains the interests and dignities of the Cross that surmounts the diadems of monarchs, and which includes both the temporal and the spiritual in its rule from so remote a date, was founded," says Hurter, in his history of Innocent the Third, "on the most just and honourable titles— namely, on the legitimate conquests of a people

abandoned by their former rulers—founded, too, on the righteous conquests of the French nation, that Italy had called to her aid, through the intervention of the Pope, and also on the vital services tendered to Italy for more than two centuries, and in the greatest emergencies, through the prudence and generosity of a lengthened succession of Pontiffs. History certainly presents very few examples of a sovereignty whose origin was so legitimate and so venerable." " Let us add," continues Hurter, " that the sovereignty so rightful in its origin is one of the most signal evidences of the Almighty's care over His Church, and of that Infinite Wisdom which makes all human institutions auxiliary to His designs. Were a Pope a citizen of London or Paris he would not be equally respected by both nations, nor would he have always free action in the duties of his administrations. It would be difficult to recognise the Pope as a common father were he the subject of any king." Thus does Hurter write, at a period when he was under the influence of Protestant feelings, in support of the sovereignty of the Papacy. To this may be pertinently annexed what Bossuet so forcibly observes on the above subject, " God wills that this Church, the common mother of all kingdoms, should not be dependent upon the temporal bidding of any rule, and that the See through which the faithful preserve their unity should be raised above partialities, which conflicting State interests and jealousies might cause." Who will not then recognise in this the Hand that withdrew the Cross from the labyrinth of obscure caverns, and finally fixed it prominently for reverence in the common emblem of sovereign power? · The kingdom of Jesus Christ is not indeed of this world as to an universal earthly dominion, which the carnal Jews looked for, and which was, when attained, to make it conclusive amongst them of the presence of Jesus Christ. Jesus Christ came to establish a celestial power, for the rule of souls, but what princes bestowed for its terrestrial independence under the wise dispensations of Providence, and watched over as the sentinels of Him who decreed and gave them sovereignty, could no more be construed into what was adverse to the declarations of truth than the title of king which was affixed at the head of the Cross beneath which was suspended the Divine Sufferer, crowned with thorns.

But it may be asked, "What suitableness is there in a priest of the altar to meet the requirements of a possessor of a throne?" Much, is the unhesitating reply, since his education comprises the affairs of earth as well as heaven. This will be seen when the respective positions and circumstances are taken into consideration of the eventual monarch as well as the

Pontiff. Docility and assiduity cannot be very readily formed in those who are fully conscious of being presumptive heirs to regal power. It is as difficult to enlighten their minds by regular and close application as to realise in some a control over vice by the fascinations of virtue. And even if, under the most happy tutorings, august pupils are inducted into scholarship, and religious impressions are attained, there will be vitally needed a considerable worldly experience to ensure in a final regal administration wide and beneficial results. From the flattery, servility, sordidness, and self-seeking of Courts, little can be derived to aid the successors to empire in the compassing of many things identified with a common and a practical good. Even among the better lived that may abide with heedless worldlings, who so thickly beset the paths of princes, hardly will one be found dutiful and courageous enough to whisper warning or information for a public or a royal advantage. However, let it be admitted that exceptions are to be made, and illustriously so, in favour of kings in securing the happiness and affections of their subjects, yet generally the successors to sceptres are under the sway of some master-passion, that monopolises for self the most vigorous and profitable of their moments, and leaves them with but a very meagre possession of what will best respond to the high requirements of their position.

However, in most lands, when princes at last come to regal dominion, religion, laws, and the prosperity of the realm are almost invariably consigned to the entire care of a minister or Ministry, that not often makes known to rulers what imperative claims accompany their anointed rank, and are to be fulfilled to ensure a blessing for themselves and the well-being of their subjects. Yet commonly there is not a very intimate relationship between ministerial counsellings and royal wills; these latter have had their impunities and their immunities in their princeships, and now these with the possessed diadem constitute privileges and rights, without the adjunct often in their exercise of the fear of God. Dying sires have, as history has made known to us, occasionally uttered last words of advice to their succeeding heirs, but whether last words have made a lasting impression is, in the main, very doubtful. A few final words of a good King may, however, be here given as pre-eminently suitable to be addressed by a declining Emperor to his eldest-born before his departure from this life to immediate judgment: "My son, love your people as a father loves his children. Be superior to prejudice, and have equity for all. Be more solicitous to preserve peace within your territories than to add to them. Reign in justice here, and you will not fail of your crown hereafter." This sound advice remembered and acted upon would enable presumptive heirs when seated on thrones to make some approach to a Josias, who endeared himself both to God and man by his just and paternal government —unlike Solomon, who preferred to be swayed by passion rather than by the wisdom which would have preserved him from the deadly perversions of which he was forewarned, and whose final fate is a problem among men.

The circumstances being thus briefly discussed which commonly attend on princes in their youth, and in what form they absolutely interfere with the well-tutoring for future thrones, in whose due administration the governing and the governed find either misery or happiness, let the usual antecedents of one who finally is elevated to the Popedom be here entered upon. The clerical student, whose descent may be humble or the reverse, will have, under the tutoring and discipline of monastery or college, superiors to instruct and watch over him who will not generally be at fault in ascertaining the ability and the disposition of the candidate for the sanctuary, and in attaining some degree of certitude as to his sacerdotal vocation by his almost daily actions. There is no danger nor peril here, in rebuke or correction, in bettering the heart or mind, and one that is actuated by mere gain has not commonly the superintendence over what has the interests of religion for a chief care. To forward the advancement of ecclesiastical students emulation is not excluded from the schools, and if successful competition has its hazards by engendering pride or giving rise to eccentricity of conduct it is sure to have a thwarting through the discernment and tact of the professors, or the ever-ready playings-off and railleries of companions. Within the walls of monastery or college, as without, vigilance rarely relaxes or wanes in her watch over order and rule. Her principal solicitude next to the fulfilment of prescribed hours for prayer and study is to exclude that which might lead to effeminacy and indolence, and to allow of that only which would contribute to vigour of body and elasticity of mind. Perversity may have a presence in the best-ordered of abodes to thwart a good by her insidious speech, as with crouched mischief in Eden, and to inveigle the virtuous into guilt, yet it has rarely escaped detection, and when detected a speedy ejection has followed. On the completion of the entire course of studies, which include a moral certitude that the heart is as much benefited as the head, the finally ordained, with an assigned sacred mission, attains an experience, under a variety of important phases, that cannot but enhance the merits and profitableness of his priesthood. As advancements may be attendant on ecclesiastics of ability and probity, especially in Catholic countries, the eyes of the scrutinising are sure to be upon them, especially when their employments are diplomatically identified with States and peoples. Here unfitness it must be conceded may secure even the title of Eminence, yet it is not so very easy to defeat the prudence and experience of the conclaved Cardinalate when the suitableness of one or other of its members is the all-absorbing consideration in an election to Papal rule, to which piety as well as erudition and ability furnishes a motive for selection.

There have indeed been some sorrowful periods in the history of the Catholic Church, already adverted to, when iniquity as subtle as powerful has eluded even the watchfulness of the zeal which glowed in the breast of David for the glory of God's House, and those have ascended to the chair of Peter with the faith but not with the virtue of the Apostle. But though the most responsible and elevated of thrones, which alone combines spiritual rule with secular sovereignty, was occasionally desecrated, it was ever venerated. It has had most commonly those for its occupants who had first learned how to obey before they began to govern—who were faithful subjects before they arrived at sovereign dominion —who brought with them to this august position the practical experience resulting from public as well as private transactions with the highest as also with the lowest of society—who progressed in charity and patience in the midst of the poor and the importunate, the oppressed and the afflicted, and who added to their courtesy of demeanour in their more extended and frequent intercourse with the elevated and the courteous. The best auxiliaries of monarchs in the administration of wide dominions have been found among the spiritual princes of the Church, who were, according to the most able, experienced, and reliable of testimonies, " men as vast in their designs as in the measure of their capabilities, as prompt in meeting present difficulties as in foreseeing future ones, whose varied and profound information rarely allowed them to be overtaken by surprise, and whose fortitude in reverses was as conspicuous as their discretion in honours." Perhaps reigns have become for the chief part more renowned and prosperous when kings have had cardinals for their ministers of State. However, notwithstanding all the opprobriums that have been so indiscriminately heaped upon them, Macaulay could speak of one as " having a conscience to control his passions, and an enlightened understanding to guide himself with, in the embarrassing and perilous paths of Courts, who, as tersely observed, was as adroit in the noble science of government as profoundly versed in the sources of national prosperity and the causes of national decay, who, in the exercise of duties which in modern times do not yield in importance to the obligations of majesty, equally maintained the august characters of the Christian and the citizen, the bishop and the minister, Cardinal Fleury." Perhaps, in what has preceded, the instructed and candid Protestant may discern and admit that there is wherewith preparatory in the Catholic Church to render an ecclesiastic somewhat equal to the assumption of kingship, which the youthful expectants of thrones are never favoured with in the entirety of its details.

But what did the millions of the earth behold in a late Pontiff and Sovereign? They beheld a successor to the chief of the Apostles, who, before he became, by temporal dominion, a brother of monarchs, and received the felicitations of the representatives of majesty, together with the homage of the hierarchy, did, under the most weighty and extensive of considerations, good service to States as well as to sanctuaries. He entered upon the highest and most momentous of rules with an information that gained him an influence equally with that of his piety. In the discharge of high spiritual as well as secular functions, he manifested an amiability that obtained the confidence of those who were officially engaged about his sacred person, and secured the admiration of those who were favoured by an admission to his venerable presence. In the language of an able writer, "He was always distinguished by the quietude of his deportment, his patience in listening, and the suavity of his answers"—a man, in the words of Scripture, "Responsio mollis, lingua placabilis, et dulcis eloquia." (Prov., chap. xv., ver. 16.) The immediate period of clouds and tempests did not interfere with the serenity of his mind or aspect. The recently ordained about to proceed from Rome to their respective missions were in their farewell interviews with His Holiness as much elated by the amenity as by the blessing of one who knew so well how to make himself all to all, and to engage all. If Pius the Ninth was not so illustrious in earthly deeds as some of his predecessors, he has rarely been surpassed by them in what makes substantial worth in the citizen, the king, and the Pontiff. It has never yet been advanced that the cheerfulness of his nature interfered with the authority of his position or the dignity of his character. Hatred to his faith has not hitherto been able to proclaim anything of moment against him as to his daily life, as to public or private conduct. The ordinary requirements of nature were met by him under the most simple and abbreviated of forms. So little was Pius the Ninth solicitous about what to eat and what to drink that it might be readily affirmed in the above respects that the most menial of the servants of his household fared as well as the august master himself. Rarely has any one approached him in trouble and who left without consolation. He ever retained tranquillity in the midst of the most fearful of trials, that made martyrs of saints without the shedding of blood. His condescension and resignation were not weaknesses; he has minutely summed up errors and denounced the abettors of them, though rulers and people have raged. In captured Rome herself he anathematised those who were at the head of pillaging and sacrilegious soldiery. But whilst with intrepidity without precipitancy he thus acted he never failed to uplift those hands to Heaven that had so often been raised in prayer for the City and the world, that those who desecrated his sanctuaries as well as those who plundered them might be enlightened and repent. Where there was such a charity it was difficult to separate father from ruler, and where there was such courage it was difficult to confound the shepherd with the hireling.

SECTION VI.

The personal qualities of a ruler, and the manner in which he exercises his sway, are invariably influential in promoting feelings either of loyalty or of disaffection towards the office he fills. And a character like that of the late occupant of the Chair of Peter, combining gentleness and simplicity with strength and dignity, winning for him the devoted affection of his spiritual children, and extorting reluctant admiration from the bitterest Protestants, must serve to diminish the prejudices even of such persons as see in the Pope of Rome a despot greedy of power, anxious to extend his prerogatives and usurp the rights of monarchs, and ready to hurl anathemas at all who presume to resist his encroachments. In this light the pages of history, falsified by Protestants, depict the representative on earth of Him who declares, "By Me kings reign"—the Pontiff to whose ecclesiastical authority, exercised for the welfare of their subjects, monarchs were wont in former times to yield respectful submission.

As to whatever amount of misconception may have

been comprised in the persuasion that he who combined like Melchisedec, priest with king, possessed a right to transfer sceptres from unjust and unmerciful hands to those who would wield them with justice and mercy, certain it is that at periods of cruel and frequent oppression a credence in the affirmative realised a confidence and an influence for the Papal throne that furnished sometimes, as indisputably attested in history, a beneficial check upon the wantonness and despotism of depraved princes and monarchs. But it is not necessary here to enter into extended discussions on the abuse of the alleged prerogatives of the Supreme Pontiff and the obedience exacted from the Catholic in their exercise, especially as to what has been so insidiously and persistently urged against the devoted loyalty of the British subject, considering the many and satisfactory expositions on a matter to which brief allusion has been already made. It may indeed somewhat add to the force of what has been already said on the above by giving here the emphatic words of Father O'Leary: " I solemnly swear, without equivocation or the danger of perjury, that in a Catholic country where I was chaplain of war, I thought it a crime to engage the King of England's soldiers or sailors into the service of a Catholic monarch against their Protestant sovereign; I resisted every solicitation, and ran the risk of incurring the displeasure of a minister of

State, and of losing my pension. My conduct was approved of by all the divines in a monastery to which I then belonged, who all unanimously declared that in conscience I could not have done otherwise. . . . It is a Catholic principle and duty at the present time, as in the primitive ages, to pray for our kings, that God will be pleased to grant them a long life and a tranquil reign, that their family may be safe and their forces valiant, their Senate loyal, their people orderly and virtuous, that they may govern in peace, and have all the blessings they can desire either as men or princes." [1]

However, Catholicity will not allow Cæsar and his legions to interfere with her spiritual administrations, which are of Divine origin. She possesses what the Apostle exercised, which was not in subjection to Sanhedrin or throne, what the miracle attested to and what the sword could not triumph over. "It is useless for many to insist upon," says a renowned prelate whose amiability won estimation for himself even at the most fierce periods of conflicts and controversies, "that the Church is within the State. It is true, indeed, that the Church is within the State, and in submission to supreme power, in all that is temporal; but she is not dependent upon the State

---

[1] Father O'Leary.

for any spiritual function. Princes, in becoming her children, do not become her masters." "The Emperor," declares St. Ambrose, "is within the Church, but he is not above the Church. The Church remains as free under converted emperors as idolatrous and persecuting rulers. In her promptitude to submit to legitimate authority the Church is not outdone, and than in her members and in her princes have not a more assured source of fidelity and aid. But should the question turn upon a spiritual administration conferred on her by her Divine Master, then she vindicates, in spite of every threat, the exercise of it, as being entirely independent of man." Between, then, the Church and the State the submission is reciprocal; the former yields to the State in what is temporal, as the latter is bound to do to the Church in what is spiritual. But when kings, with the temerity of Saul, assume to themselves what exclusively belongs to the priesthood, their sin goes beyond that of Oza, who in unreflecting haste placed his unanointed hand on the apparently imperilled ark, and instantly fell lifeless by its side. To Constantine, as with Alexander, conquest gave a near approach to universal dominion, yet he never set up his imperial arms in the sanctuaries of Christendom, before which he prostrated, to indicate the absolute " mine." If he was present in state at a General Council, it was by majesty to dignify what was summoned to decide on orthodoxy, and at the same time to preserve order in its venerable proceedings, but not to dictate or decree upon discipline or creed. Constantine well knew that his sword could never have overcome the numerous veteran legions, so inured to combat and so flushed with success, except through the medium of the Cross, that triumphed over death itself—" the sacred symbol of eternal justice and holy freedom, that has presided over all the destinies of the modern world, and is connected with all its adversities and its glories, which has served as the basis of its laws, and as the standard of its armies." [1] Not so the sceptre, which has no significance of rule within the Catholic sanctuary. When potentates come to this spiritual boundary they cease to control. Here they are silent, here they kneel and do reverence with the most lowly of their subjects. In justification for the present severe and despotic action of the German Legislature towards Catholicity within its operation, it is advanced chiefly to be the Papal infallibility and jurisdiction with which no empire, nation, or kingdom could deal under any confidence, security, or profit. " By the decrees of the Vatican Council, it is affirmed that the Pope is enabled to exercise and to substitute the Papal authority for

---

[1] Montalembert.

the local authority of the bishop. The Pope no longer, as before, merely exercises certain rights that have been reserved to him, but a complete fulness of episcopal authority rests in his hands. In principle he has stepped into the position of each individual bishop, and it only depends on himself at any moment actually to assume the episcopal functions, not excluding even the relations of a local bishop with his Government. The bishops are now only the instruments of the Pope and his officials, without any responsibility of their own. They have become with respect to their Governments the ministers of a foreign sovereign, and moreover of a sovereign who, in virtue of his infallibility, is more thoroughly absolute than any absolute monarch in the world."

"All these propositions are without foundation," emphatically declare the German Catholic archbishops and bishops. "Unquestionably," they say, "according to the decrees of the Vatican Council, the ecclesiastical jurisdiction of the Pope is that of a supreme ordinary, and he has an immediate power over the whole Church, conferred on him in the person of Peter, by Jesus Christ, the Son of God. It is therefore a supreme authority that extends directly over every individual diocese, and over all the faithful, for the preservation of the unity of the faith, of discipline, and of the government of the Church; and it is by no means an authority that consists only of certain rights which have been reserved to him. This, however, is no new doctrine, but a truth of Catholic faith, which has been always acknowledged, and a known principle of canon law, a doctrine which the Vatican Council, following the decisions of previous General Councils, has declared and confirmed against the errors of the Gallicans and the Jansenists. According to this doctrine the Pope is Bishop of Rome, not bishop of any other city or diocese—not Bishop of Rome and of Breslau. But as Bishop of Rome he is also Pope—that is, the Supreme Pastor and Head of the whole Church, of all the bishops, of all the faithful; and his Papal authority is not merely called into existence in certain exceptional cases, but it has validity and power always and everywhere, and over all. In this position the Pope has to see that every bishop fulfils his duty within the entire range of his official charge, and where a bishop is in any way hindered, or where any necessity calls for the Pope's interference, there the Pope has the right and duty, as a bishop of the diocese, to regulate within it whatever relates to its administration.

"Further, the decrees of the Vatican Council do not furnish a shadow of pretext for the assertion that the Pope has become through them an absolute sovereign, and, in virtue of his infallibility, one more absolute than any monarch in the world. In the first place, the domain to which the ecclesiastical jurisdiction of the Pope belongs is essentially different from that of the temporal authority of monarchs, and the full sovereignty of the temporal will is nowhere disputed by Christians. But abstracting from these considerations, the designation of absolute monarch, even in relation to ecclesiastical affairs, cannot be applied to the Pope, because he is subject to the Divine law, and is bound by the ordinances established by Christ for His Church. He cannot alter the constitution which has been given to the Church by her Divine Founder as the temporal legislator can change the constitution of a kingdom. The constitution of the Church rests in all essential points on Divine ordination, and is beyond the sphere of human interference. As the Papacy is of Divine institution, so is also the episcopacy, and by reason of this institution it also has its rights and its duties, which the Pope has neither the right nor the power to change. It is therefore a complete misunderstanding of the Vatican decrees to believe that through them the episcopal jurisdiction has been absorbed into the Papal—that the Pope has in principle stepped into the position of each individual bishop, and that the bishops are now only the instruments of the Pope and his officials, without any responsibility of their own. According to the constant doctrine of the Catholic Church, which has also been expressly declared by the Vatican Council, the bishops are not mere instruments of the Pope, they are not mere Papal officials, without any responsibility of their own, but elected by the Holy Ghost in the place of the Apostles, to watch as the only true shepherds over their flocks which have been entrusted to them. The Pope will remain, as in the past eighteen centuries, the companion and the head of the episcopacy, occupying his place in the organism of the Church by Divine ordinance. And the right which the Pope has at all times possessed to exercise his ecclesiastical authority over the whole Catholic world has not hitherto resulted in rendering illusory the authority of the bishops, therefore it cannot be said that the recent declaration of the ancient Catholic doctrine will tend to any such result in the future. It is a notorious fact that the dioceses of the whole Catholic world have been directed and governed by their bishops since the Vatican Council precisely in the same way and manner as before it. With respect especially to the statement that through the Vatican decrees the bishops have become Papal officials, without any responsibility of their own, we can declare with the firmest certainty that it is not the Catholic Church that will ever preach the immoral and despotic maxim that the command of a superior releases one from all personal responsibility. Finally, the opinion that the Pope has become, in virtue of his infallibility, an entirely absolute sovereign, rests upon a thoroughly erroneous apprehension of the dogma of Papal infallibility. As the Vatican has declared in clear and precise words, and as the nature of the thing demonstrates, it refers exclusively to an attribute of the Papal office of supreme teacher. His teaching extends to the same domain as the infallible teaching of the Church, and it is drawn from the Holy Scriptures, and from tradition, and from doctrinal decisions that the Church has formally given. With respect to the relations of the Pope with Governments, not the slightest alteration has been effected; since it is plain that the opinion that the position of the Pope towards the episcopate has been altered by the decrees of the Vatican Council is wholly unfounded, so also the conclusion that has been drawn from that opinion, that the position of the Pope with respect to Governments has been changed by the decrees, loses every shadow of ground or respect."

To the above forcible and lucid explanation upon matter that has engaged so much attention and given rise to so much controversy are appended the signatures of the Archbishops of Cologne and of Munich, of the coadjutors of Bamberg and Fribourg, and of the bishops of the other dioceses of Germany.

Nevertheless, it is all in vain; imprisonments and fines, banishments and menaces, still continue. Yet when the storm was at its height (so massing and heavy), though there may be now some breakage in the massed, still the cry among millions was not, "We perish!" They knew, though silent, that a Divine Being was in the midst of them, with His attributes and His promises, and that these latter will have their final fulfilment when the hush of the sepulchre shall be both on man and nature, to be broken only at the decreed moment by that voice which is to awaken all into instantaneous and bounding life, and "to renew the face of the earth." German Catholic subjects will honour the king, but they must fear God, and few amongst the priesthood will be induced to swing the censer with rebellious hands in the face of the Holy of Holies, for a pittance at the cost of salvation. Stronger chains may be forged, and a more vigilant guard may be told out than what Herod's prison comprised, but the unceasing supplications of Catholicity which possesses the faith which imparts sacredness to the obedience due to all legitimate power that comes from God alone will realise the exultation which was once felt among the assembled in prayer in Jerusalem at the sudden presence of Peter, rescued from an assured and ignominious death. However, of this rulers must be aware, that they will not find much steadfast loyalty among those who make spiritual claims secondary to temporal gains, in despite of the deepest pangs that conscience can well inflict, in a trafficking upon what involves an eternal loss.

But whilst sovereignties and empires are so immediately sensitive upon their proclaimed right they can with stupid apathy or stolid indifference witness the usurpation of territories and what they sacredly include, though, if not to be identified with the Church, yet accessory, in the disposition of the providence of ages, to her independent action and well-being. They can contemplate without alarm what imperils in precedent the future safety of their own ancient diadems. The late Victor Emmanuel, biding his opportunity, and little disturbed in his Christian peace at violating a comparatively recent and solemn convention, triumphantly marched on Rome when the last sentinel of France had hastened from his position to succour his own afflicted country. In all this he added infamy to a former insignificance. The sanction of authority for the setting up to sale, much to the gratification of the deriding Jew and the bloated voluptuary, the lands and tenements of charitable and religious institutions, soon followed. The empty monasteries and convents were promptly converted into suitable barracks for a licentious soldiery, or turned into spacious warehouses for the convenient stowage of State sequestrations against the next needy and pressing Government auction. National pride may for a time preserve the priceless contents of galleries and museums, but this will not perhaps long prevail against the ultimate threats for the most part of a poorly fed and indifferently clothed soldiery, and the eventual frantic mobbings of an oppressed and over-taxed population, to whom so much has been promised and so little given. Infidelity too may have finally her staggering and meandering mobs in the streets of Rome to complete calamity, that has as much respect for thrones as reverence for altars. On the hearing of their impious shoutings and their disorderly tramp, should his days have been prolonged to such a doleful period, which God has otherwise willed, Pius IX. would scarcely have deemed himself secure within his very limited and guaranteed boundaries from the desolating advance of commiserating Alarics and forbearing Generics. His necessary withdrawal would have been the immediate signal for infidelity to seize on St. Peter's and all that was valuable in its movables. These latter would soon be dissipated in carousings and debaucheries, and that which goes very, very far beyond Diana's marvel would be converted into a fraternal hall of nations, and within " the desecrated and mighty shrine " there would be assigned positions for a beauteous Venus, a faultless Apollo, and a fuddled Bacchus, where once stood what was dedicated to a saint, to a martyr, and to an Apostle. Infidel principles would be unreservedly developed in denying a faith where it first commenced to be widely believed, and in maligning virtue where it was heroically practised. Should this one day become a fact in Italy, as it has in some other lands, it may be asked, what is the value of humanity without the worth of religion?—a darkened mind as heretofore, and a debauched body. But should things not come to such extremes in a land where already are fast disappearing the aids to piety and education, as also the asylums for affliction and misfortune, where schools are being established which leave as little reverence for the spirit Head of Christendom as for the chief of her doctrines and her precepts, where even the enlistment of the clergy and the religious has received a majority of votes in the Italian Parliament, and thus the anointed and the professed may be shouldered together with the impious and the dissolute? Such an insult to Christianity will not be forgotten, since Protestantism as well as Catholicity has denounced so irreligious and execrable a measure, and which the late Pope subdued by profound grief supplicated might not be passed. However, what cared then the usurping Sard, who affected to reverence the hands which elevated the host in the sanctuary that he adored, and yet sanctioned a law that, if occasion should arise, constrained the ordained to level and discharge the musket on the battlefield, with an almost certitude of maiming or killing for the revolting result?

But in France a sad precedent is to be found for all that the above may finally come to, when Infidelity nearly throughout her broad domains attained a mastery, when the enduring rectitude of the creation failed of its solemn influence, and the splendours of day and the shrouded glories of night were regarded without the slightest impress of a pervading Deity. All that were known in the moral world by their Christian deeds and their Christian teachings were set down as either fools or miscreants. No sooner did Infidelity deem herself equal to the establishment of her vaunted and unparallelled providence for the bliss of man than, fantastically garbed, she strode at the head of her swaying and vociferous red-capped mob, and soon were her hands stained with the blood of majesty, priest, noble, and citizen. The throne was cursed and speedily in ruins, whilst bloated and spangled vice was elevated as the Goddess of Reason for homage on the defaced and defiled altar. With Infidelity it was from one blasphemy to another blasphemy, from abyss to abyss. All was, as well expressed, in full insurrection against God Himself. No soul, no mysteries, naught but ravings and absurdities, in their place. All was material, all above and all below, was fortuitous; on every side the reign of disorder and terror existed. To pray was insanity, to adore was treason; the one was met with gross insults, the other with condign punishment. Perils and impeachments, confiscations and executions, were ceaseless in a land once termed Christian, and where once belief and piety made confidence and merit. As heresy in Great Britain, so Infidelity in France, appeared to prevail over what Paganism with her philosophers and legions failed to confute or subdue. The devout hid their heads through fear, the weak affected to live licentiously, and the impious gave vent to their impious jeers with complacency and freedom. Infidelity had its wide rapture of supremacy for a season, when again that faith in which Clovis found victory as well as Constantine commenced to expand into a former influence, and with it civilisation, with all that makes security and confidence. Nothing, however, was omitted by the chiefs of a determined and insatiable cabal to obtain a permanent and a universal triumph. They scrupled at no plottings to insure success for their patriotic purposes, which included defiance of the Almighty, and contempt for His commandments. "Not being able to avenge themselves on God," says Burke, "whom they hated with all their soul, with all their heart, and with all their mind, they took a delight in vicariously defacing and degrading religion and its professors. They tore their reputation to pieces by their infuriated defamations and invectives, before they lacerated their bodies by their massacres "— whilst on the other hand to forward their inhuman designs a sublime imagination depicted forth the happiness of mankind when liberated from the ignominious and unnatural restraints of religion in the most fascinating colours. A ready wit ridiculed in the most facetious terms the lives of the devout and the consecrated, and a subtle intellect strove by the most specious sophistry to convince the understanding as to the opposition involved in revelation to the most obvious principles in science, and to the practical demonstrations of the profound in thinking and the deep in learning.

Yet all the irreligious plannings and persistent efforts of the blaspheming were finally in vain, notwithstanding that French Infidelity had complacently concluded that in their achievements they had gone far beyond in wisdom that of the Academy, the logic of the Lyceum, or the oratory of the Forum, and who confidently deemed, with Voltaire, their enterprising and deified chieftain, that with a strenuous and combined effort they could finally loosen unto headlong ruin the foundation on which Christianity had her build. They were disappointed. Religion, who, as if for a while under the severities of first Pagan persecutions, had sought for the secrecy of her ancient catacombs, again re-appeared to carry out her consoling and assuring providence, conjoined with one who seemed to have the commission of Cyrus to aid religion, but not to preside over it. Yet in the final return to Christianity of France, that so suddenly and determinedly, at a period, appeared to have revolted against her, under standards severally upborne by ambition, voluptuousness, lust, and avarice, it was a return to the ancient belief of the kingdom, and not to the flexible and accommodating teachings of a Luther. The late Lord Macaulay wondered at this, and thus expressed himself, with marked emphasis, "that neither the moral revolution of the eighteenth century nor the counter-revolution of the nineteenth century should in any perceptible degree have added to the domains of Protestantism . . that during the former period whatever was lost to Catholicism was lost to Christianity, and that during the latter whatever was regained by Christianity in Catholic countries was regained also by Catholicism. We should have naturally expected," pursues the learned and able writer, "that minds on the turn from superstition" (as he is pleased to term the faith of his forefathers) " to infidelity, or on the way back from infidelity to superstition, would have stopped at an intermediate point." It is not difficult to give a solution of the subject-matter of the late noble reviewer's wonderment, which is to be drawn from the Divine character of Catholicity, and which is never in contradiction with herself, and never cedes to circumstances. From her alone can be derived that vivifying enlightenment, and that efficient help, which realise a lasting conviction and a settled peace. It is therefore to this faith, as Pascal intimates, that man must turn for that vital assistance which mere reason, much less opinion, could never supply. "For," said this profound thinker, "man is the depository of truth, yet he is in himself but a mass of uncertainty." France saw, indeed, in her great Revolution, what was man when totally left to his depravity and to his passions, whilst she beheld in the fiercest and most ruthless of modern periods what was the stability of the ancient faith and the heroism of her virtues. In this beholding, history had her confirmations as to her absorbing narrations in relation to Christian woes and to Christian endurance in primitive days. France keenly felt that she had lost her Providence of centuries in the temporary absence of Catholic teachings, and the discontinuance of Catholic practices. In the gradual resumption of her former action and sway, through which she seemed to impart an additional vivifying influence, like unto that proceeding from the spreading rays of the glowing sun, which was hid for a time from the sight amid the dark clouds that lent horror to the recent and devastating tempest, France beheld also, in the countenanced national privilege of self-opinion for which Protestantism has Holy Writ for its warrant, the ultimate source of that infidelity which included the hating of God with all one's heart, and the slaughter of one's neighbour with all speedy promptitude. Sorrowed and humiliated France, with this conviction eventually so strong upon her, could not be brought to take up the convenient medium of a rational Christianity, the indefinable proceed of the high calling of a Luther, in which truth is left to the recognition of private judgment. No, she could never have adopted what would have necessitated her, in a Protestant persuasion, to fit her temples for the carrying out of a pure Evangelical creed, to do away with the altars of ages as idolatrous, to displace emblems that embellish as well as instruct as profane, to remove the crucifix from its elevated prominence, for reminiscence as well as reverence, as superstitious, that had received the last sighs of preceding generations, and then surmounted their graves devoutly to testify to the creed in which they expired—to leave nothing, in fine, but the pulpit, from whence to pronounce a hundred Christian credences as little to be understood as were the political rhapsodies vociferated from the tribunes of a

National Assembly. In the above supposition the religious houses and institutions, whose subjects, as to men or women, in the fulfilment of daily duties, realised daily merits, and who comprised every grief and affliction within their unceasing prayers and cares, would be rigorously discontinued in the adoption of a simplified Protestant Christianity. No, France, as to the almost entirety of her people, could never in a Christian profession separate from those, on opening her eyes to the merciless and revolting deeds of infidelity, whose faith upheld charity for a chief virtue, which alone is capable of extending permanent vitality to fraternity and unity.

But in the ultimate return of multitudes to the ancient and undefiled worship, what a forcible additional testimony is extended to Catholicity that she only, as assumed throughout these pages, is the Christianity of Heaven and antiquity—that she only can endure the utmost rigours of scrutiny under its widest range, whether made by heresy or infidelity, without the hazard of a flaw, and undergo the test of any contrast without a fear of being excelled ! She is not scared by any investigation, through whatever science it may be proceeded with, since whatever is identified with truth has, as already laid down, God for its common Author. When Christianity in Pagan times confuted the falsities of idolatry, and triumphed

over the passions that battled for its existence, it was
but, as thought the modern infidel, the mastery of one
superstition over another, a change in profession with
but little change in the outrages upon common sense;
were science, as argued the sneering and scoffing philosopher of the Ferney school, as sedulously unfolded
and as closely studied during the first days of Christianity as at present profound periods, mysteries
would not long have perplexed the world, and the
scourge, the axe, and the rack would have been employed only in regard to the thief, the murderer, and
the conspirator. And what laboured impeachments
at this day calculated conclusively to respond to the
allegements of the impious of revolutionary date, and
to affect vitally the belief of Apostle, martyr, and
saint, have been put forth by the scientific! They certainly have not demonstratively evinced a jot more,
under the most systematic and subtle of scrutinies,
than the most learned and indefatigable contributors
to the "Dictionnaire Philosophique" at its last revisings, that science and revelation are not in complete harmony. On this subject the late Cardinal
Wiseman has impressively laid it down that there
always will be "a strict correspondence between the
progress of science and the development of Christian
evidences." Yet it is here to be affirmed that neither
pure reason nor sound philosophy could advance man

in such a degree in respect to a knowledge of God as to enable him to frame a true, and consequently a legitimate, religious worship. Divine revelation must interpose. Nevertheless, Reason, in her investigations through science, that includes certitude, though faith soars above her, would experience no embarrassment in reference to what was, or as to what was not, of positive revelation in the formal teachings of Catholicity, since infallibility is hers, being guaranteed by a Divine promise that has its entry in the pages of inspiration, that have miracles for their warranty, as heretofore set forth. It is this Church alone, then, a necessary sequence from the above (or Christianity is of man, not of God) that has wherewith to content reason. She is as perspicuous as consistent, and possesses an olden lineage to uphold authority as well as to certify origin. She furnishes the most luminous proof of the Divine nature of the Old Law by the most obvious fulfilment in herself of its respective prophecies, in her economy, her doctrines, and her victories, and in whose mysteries and sacraments are so sublimely manifested the grandeur and the misery of man, his resources and his wants.

It is not surprising, then, that the most dogged foes of Christianity, and therefore the most staunch friends of Humanity, should have uniformly and exclusively singled out, as the most ancient, powerful, uncompromising, and majestic of her foes, Catholicity. Yet even these, like the Philistines who were constrained to respect whilst endeavouring to exterminate what Israel most revered, have been compelled, as it were in the midst of their plottings, as daring as impious, to substantiate by their several testimonies the sublimity of Catholicity's dogmas, and the effective aids to be found in her rites and ordinances. Truly the immediate hour prominently befits the setting forth of these witnessings, as frank as they are fervid, and as lucid as they are for the most part eloquent. But, primarily, what is the utterance of Rousseau in relation to the Divine Founder of Christianity, the chief object of infidel detestation? "I avow," says this pre-eminently gifted and anti-Christian man, "that the Gospel fills me with awe, and its sanctity speaks to my heart. Behold the books of the philosophers, how insignificant do they appear by the side of this, notwithstanding all their pomp! Is it possible," continues the same writer, "that He whose history it includes should be Himself a mere man? Does He assume the tone of an enthusiastic or an ambitious sectary? What mildness! What refinement in His manners! What a touching grace in His instructions! What elevation in His maxims! What profound wisdom in His discourses! What presence of mind—what subtlety and fitness in His replies! What an empire over His passions! Where is the man, and where is the sage, who knows how to act, suffer, and die without weakness or ostentation?"[1] "What blindness it is to compare the son of Sophroniscus with the Son of Mary! What a distance there is between one and the other! Socrates, dying without pain, without ignominy, readily supported his usual comportment to the last. And if so easy a death had not contributed to do honour to his life, it might well be doubted if Socrates, with all his pretensions, was but a mere sophist. He devised, it is said, a system of morals, yet, before he praised virtue, Greece abounded with virtuous men. But amongst His own, where could Jesus find a morality so elevated and so pure, of which He alone has given both precept and example? From the bosom of the most furious fanaticism the voice of the most sublime wisdom made itself heard, and the simplicity of the most heroic virtues did honour to the grossest of people. The death of Socrates, tranquilly philosophising in the midst of his friends, is the most agreeable one that could be imagined; that of Jesus Christ, expiring in torments, reviled, outraged, cursed by a whole people, is the most horrible one that could possibly be conceived. Socrates, in taking

---

[1] Rousseau, Emile.

the poisoned cup, blessed the man who wept as he presented it. Jesus, whilst enduring the most frightful of punishments, prayed for His unrelenting and savage executioners. Yes, if the life and death of Socrates were those of a sage, the life and death of Jesus Christ are those of a God. Shall we say that the Gospel was invented to amuse? It is not after such a fashion that people invent, and the deeds of Socrates, which no one doubts, are not so well attested as those of Jesus Christ. It is more inconceivable that many men should concur together to fabricate such a book than that one only should furnish its subject. Never were the Jewish writers capable of assuming such a tone or of devising such a moral, and the Gospel is stamped with characters of truth so grand and so striking, so perfectly inimitable, that the framer of it would be something more astonishing than the Hero." Such words and thoughts are scarcely to be surpassed in the records of Christian eloquence, which Chateaubriand represents as having the greatest control over the movements of the soul, and the surest biddings in silencing the importunities of the passions. Rousseau for once, perhaps, deeply meditated upon the inspired page in which virtue equals truth, and in the kindling of his glowing feelings penned words convicting those of an insult to their own reason, and that of humanity, who put forth, with all the address and force they are capable of, that Christianity, at the most, is only a specious cheat of centuries, with a succession of nations, kingdoms, and empires for its august dupes.

To the above let the following testimonies severally be conjoined, in support of some of the most prominent portions of Catholic dogma and Catholic discipline, proceeding from writers who were as conspicuous for their varied gifts as in their continuous favouring and advancing of disbelief. "In the first place," says D'Alembert, alluding to a Divine religion on earth, "God (and no one is permitted to doubt it) has made known to men the true worship they ought to render Him, and it is clear that the arguments which go to establish this worship ought to introduce into the mind a conviction akin at least with geometrical demonstration." "The most severe critic," asserts Diderot, "in the same view recognises the Old and New Testament, the most haughty reason the certitude of the facts which they narrate, and sound philosophy, resting on their authenticity and their truth, concludes that both are Divinely inspired." "Admirable thing!" exclaims Montesquieu, "the Christian religion, that appears to have for its only object the felicity of another world, yet secures happiness to us here below." "O perfect God!" exclaims Necker, "it is from You that we hold a legislation whose sublime spirit is in close relationship with our nature and with our felicity; she comes from You, and is engraven in the depths of consciences; she comes from You and leads us to You." "The aversion to having any check upon our passions, and the vanity of not thinking with the multitude," affirms D'Alembert, "have contributed to make more unbelievers than the illusions of sophistry." "I now, in verging towards the point mentioned," writes Rousseau to one of his friends as to the necessity of fixed principles, "declare to you that if I were born a Catholic I should continue one, well knowing that your Church places a salutary restraint upon Human Reason, that goes beyond her reach when she attempts to fathom the abyss of things, and I am so convinced of the utility of such a restraint that I have imposed a like restraint upon myself, by laying down certain rules of faith, from which I have interdicted myself ever to depart." "This stability, this perpetuity," argues Raynal, in reference to the indications of religious truth, "ought to be peculiar to a religion that has dogmas, a well-directed ecclesiastical hierarchy, and a supreme chief, who by his authority maintains all dogmas in their primitive state, whilst he condemns every fantasy of opinion that pride has produced or novelty adopted." "People," says Marmontel, "attack Catholics (speaking in defence of her consistency) because, as they declare, she is exclusive and intolerant. Yes, exclusive in the persuasion that as to dogma and belief the truth is one, and that it is in the possession of him alone who professes it without alteration or admixture of error; hence arises the intolerance of Catholicity, or a stern refusal to unite her hopes with those of any one who has not her faith." "These people (unbelievers) have well known," lays down the same writer, " that Catholicism was the profession of all the maxims which they have striven to induce mankind to abjure, the friend of all virtues which they have been anxious to banish or proscribe."

In speaking upon the two great sources of holiness in the Catholic Church, Confession and the Eucharist, Voltaire observes, in reference to the former, "that it is one of the most efficacious of means for the controlment of secret crime;" and as to the latter, he declares it to be one of the greatest restraints possible, "for who," asks Voltaire, "believes that he possesses the Divinity, and yet can readily sully his heart by injustice or impurity?"[1] As to the advantages of ceremonies in stimulating devotion, Montesquieu remarks that when an exterior worship exhibits an imposing magnificence, it moves and pro-

---

[1] Dictionn. Phil.

duces within us the most lively religious emotions. Another writer, already introduced, inquires: "But what can symbols of modest and engaging virtues comprise of scandal or of detriment? What can there be of alarm, either to morals or laws, in examples of humility, of patience, of forgiveness, of self-denial and universal philanthropy? For why, specially, should the emblem of the Cross be forbidden to be displayed by Catholics on their festivals and their funeral solemnities? It is significant of their faith and their hope, it is their pledge of immortality, it is their sign of the love of God and His devotedness to the salvation of man." In defence of those who have for their sublime and arduous object the steady fulfilment of the Evangelical counsels, the chieftain of disbelief is compelled to avow that within the cloister, which, indeed, cannot be denied, there have existed great virtues—there is scarcely a religious house which does not contain some souls worthy of admiration, and who do honour to the human race. Vividly impressed, when at Rome, with the august and venerable form in which Religion presented herself in material things around him, Volney, with rapturous earnestness, exclaimed: "I salute you, ye abandoned ruins, tombs of saints, and solitary walls; it is to you that I address my prayers! Yes, while your aspect repels, with a secret awe, the looks of the vulgar, my heart experiences, while contemplating you, the charms of the most profound sentiments and the most elevated thoughts."[1] Such are a few of the testimonies in favour of the faith of ages, her solemn rites, and her sacred usages, selected by an able hand, and published at a period which best responded to the needs of religion.

But one more testimony, though lengthy, yet remains to be put forward, and that in this instance of the final conversion of a disciple of Voltaire, who with as much acuteness as judgment has criticised the works of the most celebrated writers, both ancient and modern, and whose own productions have, for the principal part, so greatly added to the worth and correctness of the highest order of literature. La Harpe, after so close and long a tutoring in the then-prevailing infidelity, thus eventually expressed himself in favour of a faith which the wretched De La Mennais once pronounced to be the centre of all that is fixed and general in human evidence: "A man has been so miserable as to forget for forty years the law of a God whose existence he recognised, and to blaspheme a holy religion which this God came Himself to deliver to men. This same God touched

---

[1] Les Ruines.

him in a moment whilst perusing the inspired volume which he had always neglected. God enlightened his spirit, and spoke to his heart. The veil has fallen, and he has become a Christian, and a contrite Christian. He feels that his life has been one continuation of the most shameful and guilty wanderings. Even before man himself he raised his eyes to heaven, and compared so extended an obstinacy with the goodness of God, who has freed him from it, and who promises him forgiveness should his conversion be sincere. This contrast affrights his reason. He cannot comprehend how it is possible to obtain a pardon of which he feels himself so utterly unworthy. In reflecting on the justice of God he is ready to doubt of His mercy, but the Gospel replies to him, by the voice of its Apostles, God has so loved men as to send His only Son to them, and to deliver Him to death for them. It is this, then; the penitent sinner comprehends the ineffable mystery; his proud heart and his blind reason had rejected it, his sorrowful and his humbled heart profoundly feels it. He believes because he loves, he believes because he is grateful, he believes because he sees that the entire goodness of God the Creator is proportioned to the miseries of the creature." "O my God, all Thy mysteries are of love, and it is for this they are Divine. Man does not thus invent, it is beyond his powers. A God alone can thus speak, as a God alone can thus act. If man refuses to believe, it is because he is ungrateful, and he is ungrateful because he is blind. O God, You who have so loved man, enlighten the eyes of the blind, and soften the hearts of the ungrateful." Thus does a philosopher here address the world whose Christian and intrepid avowals startled the disbelieving and animated the faithful. They are as clear and energetic as his former opinions and conduct demanded.

In all this is strongly substantiated what Diderot himself asserts of Religion, that she destroys not the man, but converts him into a saint. A special providence aided La Harpe in freeing himself from a most calamitous position, that of Deism. In what this differs from Atheism may be considered as well understood. The latter implies the rejection of all credence in a supernatural Being—the former, the bare admission of the existence of a Deity. Many demur as to the reality of a *bonâ-fide* Atheist. Nevertheless, it is undeniable that Atheism, as well as Deism, has at this day, as heretofore, an existence, and exercises a broad and a fatal influence. She has as much solicitude for the diffusion of her deadly lie as in some respects the Apostle had for the spread of life-giving truth. Well, indeed, may she at once be met here in the following brief form of address: "Is death, then, the termination of every woe, as well as every bliss? Has hope, then, the earliest and the latest friend of man, without which life could not be enjoyed nor pain endured, no warrant for existence beyond the grave? Is history but delusion when the perfections of the Deity give interest and sublimity to its pages, or when what is supernatural constitutes its fervid matter? Is the feeling that witnesses to the most absorbing and momentous of considerations, an eternity of being, but the proceed of a fiction to bring minds into debasing thraldom? Is it against common sense to confide in the beneficial conclusion that are deduced from an evidence which in earthly affairs has ever made up the convictions of the universe, and furnished, in undertakings as important as extensive, the best surety of mankind? If man is born for society, where is there a better detailing forth of his rights and privileges, or stronger arguments to enforce them, than in that religion which at the same time testifies to salutary laws as the emanation of a Supreme Being, and their legitimate administrators as the representatives of His infinite justice, wisdom, and power? If man is born humane, what has unfolded more lively motives to stimulate what is inherent in him, on each pressing and affecting occasion, than religion, which has so well described the subtle and influential impulses of his own mysterious heart?"

Can it be possible to reply to all this conclusively, and yet not confound men upon what best constitutes their dignity and promotes their mutual and common welfare? Is it credible that those can have truth with them who maintain for a fact what must consequently leave but a few advantages to man beyond what instinct yields to the beast of the field, for the conservation and the good of its being? What confusion would be the sure attendant if the hearty and entire credence of mankind were given to specious sophisms, unstable opinions, and chimerical hypotheses! It is said that an infinite perfection could scarcely actively pervade all things, and yet virtue be oppressed and vice be triumphant. But without trials religious heroism would never have had its manifestation. Mankind has its probations before the awarding of crowns, and certainly it is justly the prerogative of the Creator to ordain His taskings ere He encircles with glory. Again, not to recognise the immediate Providence of a God in the midst of the undeviating movements of the heavens, and the uniform results of nature, would give rise to as great a bewilderment for the understanding as, it is alleged, mysteries comprise. All this would tend to make a nullity of conscience, though a continuance of honesty would be looked for amongst men in the various transactions of life. It would be to deny the efficiency of arguments that ought to ensure a ready assent, and still to be confident of possessing ample means of showing things to be obviously undeniable. In fine, it would be that in professing which, assimarily remarks Bossuet, would include such an utter departure from every feature of reason as would give rise to as great a difficulty in finding an adequate term for it in language as for the body when by gradual decay it has completely passed away from every distinctive outline and form which the Almighty had imparted to it.

In like words, at least in substance, has the Atheist been often addressed, and what a nothing does he not make of man in the midst of the creation in the complete marring of what is rational within him, and in giving him for existence but the mere span of time that intervenes between his first breathings and eventual annihilation! Verily, he scarcely leaves a single thing inherent in man which is so exquisitely constituted to move the affections of the heart, and to give an impetus to the powers of the mind, as to its main purport, unquestioned. A disbelief is not only kept up in what a contrary conviction makes the chief joy and energy in man's being, but also the religion that first so sublimely demonstrated order and unity throughout the creation is persistently represented as the principal obstacle to the progress of science and art, though in her, again to be repeated, as history testifies, they had their first fosterings and a solicitous guardianship in the most barbarous and the most unsparing of times.

Nor is Deism very far apart from Atheism; indeed, as to results it may be ranked as one with it, for though by Deists a God is proclaimed, it is akin somewhat with Robespierre's comprehension of a Deity, since with them the Deity is considered as taking but little interest in sublunary matters, and consequently they can have but a very scant appreciation of His presence throughout nature or in the midst of themselves; they have, consequently, much about Herod's adoration for their lolling Deity in the skies, which is neither very profound nor sincere. The virtue that has astonished by its enterprise and endurance or inflamed by its disinterestedness and devotedness has had in their blank view of things its primary impetus in what is visionary. In their dreary creed, which admits of nothing supernatural, there is little to enlighten or to coerce a corrupt and wayward nature. Revealed religion with them is a well-contrived fraud upon men, and the miracle, the principal warranty of its truth, is at the best but an adroit and successful juggle. "To supply for this decried and rejected Christianity," says Bergier, as summarily as cogently, "they ostentatiously put forward this mere belief in a Divine Being whom they are totally incapable of defining, and for whom they have a worship that is not very easy to comprehend. They uphold a system loosely concocted, and which, indeed, is only a palliation upon Atheism, that includes the privilege of thinking as you like and doing as you like." "In all this," declares the Deist, "there is wherewith to form the honest and the benevolent man, and which is to supersede a religion which is emphatically pronounced to be an imposture, but it is nevertheless a sublime philosophy which demonstrates the order and unity of nature, and happily elucidates the enigma of the human heart, which comprises the most powerful motives to incite man to good, by placing him directly under the eye of the Divinity, and which acts with as much empire upon the will as upon thought, whilst furnishing a supplement to conscience, and thus strengthening and perfecting every virtue." It is for the Deist, impartially and patiently, to consider this, who has the most sublime of his sentiments, and the most practical of his humane devisings, from writings which he studiously contemns for their simplicity and incredible narrations, accompanied with a solemn shake of the head, and a grimace of affected pity for the deceived. Should the Deist, however, persist in a prudential and a deep thinking, he must come out of chaos upon a work of perfection, that the creation does not outvie in the wisdom and endurance of its construction. He must be convinced that no man was equal to such a pronounced cheat upon man, and that there could be no certain good, nor assured reliance, in any home or society without the succour of Christianity.

People may remark that the alleged dire results of Atheism or Deism are not so very obvious in society at large. This, indeed, may be plausibly advanced, yet it is to be readily replied that the maxims, usages, laws, customs, and religious practices of Christianity counteract and conceal the mischievous tendency of the principles of Atheism and Deism. But let order in any Christian land be completely disturbed, and then the principles of Atheism and Deism will commence to display themselves, both speedily and conspicuously, and will eventually be seen in the plenitude of their calamitous character in the light of the fired temple, and palace of the Courts of Justice, and the State prisons; and as history tells us, either as to the staying or repairing of the expanding and startling ruin, Catholicity, among all the numerous and embarrassing pretensions to an Apostolic Christianity, has best at these epochs of visitation befriended affrighted and afflicted society. She alone remains unchanged and self-possessed in the midst of political revolutions which have gradually but surely brought nations to utter misery and desolation. Nor can she, as hitherto insisted on, be counterfeited. Ingenuity may, with wondrous fidelity, fashion forth falsehood after her fair form, imagination may deck out the imposture in her most dignified robes, and passion may, with her numerous auxiliaries, elevate it upon one of the most lofty and costly of pedestals for veneration; but it will after a period, as with the citadels and the strongholds of nations and empires, have its eventual decay and finally disappear, whilst Truth, though lost to sight, and under the tramp of ages, identified with the pledge of the Most High, will again, in her prevailing might, make herself visible in all the freshness and loveliness of immutable being.

As earlier and briefly touched upon, to what an extent has not this been evinced here in regard to Catholicity! In this empire Catholicity had the closest of approaches to the almost imperceptible seed of the Gospel, and though prostrated her vitality was not to be stamped out, since she could not forfeit the chief care of Heaven. Those, at last, in a Divine willing, came to her succour that had had in her profession to endure what the Apostles underwent in her propagation, and from Ireland as well as France came this timely intervention. Ireland, for a first reference, oppressed by statutes, and harassed by poverty, and degraded by exclusions, made an effort to free herself, much in the same manner as when a Red Indian might rush upon his surrounding and deriding tormentors in the madness of desperation to open a way from deepening and protracted pangs. She failed to do so, though she astounded by her heroism, and additional woes were the dire consequence. All was well-nigh lost to her, except the faith that whispered consolation to the martyr on the rack of ancient days, and which she would not barter for the favour of the wealthy and the titled who falsified her creed, and aggravated her burthen, with all the persistency and obduracy of Egypt's chief. God, however, did not withdraw Himself from Ireland's fidelity. He was with her as He was with his Apostle whom He afflicted with evils for the realisation of future blessings. The many trials of primitive Christian days that Ireland's people had to endure prepared them for missions of Divine purposes, both as to the diffusion and influence of inspired truths. Without their unceasing pressure they never would have quitted their cherished hearths and fields for settlements that commerce then had hardly ventured near, and where death, as rumoured, was a certainty in any casual confronting with the fierce and savage tribes that constituted almost entirely the scanty and roving population of the comparatively unknown world. But Ireland's faith, conserved at every cost, and conjoined with the Apostle's confidence, in every peril by sea and by land, comprised fortitude and victory. The voice of busy civilisation at length broke the monotony of the vast wildernesses that were first cautiously treaded for a frail home, and speedily, where nearly all once was unstaidness and entanglement to the footing, villages began to increase about, and branching and expanded roads commenced to exist, made firm for frequent and profitable traffic. Amid boundless and mysterious forests, with hardly anything to procure substantial sustenance for life, except what resulted from indomitable energy, matchless patience, and an unflinching will, populations increased in importance, and Ireland's dispersed sons may indeed be justly reckoned among the most prominent and determined of the pioneers that made an opening for America to a prosperity and an influence now unsurpassed by the olden empires of the earth, undeterred even by fevered swamps and scalping Indians. In all this Heaven has had Her merciful and wise designs principally replied to by the establishment of a Christianity, with its altars and its sacrifice, where humanity was as revolting in its doings as scaring in its habiliments. In the land where this has been effected there is now among its almost innumerable and diversified inhabitants a wide mingling of that blood in the shedding of which

Great Britain has counted many a success, and which came from hearts that were true to what goes beyond patriotism in the faithful and eternal records of merit, to a one and undivided faith.

Numbers also of Ireland's people, to alleviate their severe and many miseries, sought even the unfriendly coast where persecuting heresy was dominant, and where orthodoxy, overpowered, had no appellation but what implied insult. However, though the suffering had to stoop under an oppressive load, they had not quite to sustain Egyptian burdens, as in their own nation, under a ruthless and unsympathising administration. To their daily toils London, the most imposing of Christian capitals, chiefly owes her present magnificence, and from the little that they could well spare out of the pittance of their hazardous labours arose the chapel, which if not in the stateliness of the mansion of the peer, yet did honour to Him in the zeal which commenced and completed it, even amid persistent persecution. Within this holy edifice, when completed, the sons of Erin were freed from the jeers and revilings so often heard without. "Within it," says Gustave de Beaumont, "then the downcast look and the lowly bearing no longer existed, and the sons of mourning Erin became elevated in demeanour and animated in countenance, and with eyes uplifted to Heaven they appeared to have repaired their dignity as men." They felt there was nothing stable or sovereignly true in this world except their faith, which they kept, though in doing so they lost their country and parted from all they so dearly loved. But Job's sufferings had their limit. A gradual lessening in penal laws came on; one great and unjust grievance still, however, remained—the exclusion from the Senate House of Ireland's faith, the faith of united millions, unless denounced on oath. The House of power and eloquence at length heard a voice at her palatial doors claiming admission. A refusal was given, but the righteous demand for entrance was soon attended to in the ruling of that Providence "by which kings reign." What the Roman edict could not prevail against British might, which the world feared and sought alliance with, had to cede to, and the Maccabeus of an aspersed and an oppressed people took his dignified way into the midst of the legislative of a former exclusive and ungrateful empire, to oppose, now without treason, enactments that justice could not weigh in her scales without a blush and a shudder. In all this is to be witnessed how futile are the efforts of heresy against the ultimate prevailing of truth. At the period, too, when in Great Britain Heterodoxy seemed to have Orthodoxy under her foot, there was also a full and calamitous dominion for Infidelity in

France. Christianity, in a kingdom styled Christian, was inveighed against and persecuted with all the vehemence and rabidness of paganism, in its most thrilling and unsparing of times. Person and property were at the utter mercy of tribunals whose decrees, in the revolting deeds consequent upon them, went beyond the appalling visitations of an Eastern plague. Unable to dwell with safety in a country where a curse or a trample on the Cross signalised the patriotism and manifested the worth of the citizen, whilst the slaughter or the tortures of the priest made the pastime of officials, many of the French clergy fled to English shores, not to meet there, on their landing, a sure doom, as it was in Elizabethan periods with the ordained British subject, but to receive an hospitality and a protection which rendered England as worthy of eulogy as her victories. Admired for a Christian fortitude which was tested through equal perils and sufferings that constituted Apostolical merits, their ancient belief did not, as hitherto in Protestantised England, prevent a close intimacy with families of distinction, repute, and wealth. They possessed, too, an influence in their engaging manners and their finished education, in addition to their consistency and firmness in Christianity's cause, that could not but bring about a benign result, in inducing the higher class of the English people to reflect upon and to discuss, with less bitterness and asperity, the creed of their forefathers. Catholicity commenced in those to have her rapid forwarding who had so well and so perseveringly fought the " good fight."

In reference to the French clergy, the celebrated Edmund Burke thus speaks: " I saw among the clergy at Paris (many of the description are not to be met with anywhere) men of great education and candour, and I had reason to believe that this description was not confined to Paris. What I found in other places I know was accidental, and therefore to be presumed a fair example." In personally alluding to the higher clergy, he says: " They seemed to me beyond the clerical character liberal and open, with the hearts of gentlemen and men of honour, neither insolent nor servile in their behaviour and conduct. They seemed to me rather a superior class, a set of men among whom you would not be surprised to find a Fénélon."[1] Upon the like men as these, that England received with a welcome that procured honour for herself and cheered the afflicted, whose courage would not have quailed at the roar of the uncaged ferocity in the Roman Amphitheatre, the blessing came down in which St. Peter reaped his thousand-fold. Not less did the Lord co-operate with the

---

[1] Reflections upon the French Revolution.

faith and toil of Ireland's people than with the virtue and learning of the anointed of France, and thus Catholicity in this kingdom, where so many of her faithful made their exit from this world with the ignominies and throes of the murderer or traitor, had a sudden and broad spread beyond that of Tertullian's early Christianity. And what is the registry at the present moment in this country, not surpassed on earth in science and learning and invention, of Catholic chapels, churches, seminaries, colleges, and religious institutions? A marvel indeed in their respective amount to those who are daily taught that Catholicity makes the pre-eminent wrath of Heaven by her abominations, but which evinces the intervention of this Heaven in the altered views of those who once reprobated Catholicity, and who once made the principal reference and the chief exultation of Protestants for the earnestness of their lives as well as their respective gifts and great acquisitions. "From the time that I became a Catholic," declares Cardinal Newman, "I have no further history of my religious opinions to relate, and have been in perfect peace and contentment. I never had one doubt."[1] Thus speaks one who, as St. Augustine, "for a time was separated from the

---

[1] Dr. Newman's General Answer to Mr. Kingsley.

unity and lost in the multiplicity," and who alone could find in Catholicity conviction for his intellect and tranquillity for his conscience. Hundreds are now conjoined with Cardinal Newman in the declaration just given who were for a lengthened period the dupes "of statements made up from rumours, false witnessing, morsels of history, and morsels of theology, dark suspicions and romantic scenes." These also with St. Augustine have their lament at the tardiness of their conversion to Catholicity, and exclaim, "Too late have I known Thee, too late have I loved Thee, O beauty so ancient and yet so new!"

And after what form do present distinguished Protestant divines view the above (it may here be inquired), who for the most part were once in intimate friendship with themselves, and equalled them in intelligence and science, and in regard to the Christian were not their inferiors in devoutness and benevolence? As men, do they view them, reposing in surety in their own fond inventions, or those of others, or as tranquil in the certitude of the orthodoxy of their final belief—as men certainly, as it ought to be, that have bade adieu "to the logic of the passions," and that have found what can alone satisfy reason and find acceptance with God, the One Holy Catholic and Apostolic Church, the true Christianity of celestial origin, and to which Dryden in his eventual fixed orthodox convictions thus fervidly alludes—

> "Where but from Heaven could man, unskilled in arts,
> In several ages, born in several parts,
> Have agreeing truths? or how or why
> Should all conspire to cheat us with a lie—
> Unasked their pains, ungrateful their advice,
> Starvation their gain, and martyrdom their price?"

Were it not for the conservative influence of Catholicity, Protestant reforming would indeed, ere this, have made of Christianity a complete deformity. Impressed with the features of authority, that need not a glow from the fires of Sinai, it is impossible for Protestants generally to fix their eyes upon Catholicity with due attention, and then to contemplate the outrageous and abominable follies that are continually set up for the reverence of the fickle and insubordinate multitude, without some recoil. The Puseyites, indeed, in these progressing, freethinking times, to strengthen their Protestant Christianity against imperilling opinions and monstrous devisings, could discover no suitable aids except in taking up with the several leading teachings of a Church that has no halt in her Providence, and upon whose recognised brow ages cannot effect any change—within which neither the corruption of men nor the malice of demons has interfered with the promise of Him, as to tenets and holiness, whose omniscience allows of no surprise, and whose omnipotence is equal to every assailment. "As well might an attempt be made" (as a member of the House of Commons some years ago observed) "to pluck a beam from the sun as to remove any doctrine from the registry of Catholic dogmas." But if the Almighty ceased in His care and watch over His Church, which once, as admitted, possessed His pledge ever to succour and enlighten, that makes it an impossibility, at what period did the calamitous stray into the paths of heterodoxy and perdition take place in regard to Catholicity? Some Protestant writers, after, as it may be piously deemed, fervid supplications for enlightenment, and the thumbing of scarce works, have confidently essayed to meet this little difficulty; however, it must be here remarked that as with their articles of belief, they are not quite in harmony with each other as to periods when the teaching became that of man and ceased to be that of God. Bulington thus pronounces— "The invocation of saints was introduced in the year 700, the supremacy of the Pope in the year 1215, the Apocryphal Books in the year 1547, and the sacraments at the same time." Puaus, in his chronology, puts down the introduction of the worship of saints in the year 375, the primacy of the Pope in 600, Apocryphal Books in 1564, and the sacraments in 1160. Others have ventured on statements with more circumspection, but with as little agreement as the foregoing in reference to respective averments. " Nevertheless, under every untoward circumstance, Protestant divines will cling as tightly to their several assertions as to their livings, and prefer," as Bossuet remarks, " to risk all rather than constrain themselves to examine deeply into the truth of their statements, and who love better to persist in their ignorance than to avow it."

However, though the passage of time frets away the deepest gilding, and manifests the worthlessness of what it concealed, yet Protestant avowals must be maintained, since one retraction under as serious as broad an importance would well-nigh go to affect the credit of the entirety of what has been charged upon Catholicity. Hence it is not surprising that at the period when the Catholic hierarchy was re-established in this country, a period when Guy Fawkes recovered his lost honours, and a Wiseman had to exercise a cardinal virtue for the safety of life, a Protestant hierarchy considered themselves to be politically bound thus to make known their due appreciation of the existing Apostolicity of the olden faith—" She is anti-Christ, blasphemous, unclean, an apostate, arrogant, profane, pestilent, sorceress, satanic, degraded, dishonest, false, tyrannical, offensive, selfish, contemptible, artful, wilfully blind, shameless, scandalous, disgusting, ignorant, cunning, audacious, ungrateful, domineering, gross, cursed, insidious, revolting, pagan, malignant, infatuated, corrupt in doctrine and idolatrous in practice."[1] In the above aggregate of conscientious and well-considered epithets, there is something appallingly definite with regard to Catholicity, not often to be gathered from the language of Protestant prelates when addressing sectarian minglings in palatial halls, for then it suits a purpose

"Spargere voces
In vulgum ambiguas."

---

[1] Serjeant Bellasis.

SECTION VII.

In immediate contrast to the aggressive spirit exhibited by Protestant leaders, and their unscrupulous vituperative utterances against Catholicism, a spectacle of widely differing nature, illustrative of the majesty and unanimity of the Catholic Church, may be well referred to, which had its place in the Basilica of the Vatican, on the occasion of the Immaculate Conception being solemnly proclaimed an article of faith. On the simultaneous rising of the assembled dignitaries from all parts of the Catholic world to join in the *Te Deum*, which the now departed venerable head of the Church intoned in joy and tears, a representative of one of the leading daily journals of London[1] was so overcome by the solemnity and grandeur of what he witnessed that he grasped the bench on which he sat, and was forced to avow that in what he beheld was the faith of ages and of nations. On the immediate finishing of so imposing and unanimous a thanksgiving for a dogmatical definition that made for Christianity the Immaculate Conception an article of belief, let it then be supposed that several of the most distinguished

---

[1] The *Times*.

of the Protestant hierarchy suddenly presented themselves before the assembled distinguished prelates and launched out against them some of the most opprobrious of foregoing epithets. At their vehement utterance by those dissimilar in lineaments, deportment, attire, and speech to the addressed, a deep sensation would, doubtless, have come upon even the most adverse Protestant, who had transfixedly beheld religion and truth honoured with a grandeur that no crowned potentate could realise, and naught but a spiritual headship could assemble. If the justifiableness of the vilifying terms was conceded with which the representatives of the virtue and faith of Catholicity were greeted, there would be a full warranty for the instant casting off, however preposterous it may sound, of vestments, the overturning of tabernacles, the defacing of pictures, the destroying of statues, the extinguishing of lights, the removal of religious emblems, and the displacing of crucifixes, leaving little, in fine, that was indicative of Christianity beyond bare walls, as best responding to an Apostolic piety and an Apostolical purity.

But upon what foundation do those stand who thus, as supposed, have assailed the purity of a Church, in the most revolting terms, that keeps and has kept millions for ages in doctrinal union and severity of discipline, notwithstanding the most fearful aberrations from truth, as so alleged, and which so immediately and vitally impeach the decrees of Councils, the unanimous teaching of the Fathers, supported by the tradition of centuries? Before replying it is to be observed that the Greek Church does not here escape unscathed, and certainly the Puseyites cannot expect to have a better fortune, that devoutly cling to not a few of the anathematised " Romish blasphemies." However, those who assail in the foulest of terms have no foundation to stand on for what they utter. Private judgment cannot yield anything of a stable nature. "It gives rise," says an able polemic, "to an unbounded licence in disputing on Divine things, without end, without rule, and without submission, and which, without Catholic authority, no prudence, no mildness, no firmness, could withstand."

Upon the breaking up of the venerable assembly within the Basilica, it might now be timely inquired what was, on the return to their respective positions and rulings of the many high and distinguished prelates that composed it, the acceptance given to the dogma of the Immaculate Conception by their spiritual and diversified flocks? An acceptance was given with the promptitude with which the subscription was given to its orthodoxy by the august assembly at Rome, in conjunction with its Supreme Head. If it is here urged that it was not so with the recently proclaimed dogma of Infallibility, which in these pages, as to its relative nature, has had its lengthened and lucid reference, it is to be replied that the secession of Catholics on this occasion, exceptionally termed by Protestants "Old Catholics," as to their number, was of a very scanty character compared to the myriads which remained faithful and believing. Separated from the unity, soon Old Catholics commenced to take up new doctrines which have entirely confounded them with those who might well exclaim—

> "As long as words a diff'rent sense will bear,
> Each one may be his own interpreter.
> Our airy faith will no foundation find—
> The world's a weathercock for every wind."[1]

Such is the sure consequence attendant upon a separation from the authority of the chair of St. Peter, which has so clear a warrant for its foundation in the Gospel, and such an unimpaired evidence in tradition. St. Paul, who foresaw and lamented many things, had his chief and deep grievings in those that would frame their own creeds and accept of none—men, as the Apostle so pronouncedly describes them, "lovers of themselves, proud, puffed up, disobedient, covetous, stubborn, without peace, having an appearance indeed of godliness." (2 Tim. iii.) "The Doctor of nations," as pertinently observes Neuville, "beheld

---

[1] Dryden.

all these passions under their most deadly form, of pride and loftiness, of vanity and presumption, of obstinacy and indocility, of cupidity and ambition, of haughtiness and disdain, of hatred and jealousy, arm themselves against the faith and venture upon the most hardy and unseemly assertions. He saw them signalising themselves by audacity, obtaining influence by calumny, gaining respect by an affectation of reform, captivating the populace by novelties, swaying them by adroitness of speech, and dazzling them by a manifestation of science, embarrassing them by a subtlety of reasoning, leading them astray by propounding and discussing questions to which neither their capacity nor information were equal." The Apostle witnessed all these calamitous and inevitable proceedings of heresy, and he groaned, not, as said, for the Church, in whose stability he had as much certitude as in the revelations of the third heaven, but for the dire mischief that would arise in after-days from the workings of the vain, the conceited, the sensual, the insubordinate, and the wilful. Surely what Protestant dignitaries beheld at Rome, as supposed, an assembly beyond in majesty "the sons of Aaron bearing the oblations of the Lord in their hands," the representatives of a Church that made the principal interest of history before Protestantism became an historical event, and whose foundations have remained unshaken and uninjured amid the decadence and the fall of empires that she had in spiritual subjection, or combatted as determined foes —an assembly, by its unity in creed, its sanctity of demeanour, and its dignity of rite, swaying the sternest of prejudices, and ensuring the reverence of the most obstinate in credulity—could never, though stigmatised as "abominable" and "idolatrous," have been included in the revelation of the future spiritual evils of Christendom that sorrowed the soul of the Apostle of nations. Such is at this period the condition of Protestantism generally that though the name of Christian is sedulously upheld, the diffusion of error, and of such an extreme character, which renders this quite consequent enough where all is arbitrary, that the reformed Christianity here is a complete inanity as to the fact of doctrine, and as to any controlling action. Mahomet may now be crowned with laurels without a failing in fidelity to the crown of thorns; and what makes the "world's priest is learning, guiding it like a sacred pillar of fire in its dark pilgrimage through the waste of time."[1] Truly magnificent, but scarcely comprising what would be fully adequate to constitute a safe conduct in Christianity to the promised land, since this guiding fire, in its course athwart the

---

[1] Carlyle.

treacherous waste, has incidentally, at least, evinced something akin to the erratic movements of the Will-o'-the-Wisp, which have brought about a little floundering confusion among the enthusiastic and confident following.

Nevertheless, the renown that is attached to genius, learning, and even to extraordinary Gospel feats in whirling and jumping, will rarely fail of a fascination and a leadership; it lends an influence of exceptional force, under a religious aspect, which is often extended to the most extreme of displayed follies, and dignifies them in worth even with the very pith of an inspired purport. Productive as this infatuation is in polemical considerations of variations upon variations within Protestantism, it gives rise to no misgivings in the thoughts of the chosen—it is in perfect consonance with Gospel liberty, and therefore with Gospel truth. In these differences there is to be found a free but a more exalted mind, a free but a more decisive will, which contribute something more to make the legitimate Christian in these modern days than the constrained and stereotyped teachings of the first ages, that formed both Father and saint. But thus writes the celebrated Channing in commendation of these variations, and as having most providential results. "Every sect," he sets forth, " has embodied a religion, a form, suited to some large class of minds that have met, somewhat answered some great principle of the soul, and thus every new denomination (whether Johnsonian or Dunker) has been a standard under which to gather and hold fast hosts against Rome." Against Catholicity, against a Church that makes the history of an uniform Christianity, and alone constitutes its being, its longevity, and its value—a Church proclaimed and manifested by her distinguished men, whose minds were as enlightened as profound, as being the true Church, the mother and the ruler of Christendom, with whom nothing can be met comparable in empire and authority, to which, in spiritual matters, an absolute submission must be rendered, and without which the Christian has nought of right to participate in her graces and merits, whatever deference the world may give to probity, title, or intellect. She it is who has been proclaimed by her gifted and learned adherents to be a Church that can alone furnish constancy to conviction and surety to reason, and whose virtues, in the heroism of their exercise, are not in confliction with the Divine declaration, "My yoke is sweet, and my burden is light." Certainly she excludes, and she anathematises. She, moreover, cannot call on her subjects to adore "in spirit and in truth," and permit them approvingly to smile upon innumerable religious professions, whose respective founders, the descendants of Luther, Calvin, and

Socinius, had their reveries for inspirations, though they should comprise " what is suitable to some large class of minds, and respond to some great principle of the soul."[1] Such is at this time the diversified character of doctrinal conceits, which makes Channing's providence for Christendom, a period indeed in which all is not in complete unity even between bishops and their selected theologians, when Protestant State authorities consider it to be of peremptory importance, and the height of prudence, not to sanction the summoning of any formal assembly to draw up a common symbol for acceptance and credence.

On this subject it is scarcely necessary again to advert to what history records, that when the first reformers congregated together to determine upon their Christian creed, opposite opinions might almost be counted with heads. Nevertheless one historical reference in connection with the above might here be pertinently introduced; it is the Conference at Worms, assembled under the auspices of King Ferdinand. It was composed of twelve Catholic and twelve Protestant theologians. The most able theologian among the Catholics was Canisius—among the Protestants Melancthon. The first thing proposed at this celebrated meeting, as narrated in the life of Canisius, was to lay

---

[1] Channing.

down the basis of the dispute, for if all were not agreed on some fixed point that might serve as a rule to both parties it would have been in vain to expect that they could ever agree. To this the Protestants assented, saying that the pure word of God ought to be this rule. The Catholics promptly admitted that the word of God was the rule of truth, but that it was not indiscriminately granted to every one to interpret it. It was required in the first place that the entire canon of the Scriptures, such as had been universally received and approved of in the Church for one thousand years, should be accepted; secondly, when no agreement could be come to as to the real sense of the Scriptures, it should be decided by a reference to the common opinion of the Fathers of the ancient Church. These advances led insensibly to vain arguments, and the Catholics perceived, even at the commencement, that their adversaries would in nowise agree with their doctrine, and that they belonged to different sects. This is the reason why it was required that since the liberty of dispute was only accorded to those who held the Confession of Augsburg, all those should be excepted from the Conference who were separated from it, either by adding to or changing its articles, as they had done on several occasions, which was the prolific parent of such a strange diversity of opinions among the Lutherans.

This blow, which they had not foreseen, as stated, stunned them, for here lay the weak point of these reformers, who were never cordially united among themselves, except in their constant and violent hatred against the Church of Rome. "Thus," as Canisius expresses it, "was seen how foolishly the giants laboured to build up the Tower of Babel, since God had struck them with the spirit of confusion, that they might contend among themselves." "This division," as the narrator continues, "having sprung up among the reformers, disputes, reproaches, invectives, and replies, both by word of mouth and by writing, was the result, so that the Conference could not be carried on with men who could not agree among themselves on any point, although one and all maintained that they belonged to the Confession of Augsburg." The reformers having left Worms, one after another, under various pretexts, returned to their own several countries, with hearts filled with bitterness and animosity. Thus ended the Conference of Worms. The unity of the Catholic Church was here most happily displayed in the contrasted disunity of the gathered reformers, who were, as the author of the life of Canisius observes, as much in dogmatical conflict with one another as with Catholicity herself.

This disunity yet exists in the Reformation, and in no nation again to be alluded to under so extreme and wide a form as in this kingdom. The Reformation, here so prolific in diversities, owes chiefly its introduction and dissemination to Cranmer. Burnett holds him in estimation with an Athanasius and a Cyril. Other Protestants of high rank and clerical position and erudition set him forth in the aggregate as forbearing and honest, as a lover of truth and an enemy to falsehood. "But what kind of Christian was one," asks Bossuet, "who, being a bishop, was at the same time a Lutheran, who was secretly married, and was finally consecrated Archbishop according to the Roman pontifical—who affected to have the most profound reverence for the Pope whilst inveighing against his spiritual rule, who continued to say mass, and permitted others to do so also, without a belief in its efficacy." "He professed Catholicity," declares another judicious writer, "to save his life, and he died a Protestant in order to avenge himself on those who would not grant him his life." But thus does Macaulay detail forth the conduct of Cranmer of saintly memory, who, as with Luther, had the broad road for the direct and safe way to heaven, in which the striding and bluff reformer made no halt, to give assurance to Christendom that he had his calling equally with Saul: "Cranmer rose into favour by serving Henry in the disgraceful affair of his first divorce. He promoted the marriage of Anne Boleyn with the King; on a frivolous pretence he pronounced the marriage null and void. On a pretence, if possible, still more frivolous, he dissolved the ties which bound the shameless tyrant to Anne of Cleves. He attached himself to Cromwell while the fortunes of Cromwell flourished; he voted for cutting off his head without a trial when the tide of royal favour turned. He conformed backwards and forwards as the King changed his mind. While Henry lived he assisted in condemning to the flames those who denied the doctrine of transubstantiation; when Henry died, he found out that the doctrine was false. He was, however, not at a loss for people to burn. The authority of his station and his grey hairs was employed to overcome the disgust with which an intelligent and virtuous child regarded persecution. . . . But his martyrdom, it is said, redeemed everything. It is extraordinary that so much ignorance should exist on this subject. The fact is, that if the martyr be a man who chooses to die rather than renounce his opinions, Cranmer was no more a martyr than Dr. Dodd. He died solely because he could not help it. He never retracted his recantation till he found that he had made it in vain." The circumstance mentioned by Burnet, the great admirer of Cranmer, of having thrust forth his right hand into the flames, at the same time exclaiming, in reference to the signing of his recantation, "Thou unworthy hand!" is questioned, as Cranmer having been probably bound to the stake, both as to hand and foot, it was not quite certain that such an edifying and interesting event should have come to pass.

But if the preached-up immaculate character of Cranmer were here brought into contrast with that of the Venerable Bede, styled by Camden a shining light, whose learning at a most barbarous period enlightened this country, and which would do honour, even now in the most prominent and practical of its branches, what a reverse in Christian worth would manifest themselves! Who could in calm reasoning, and with an approving conscience, turn from purity, simplicity, charity, piety, and obedience, under the most tasking discipline, which gave a position in history to the Venerable Bede beyond the consideration of his mental capacities and literary attainments, to supplicate on bended knee the blessing, in preference to a saint, of a prelate who was, as Macaulay asserts, equally false in religious and political obligations.

That which Cranmer anathematised in the sixteenth, Bede in the seventh century believed and taught, and which preceding saints and martyrs conjoined with truth and eternal life. In his teachings were comprised tradition, and the supremacy, the excellency of religious orders and institutions, the merits to be derived from fasting and perpetual chastity, the profit to be gained by the veneration of relics confirmed by miracles, as also the salutary practice of invoking the saints and praying for the dead. To these are to be added the ineffable helps to salvation comprised in the Holy Sacrifice, the Eucharist, the confession of sins, and finally, the advantages which arise from the use of holy pictures and images. These, set forth as the most prominent matter of Protestant controversy, were not only sacredly held by Bede, but also all that which Catholicity taught and practised had, without any ambiguity, his fervid and conclusive assent. But Protestants, for the most part, would rather be in religious federacy, although at an eternal risk, with the New Methodists than either saint or Father, with those who have somewhat of a notion that nothing in the way of ordination can come from empty hands, though from the shadow of the Apostles proceeded instantaneous blessings, as vouched for in inspiration, or even with the Baptists (New Connexion), who in their Christian pretendings affect to claim the chief references of olden Christianity, as to saint and Father, in regard to virtue and doctrine, entitlings appended to the name of Bede in the early times of this country, the highest conferrings of antiquity to ensure honour and confidence for orthodoxy and sanctity. This, however, does not much recommend or enhance virtue or creed in these brightening Gospel days of indefatigable and untiring doctrinal betterings, whose respective denominations have often a more apostolical sounding with the fanatical many in proportion as they may be more quaint, absurd, or even monstrous. Indeed, the signification of "saint" is not very well apprehended now by those who think so intensely and know so profoundly, and consequently fails at its utterance to make so lively an impression commonly as the widely lauded name of a genius or a hero. As to the epithet of Father it is usually and promptly complimented on the hearing with derision and contempt. But firstly, again referring briefly to the term "saint" in the Catholic Church, it designates one who is not only ardent in his faith, but also heroic in its practices, though there may not be an entire freedom from every imperfection. It is a name that had its place in first ages next in appreciation and confidence to that of martyr and Apostle, and has miracles to confirm its august reckonings in the Book of Life. It will be found in history to be identified with the valour of the battle-field, the wisdom of the politician, the sagacity of the judge, the knowledge of the scientific, the reasoning of the logician, the industry of the merchant—in fine, with inventions and discoveries that have enabled men better to comprehend the grandeur and rectitude of the heavens, and to facilitate their beneficial and enterprising undertakings on earth and sea. It has yielded more influence to majesty than the crown, and makes the titling of many Protestant churches, whilst, as record attests, implying in this entitling, as to what is taught and practised within them, the very reverse as to doctrines and rites. Protestantism may indeed totally discard the designation of "saint," and take up with, for her diversified places of worship, the several names of the Apostles, but in so doing it would give greater conspicuousness to what is consummately ridiculous, and to what private judgment has led to in jumping Paulites, who have not as yet reached their third heaven, and in Matthewite Seekers, who have not hitherto discovered the holy nook in which their sought-for Saviour is still hidden.

In alluding here once more to the term "Father," which indeed has had its reference already in some detail, it implies one, whether Greek or Latin, whose writings and teachings constitute what is known under the name of tradition, on which rested Christian belief ere the Scriptures were penned by the inspired. It manifests the fixity and perpetuity of the faith in all ages and in all Churches, from the time of the Apostles to this immediate period. "It is that which evinces," says St. Vincent of Lerins, "what has been always taught by all, and in every place." To step out of tradition is to find one's self in a labyrinth. The inspired Writings do not speak, and in a contestation upon Catholic doctrine it is necessary to consult the Fathers of the Church as to what they thought and taught upon the subject in dispute. But thus does Bossuet speak of the Holy Fathers, in his treatise upon them and tradition—" Whoever wishes to become an able theologian, and a solid interpreter of the Scripture, let him read and re-read the Fathers, and if frequently you meet with more of detail in modern writers, you will often find in a single book of the Fathers more of principle, more of the very sap of Christianity, than in the many volumes of modern divines." " These great men, the Fathers," continues Bossuet, " were nourished on the wheat of the elect, and filled with their primitive spirit, imbibed at so Apostolic a period, whatever came from their plenitude has not been surpassed in sublimity and utility by what has been the proceed of the most profound meditation." On the foregoing subject ecclesiastical writers say, and which may be here very pertinently introduced, that all the Fathers are comprised within the Doctors of the Church, but that every Doctor of the Church is not included among the number of the Fathers. Strictly speaking, those only are to be classed with the Fathers who have been elevated to the priesthood, and after death have been enrolled among the number of the saints for the perfection of their virtue, as well as the soundness of their belief. The most distinguished of the Fathers, as to the Greek Church, may be set down as St. Athanasius, St. Basil, St. Gregory Nazianzen, and St. Chrysostom—those of the Latin Church, St. Ambrose, St. Austin, St. Jerome, and St. Gregory the Great. Those, whose victories over their passions went beyond the triumphs of the renowned in the subjugation of towns and cities, kingdoms and empires, filled with the assurances of Heaven, that they so faithfully served, as well as the powers they owed obedience to on earth, never at the sacrifice of their conscience evaded a menaced torment, or at such a cost freed themselves from a continuous oppression. They possessed here their beatitude in humility, in meekness, in the exercise of mercy, and in the endurance oftentimes of persecutions for justice's sake. The greatest orators of ages, in praising majesty and its deeds, have always had a more sublime and influential theme for eulogy in the Fathers. Yet, whatever may have been the perfection of their lives, or the orthodoxy of their teachings, confirmed by General Councils that have now an ecclesiastical authority even with Protestants, they are nevertheless characterised by their persistent and unscrupulous enemies as " the Christian Doctors educated in the schools of orators and sophists, that practised dissimulation, craft, and trickery, in order to triumph over their adversaries." " The great confusion in their ideas matched with their profound ignorance on fundamental articles of Christian belief, their superstition was as excessive as their extravagance in religious worship—in fine, they were simple and credulous men, not very judicious in their criticisms, and often visionary in their ideas."

Yet, strangely inconsistent and contradictory enough, these traducers of the Fathers of primitive times, that edified Christendom by their virtue, and swayed it by their learning and eloquence, are thus referred to by the most staunch of their foes. " Their writings," says Daillé, at the close of his work entitled " De Vero Usu Patrum," " comprise lessons of morality and virtue capable of producing the greatest effects. Many things are therein contained that go to strengthen the foundations of Christianity, and also many observations under the most judicious form, in order to arrive at a proper understanding of the Scriptures, and the mysteries which they include; their authority went very far indeed to prove the truth of the Christian religion. Is it not a wonderful phenomenon that endowed with every capacity, and with every possible talent—born at different periods, and in diversified climes, during a period of fifteen centuries, with inclinations, manners, and ideas so different—they should be, nevertheless, in agreement in receiving the evidences of Christianity, in giving their common adorations to Jesus Christ, in preaching the same virtues, in hoping for the same recompense, in accepting the same Gospel, and in discovering there the same mysteries? . . . Is it very likely that so many men, celebrated by the sublimity of their genius—by their expanded and penetrating lights, whose worth is proved in their works—should have been so foolish as to found their faith and their hope upon the doctrine of Jesus Christ—to sacrifice to him their interests, their repose, and their life—without having deeply felt His Divine power? Shall we prefer to the unanimous suffrage of these great men the prejudices and clamours of a handful of disbelievers and Atheists, who calumniate the Bible without understanding it—who blaspheme that of which they are ignorant—who bring upon themselves much odium by the irregularity of their lives, and the limited nature of their information?" To this may be subjoined what Mosheim, in his dissertation on the Church, says: "I have scarcely any patience with those who do not cease to deafen us with their clamours against the Fathers—who tax them with ignorance, malice, sordidness, and ambition—as if these ancient and venerable men had never been of good faith—as if they had always acted and spoken under the influence of vicious motives, without shame, and in direct opposition to the voice of their consciences." "How little should we have known of the doctrines of the past," others admit, "without the enlightenment and conservatism of the Fathers!"

But what have the successors to Cranmer in orthodoxy and holiness effected here in the full sway of Protestantism during the hush upon Catholicity for such a lengthened period, or brought about by banishment and imprisonments, by fines and confiscations? These motley successors have made a chaos of Christianity, as including nothing definable, for what definition can be framed on the whim of opinions and the jargon of the passions? However, this Evangelical state of things troubles but little the Protestant mind, though it is pervaded with horror in reflecting on the alleged gross perversities of Catholicity, which, nevertheless, will not induce Catholicity to seek for an Apostolical character by fusing with the salutary Biblical certitudes of Baxter or Wesley, of Irving or Spurgeon, whose doctrines, in the aggregate, would be as unknown as their names to the Cyrils, the Basils, or to the Seven Champions of Christendom. Exceptional Puseyism, which comprises such an amplitude in ancient doctrines and practices, and such a largeness of discipline and rite, which Protestantism, since the Reformation, has never been so absolutely enlightened and ennobled by, must, through its very Catholic professions, concur with the foregoing. But, alas for Puseyism! however distinguished by erudition, piety, discipline, rites or tenets, it is yet without a supreme spiritual rule. No sure mooring can be effected to resist every sweeping billow and fitful blast, by the hands of man, on the exterior of the rock upon which is founded what is of Divine construction, and which ever after the impetuous whirl of winds and waters around it, stands out and glows in greater strength and majesty in the serene and returning ray. In other words, Christianity, which has its providence with the Ark "that alone rode amidst darkness and tempest on the Deluge, beneath which all the first works of wisdom and power were entombed," on the termination of the Old Law, had its build upon what was so pre-eminently significant of safety, combined with a sacred pledge of continuous preservation, which was not vouchsafed to the heavens themselves, that will be outlived in the complete fulfilment of the Divine promise. Up to this moment Catholicity, identified in truth with Christianity, has fully responded to the Divine promise in existence, integrity, and triumph. "What is there," exclaims an eloquent prelate, " to be feared? Catholicity has prevailed over every obstacle, successfully resisted every heresy, confronted the most hostile of philosophical opinions, and mastered the most shameful of the passions. The sciences have been arrayed against her, she has faced them and contended, and they have been severally compelled to bend the knee before her, and to hail her as of Divine origin." "All has been ultimately overcome by Catholicity, though not destroyed." "For if," says Montalembert, in quoting Lacordaire, "everything was destroyed productive of evil, nothing on earth would be left standing, not even religion herself." But let the great and distinguished of this land, who are the august representatives and possessors of ancestral houses and castles, who have abjured the faith of their illustrious ancestors to secure salvation in Protestantism, search into the most remote of piled records within their archives which refer to the primitive risings of their families, and they will discover bishop, priest, and religious of the olden belief to be almost in complete concurrence with their forefathers in the advancement of their early prosperity and their ultimate greatness. Within their extended and broad galleries of famed paintings, chiefly the production of Catholic genius, and models in their kind for the gifted of the immediate hour, they will behold vividly displayed piety and adoration at the altar of sacrifice; they will witness enthusiasm, if not heroism, on the field of battle among the anointed, upholding the Cross amid banner and sword, that the God of armies had been invoked to bless in a cause deemed just and holy.

"Nobility," says Edmund Burke, "is a graceful ornament to the civil order; it is the Corinthian capital of polished society." And when, in connection with foregoing matter, hideous and smouldering ruin has been pent up about it, as in successful infidel days, what power has been more prompt and efficient in preserving this symbol of grandeur from being entirely overturned, and confounded with the devastations of impiety and fury, than that with which the throne has found its safest league, and "which has conquered," says St. Prosper, "when arms have failed"? This power is Catholicity, with her hierarchy, that is based upon that order which prevails among the celestial hosts in the superiority of some and the subordination of others; it is of Divine origin, and admits of no equal. It will denounce and resist when the federacy of kings will be defied. It will survive the empires and nations that it spiritually directs, as well as those that strive to bring it within their royal bidding. In the various grades that constitute it, Catholic society has an unshaken confidence, and the intimacy of its members with the lowest ranks does not militate against their respective dignity. From amongst them the barons selected Stephen Langton to present to John for signature the Great Charter, which so largely wrested from the wanton despotism of a monarch the vital rights of a subject. Is it possible that the representatives of ancient house and castle, in searching into their remote records, in viewing depicted deeds as animated as true, should, under lively religious impressions, the last to be effaced from the mind of man, finally contemplate the portraits of the founders of their fortunes, their titles, and of still-existing charities, and then execrate their faith whilst venerating their virtue? It is scarcely possible. The genuine virtue that merits with Heaven is one with her truths, that exclude disunity, and could not preserve her present features amongst a monstrous assemblage of incompatible and unstaid tenets, that are unceasingly resolving themselves into a more profound enigma. All this, again to be insisted on, is the sure product of opinion, the idol of the infidel, who in the world of nature cannot discover a complete harmony and accord which proclaims a Divine intervention in all things, no more than Heresy in the world of grace can be convinced of the impossibility of an abiding truth among the contradiction of her sects— or, in other words, considers that she has an unexceptionable countenancing for all divisions within her through the Divine presence. "Lo! I am with you all days unto the end of the world" (St. Matt. xviii. 20). This most inconsistent persuasion yet goes to support her in an untiring and unscrupulous effrontery in resisting the claims of Catholicity to exclusive orthodoxy, and also to embarrass many conscientious and thoughtful Christians, by the assurance with which Protestant fictions are reiterated. With this conflict of feeling within them, though yearning for the manifest peace and unity combined in the Catholic belief, " they are like unto those" (as beautifully and forcibly expressed) " who externally gaze upon the storied windows of some venerable abbey, perplexed with their seemingly comprised incongruities, but on entering the sacred edifice all that seemed embarrassing to comprehend suddenly displays itself to be in perfect harmony, and glows in charms that the beam from heaven alone can so enrapturously impart."

With such a consolatory and vivid appreciation of facts are those imbued on eventually entering the Catholic Church; then every harassing misconception and early prejudice disappears. They are assured that they are within a genealogy that has no severance to let in confusion, and which includes the Patriarchs and Prophets, unto the first workings of a merciful

Providence that ensured the crushing of the head that devised the first mischief, the fall of man. They feel that they think and reason, not with Evangelical this, or Apostolical that, but with the heroic and uncompromising defenders of the faith, especially at the periods when Arius, Nestorius, and Macedonius denounced and maligned a Church that is named Catholic in the most early of symbols. They possess the peaceful conviction that they are in full relationship with those that adorned their one faith, not only with their virtue and their erudition, but also witnessed to its Divine nature by their blood and their lives. The books that Catholicity extends to them to nourish and quicken these salutary impressions are not of that complexion which has the approbation of Protestant authorities, in which Christianity is set forth under such diversified forms and extravagant representations as to bring it very close in similarity with the idols of the East, so distorted in feature, so misshapen in body, and so twisted in limbs that only the most stolid or infatuated could be induced to prostrate in adoration before them with religious convictions.

But as to Catholicity it is not possible for her, though so assiduously misrepresented, and delineated under the most repulsive features, to be put forward at any period as a mere thing of grotesque jumbles, for public gaze and conjecture. Her attributes give her the conspicuousness of a majestic and unimpaired building upon a mountain's elevation. The continuous denouncements of those that are without her precincts invests her indeed with an exclusive distinction, and which unceasingly challenges the blustering indignation of the members of a Christianity whose phrasings upon inspiration to-day are bettered in the Apostolical to-morrow. She holds her own now intact in doctrinal integrity, as when Tertullian defied the philosophers to convict her of crime or folly, or the heresiarchs to prove the legitimacy of their mission, or evince Christian suffrage to be on the side of their rapid and irreconcilable novelties. Within the library of a museum (to which, in comparison, Alexandria's marvel was insignificance) that is stored with much that is now lost to nature, and which possesses in perfection the interesting relics of empires whose respective sites have as utterly passed away as that of Jerusalem's Temple, volumes upon volumes are here kept in watchful custody, whose Christian teachings of the earliest periods will be found to be in perfect doctrinal harmony with the most recent of deposited Catholic works within the almost countless shelves that contain the literary and scientific works of the ingenious and gifted of ages. This indicates somewhat of a Providence in alliance with that which has ensured a virtual triumph in Great Britain for

Catholicity. But Catholicity or the one Christianity needs no attesting records for her absolute vitality. She existed, and was believed in without dissent, before the entry of her authoritative truths gave to books their chief value. Omnipotence is combined with tradition, which held guardianship over Noah and his family, that remained to witness to what in detail made prominence in the belief of their forefathers, the creation, the fall of man, and a future Redeemer, when every vestige of the mighty and their histories had disappeared from the face of the earth. The very language that the Catholic Church has retained for centuries in daily usage among her clergy, and within her sanctuaries, preserves for her an incontestable evidence of the antiquity of her teaching, and best responds to a Church of fixity of doctrine. It facilitates official communication on every side; it frees from the expensive and inconvenient necessity of revising rituals and missals. For if in the vernacular tongue much of their wording would have become obsolete or reversed in meaning, and there would no longer exist that ready facility to the ordained, into whatever parts they might journey, of offering up the Holy Sacrifice, which, according to the prophet Malachi, was to be unceasing in its celebration from the rising to the setting sun. It is a majestic language, and enhances education in its acquirement, and is venerable in the eyes of Christianity, since it was the chief medium of its diffusion throughout the world-wide conquests of Rome. It is the language, too, in which the converted from idolatry first chiefly learnt their lessons of virtue, and in which, when expiring on the blood-soaken sands of the arena, they proclaimed their faith, the one faith of the present hour, and then commended their souls into the hands of a God that was but little known. It is a language which in its ancient and continuous use presents as much of a Providence as the conversion of the city of cities itself to Christianity.

But if the Catholic or Universal Church has given a preference for its venerability, and its wide extension among the nations of the earth during the Roman ascendancy, in the exclusive retention of the Latin tongue in her offices, rites, and sacrifice, the Greek tongue is not to be overlooked, which was largely in use for centuries. The Books of the New Testament are written in Greek, and a moiety at least of the Acts of the first General Councils are written in the same tongue. The Fathers of the Greek Church, who number many, are not to be read with less advantage than the Latin Fathers. They constitute a portion of tradition, and are the depositories of doctrinal truths as well as the Latins. In some instances their accuracy in defining supersedes the Latin Fathers.

But well here may be introduced the observation of the profound Bossuet relative to the two Churches in his "Defence of Tradition and the Fathers," that "it would be futile since the schism to urge the sentiment of the Greek against the Catholic Church, which, since the above sorrowful event, has been always looked upon as the Universal Church. However it is of importance to know that during eight centuries the Greek Church formed a part of the Catholic or Universal Church, so that it is essential to combine the Latin and Greek Fathers together, and thus to ascend to the times of the Apostles themselves." As to the separation of the Greek from the Catholic Church, schism first brought it about, by disclaiming the spiritual supremacy of the Pope; to this succeeded heresy, by the denial of the procession of the Holy Ghost from the Son as well as the Father. A reunion was eventually effected between the two Churches, by the recognition, through the authorised representatives of the Greek Church, of the spiritual supremacy of the Pope, and in professing that the Holy Ghost proceeded from the Father and the Son. This union, however, was not lasting; it had its interruptions as well as its renewings, and finally, through a powerful and prevailing faction among the Greeks at Constantinople, it entirely ceased. It was followed as if through a visitation upon persistent perversity by the complete breaking up of the Greek Empire on the capture of its chief city by the Turks. The Greeks have now continued for centuries in their schism and their heresy, and though but little changed as to teaching, if otherwise in discipline, their influence among Christian or pagan nations, through the intrepidity of their zeal in the propagation of their creed, or the heroism of their virtue in evincing its worth, has indeed been of a very limited nature. Russia's Emperor, invested with a religious supremacy, and of the same doctrinal persuasion with the Greeks, and one with them in details of Divine worship, has recently given his assent to his grandchildren being baptised and reared in the Lutheran belief—a belief which anathematises his credence that the Holy Ghost does not proceed from the Father and the Son but from the Father only. In contrast to this truckling Christianity, the conduct of the late Pontiff, Pius the Ninth, might here seasonably be adverted to, who could recognise no compromise that trenched upon conscience. With but little remaining of all the several domains that a special Providence during centuries had secured to the Popedom to make independence for the most august, ancient, and responsible of rules, majesty and sway still continued with the Supreme Pontiff, and to him from the uttermost parts of the earth deputations were constantly arriving to reverence his virtue, and to give their homage to one who united in himself, with such piety and dignity, both the priest and the monarch. What was tendered to him by the hand of usurpation he ever firmly refused to accept, being the product of sacrilege, and for that which he so conscientiously refused, considering its source, he ever found an equivalent in the spiritual loyalty of the Catholic nations of the earth, in their becoming so munificently subsidiary to his wants. Though stricken with years and infirmities, though environed by the hostile, who had the crowned for their partisans, and influenced by those who shrunk not from forwarding the most iniquitous of expediences to attain political ends, Pius, as before dwelt upon, undeterred by the sovereign positions of the adverse, denounced deadly errors fearlessly, as well as secret associations which towards the end of his Papal supremacy began to swarm into wide and destructive life. In this he continued the provident care of his predecessors, in allowing no age to pass by without furnishing to Christendom a summary of the fictions of man in contrast with the truths of God. Heresiarch has succeeded to heresiarch, and sect to sect, but they have had no interminglings as among themselves with the Catholic faithful.

Catholicity has no admission within her precincts

except for doctrinal unity, assured upon a solemn affirmation which also comprises with articles of belief a credence in the word of God in its entirety. It is this authoritative proceeding that makes a surety and an exclusion which heresy will never be able to insist on or obtain. Opinion lays open a free ground for the pitching of a myriad tents, which certainly, had Balaam had the opportunity of beholding the random that pervaded their disposition, surmounted by standards of every hue and shape, he would not have experienced much of the transport that filled him in contemplating the regularity that so harmoniously prevailed throughout Israel's Divinely dictated encampment. This may not very probably disturb the complacency of self-opinion among the generality of Protestants. However, one fact ought to give rise to serious consideration, that the Christianity so contemptuously upheld as a religion of the Dark Ages should have attained in these boasted times of enlightenment such an influence that she should, in a clearer view of her nature, by her beauty, symmetry, and order, have mastered prejudice, imparted confidence, and have so largely received into her communion the once lauded and the most staunch of Protestantism. These are now convinced that they are united with one that is the centre and constitutes the keystone that makes all secure, and on which no pressure can effect a sudden collapse—the Sovereign Pontiff, the vicar of Jesus Christ. Puseyites or Ritualists, you will not have this man for a spiritual ruler over you—be certain then at some or other period you will have false prophets rising up among you, to divide and enfeeble. On this subject, further prolonged, nothing can be met with in history to justify a hope that even the most detailed profession of Catholic tenets, combined with a minute adoption of Catholic rites, without Catholic authority, will long continuously hold together.

SECTION VIII.

THERE is then no future for Ritualists, except such an existence as they may drag on in a state of separation and isolation. Freed even from doctrinal disputes among themselves, for the present, they have at intervals to withstand the concurrent pressure of the most extreme of sects, indirectly hailed on by the Legislative.

But beyond the occasional assailings of the united of differing creed, and the incidental countenancing of the Administrative, Puseyism or Ritualism has much to fear from the hostile efforts of some of the leading journals of the period for its eventual stability. Journalism comprises a power which empires court, and certainly, if this power has rarely made or unmade kings, it has had a very decided influence on their several fortunes. Not often is a widely influential journal in its purpose fairly baffled, except when in antagonism with some one equally powerful contemporary. Its information comes from the ends of the earth with lightning's suddenness, and the stirring events of yesterday's world are in its numerous impressions on the early morrow at every one's door. Its comments upon all the myriad matters of sublunary moment and interest generally include ability, erudition, research, and experience, which rarely fail to arrest attention, and variously direct and counsel the busy and diversified reading millions in their multifarious pursuits of the day. But though journalism elevates humanity by imparting knowledge, and befriends it by expatiating on the immediate position of things, by defining its rights and defending them, by making widely known its afflictions, and pleading for instant succour, by extending education and advancing refinement, by supplementing efficiency to the laws, and by extending to public proceedings order and security, and ensuring for it justice by discussing the verdicts of Courts and the legislation of Senates, yet, withal, it possesses a pre-eminent power for mischief as well as for good. It has wrought by misrepresentations distrust among kingdoms to suit and forward a policy, and precipitated them eventually into deadly strife. It has helped to unseat ancient dynasties, and thus countenanced what has made the chief woes and laments of history—" might not right." As journalism generally has its life in party, it has often, in order to preserve existence, bartered principle for gain. The sure consequence of this has been frequent cabals, which have constituted the first movements of rebellions in which the voice of religion and the whisperings of conscience have been equally little heard or little heeded. In the columns of journalism at large reasoning has frequently an approval at the expense of revelation, and the glow of genius has sometimes been made to halo the heads of those in whose hearts there is little sympathy with Christianity.

But in regard to the foregoing, if there is one country to be especially adverted to that superabounds in journalism, it is Great Britain, and among the daily published and speedily distributed journals throughout her generally educated and thronged domains, the *Times* has a precedence beyond others, under a leading view, and has a most pronounced sway. It has been on this account significantly denominated the fourth estate of the British Empire. In foreign lands it commands a circulation and a consideration with which no other imported journal can compete. Its early and important intelligence, occasionally secured at a cost which, in the adding up, amounts to a modest fortune, combined with its prompt and pertinent articles, often as deeply absorbs the attention of the ministers of rulers as the princes on 'Change. It is the chosen monitor of thousands far and near in secular affairs, and the oracle of many in religious matters. Its criticisms on the fine arts have often proceeded from those who have done most honour to them by their own exquisite performances as well as the judicious selection of their matter. Yet even Genius herself, with her innumerable, diversified, and fascinating gifts, can hardly sometimes, with any absolute success, confront the adverse judgment of a journal that has so broad a control in its decisions in all that mankind, under such a varied reference, is actuated by a resistless impulse to effect, and feels so pre-eminent a joy in its accomplishment.

But though this distinguished and widely appreciated journal has had subsidiary to its purposes art, science, and erudition—wealth and titles—for so extended a period, and almost universally so when the interests of Protestantism have principally occupied its columns, it has, notwithstanding all its exceptional and influential aid, conjoined with its continuous and strenuous opposition, failed to bring Catholicity to a stand in this empire, or even to make a partial halt in her steady advances—the faith that the masters of the earth, with their legions, could not conquer, or oblige even to retrograde, and which now, as hitherto, denounces secret societies that affect with fears leagued princes—the faith that retains history as the chief witness to her origin and her triumphs—nor can she be blotted out from history's records, nor dwindle in the slightest form as to a profound and monopolising interest within her pages. History details the ordeal she has gone through during past ages from tyrannical legislations, and from the conspirings of the heretical, and the fierce hatreds of the blaspheming and the disbelieving, but ever concludes with her victories. Ponderous volumes have been published upon others equally ponderous, having names appended to them of wide renown in science, art, and literature, in conflict with Catholicity, as if the respective writers thereof, in contemplating their several labours "as gigantic, could contend with truth and heaven." Yes, they can contend against the Church Divinely established, but they will not prevail; their failures will be as consecutive as those of Satan from his first impious and calamitous enterprise against the Supreme Author of his being. Pamphlets, magazines, reviews, and journals, with untiring assiduity and astounding assurance, nevertheless still continue to advance against Catholicity what might be said to make some approach to the accusations of primitive persecuting days as to their extravagant and reckless nature. The veracity of all this, however, has been of late most seriously affected by the conversion of those to Catholicism, as already touched upon, who, considering their education and their lives whilst abiding in Protestantism, could never, with hushed consciences, speak out so loudly in defence of deceit and abomination, being at the same time so fully and deeply persuaded of the contrary. It would, indeed, be as a moral miracle—something in the nature of the marvellous, or rather even of the stupendous. Whatever gloss or interpretation may be put on things, the preceding observation has had at this hour an ultimate influence upon some of the most inveterate in their opposition to Catholicity. If it has not done away with all rabid hostile feeling, it has certainly, to a considerable extent, repressed what was once as extreme as revolting; and those who formerly could scarcely bestow a mere passing glance upon anything Catholic without experiencing the deepest emotions of a violent antipathy can now drop the fierce term of the "damnable," and adopt one less objectionable. Even the prominent and dominating journal of the period, the *Times*, unable to resist such a host of confuting testimonies in the persons of those that have joined the so-maligned one faith, that were once of such good report within its columns, has been induced finally, though late, to admit within its orthodox precincts the "Requiescat in pace"—that is, employ a discreet silence upon many outrageous advances against Catholicity, which could not now, as heretofore, be put forward with confidence without seriously compromising the honesty or judgment of those who, in relinquishing Protestantism, have not parted from the ardent attachment of the gifted many whose friendship in the world of science and literature is felt as marking an exceptional distinction for themselves in the ranks of life.

Perhaps, for the many to arrive at a clear and solid knowledge of the nature and value of Catholicity, her Catechism may here most appropriately have a principal consideration. In this careful and exact summary upon doctrines and morals, all is to be identified with a God of truth and sanctity. Within this compendium for the instruction of her youth, and the information of Christendom, there can be no rescinding in doctrines, no amending in morals. In its brief pages it refers to a Being infinite and eternal in His perfections, the Creator of all things, who made man to His own image and likeness, which exists in his immortal soul, and upon which the entire economy of religion is founded; also the fall of man; original sin; the necessity of a Redeemer; the incarnation of the Son of God, born of an Immaculate Virgin; the mysteries which are the objects of Christian faith; the division of sin into mortal and venial; the nature of grace, and its necessity; the seven Sacraments; the Commandments of God, and the precepts of the Church; the eternal recompense of the good, and the everlasting award of the wicked; the temporal expiation of sin in purgatory, prayers for the dead, and the intercession of the saints; the moral of the Gospel, and the necessary means for the sanctification of souls. Such in substance constitutes the Catholic catechism. In it, though all is brief, all is instructive; in it, though all is simple, all is grandeur, throughout its diverse references. There is herein not only wherewith to enlighten the ignorant, to correct the perverse, but also to elevate into the saint. Here nothing is scant or dubious, as in the Protestant Catechism; all is ample and defined. There is no entire prescinding from what makes the heroism of virtues, from what ensures in their practice blessings on earth as well as rewards in heaven, and, finally, from what in their commission draws down upon man the direst anathemas of his Creator.

Now, if in the supposition the two catechisms, that of the Catholic and that of the Protestant, were presented at a deemed Apostolical period to spiritual authority for a decision upon their respective orthodox and moral worth, it might be asked, which of the two would more probably meet with a rejection or an acceptance? According to some celebrated reverend divines that are occasionally rapt into prophecies that are as little countenanced as their fulfilment is looked for, Romanism, as so distinguished from Protestantism, would receive its instant rejection, with its sacrifice, sacraments, prayers for the dead, invocation of the saints, and its evangelical counsels. But the utter improbability of such a decision being come to by the authoritative of generally admitted times of purity of faith and soundness of morals, may be well founded in the several testimonies, as already adduced in these pages, of eminent Protestant bishops and divines in favour of the most prominent controverted teachings of Catholicity. They had their guarantee for the truthfulness of their several vouchings in the ecclesiastical records of the early periods. Even Infidelity, as already in detail shown in connection with the foregoing, has, under the brightest names on her roll, discoursed upon the principal tenets of Catholicity as logically as enthusiastically, and has sedulously unfolded a Providence in her morality, for the promoting and ensuring the welfare of man, which Liberty, Equality, and Fraternity have never yet shown forth to the disparagement of a religion of Authority, Order, and Charity. These exclusively proceed from the Divine nature of Catholicity, which she has possessed from the beginning, and she retains them in their respective perfections, and which she has unfailingly developed in all their several salutary amplitudes after many dire revolutions, whose most prominent calamities were principally consequent upon the heartless and frantic proceedings of Liberty,

Equality, and Fraternity, an aggregate of terms that imply a confederacy for the entire destruction of Christianity and the utter ruin of society, and which the recently returned from banishment to their grateful country, under the decree of a commiserating and patriotic ruling, if continuously fostered in their conscientious and disinterested purposes, will most widely and calamitously evince. Catholicity, it is here to be remarked, manifests, not only in her extended existence and unimpaired vigour, a Divine Presence, but in her every formal act, although of a varied purport, since it has its immediate source in a principle that makes one with her very being. It would be therefore as difficult to battle with success against the authority, the order, or the charity that lives throughout Catholicity, as with this term itself in its complete extent. "This is our victory, our faith," which alone has been proved to be identified with Catholicity, that has ever come forth intact from every combined assailment.

But here again may Macaulay be quoted with instance in reference to Catholicity, in emerging from what was overwhelming, and in which what was merely human must have perished: "It is not strange that in the year 1799 even sagacious observers should have thought that at length the hour of the Church of Rome was come. An infidel power ascendant, the Pope dying in captivity, the most illustrious prelates of France living in a foreign country on Protestant alms, the noblest edifices which the munificence of former ages had consecrated to the worship of God turned into temples of victory, or into banqueting houses for political societies, or into theophilanthropic chapels, such signs might well be supposed to indicate the approaching end of that long domination. But the end was not yet. Again doomed to death, the milk-white hind was still fated not to die. Even before the funeral rites had been performed over the ashes of Pius the Sixth, a great reaction had commenced, which, after the lapse of more than forty years, appears to be still in progress. Anarchy had had its day. A new order of things rose out of the confusion—new dynasties, new laws, new titles; and amidst them emerged the ancient religion. The Arabs have a fable that the Great Pyramid was built by antediluvian kings, and alone, of all the works of men, bore the weight of the flood. Such as this was the fate of the Papacy. It had been buried under the great inundation; but its deep foundations had remained unshaken, and when the waters abated it appeared alone amidst the ruins of a world which had passed away. The republic of Holland was gone, and the empire of Germany, and the Great Council of Venice, and the old Helvetian League, and the House of Bourbon, and the Parliaments and aristocracy of France. Europe was full of young creations—a French Empire, a kingdom of Italy, a Confederation of the Rhine. Nor had the late events affected only territorial limits and political institutions. The distribution of property, the composition and spirit of society, had through a great part of Catholic Europe undergone a complete change. But the unchangeable Church was still there."[1] On the subject of Catholicity and her final successes the name of Chateaubriand may be well subjoined to that of Macaulay. His "Génie du Christianisme" ought, though he professed Catholicity, to obtain for him some consideration among Protestants for his luminous and fervid expositions upon the excellencies and the vitality of the Christian religion. Indeed, his thoughts, his reasonings, and his embellishments, for which Christianity gives the most felicitous of opportunities, cannot but engage in her sacred cause both soul and heart. Whilst the devastations of infidelity far and wide still remained on the land of France, when all the elements of society were yet in a confused state, when amid the ruins of the temple, the church, and the monastery, without a sigh or a shudder, people promenaded or sauntered for pleasure or curiosity, Chateaubriand, with the deep lament of

---

[1] Macaulay's Essay on Ranke's "Lives of the Popes."

the prophet, contemplated his own country "made desolate with desolation." But he found consolation in the conviction of making eventual way for faith by the overthrow of infidelity, that spat upon apparently prostrated Christianity, and then with assurance and defiance looked up to heaven. He at length gave to the world that which superseded in interest what had so calamitously fascinated it. Read by Napoleon, whose every conflict then with nations was victory, he openly avowed that there was a triumph in words as well as in arms. The Bible regained a worth beyond the Encyclopædia, and the people of France found again a witnessing therein to the Christianity that their forefathers professed, which was Catholicity. Chateaubriand, in his great work, demonstrates, in language as persuasive as captivating, that Catholicity, the Christianity, with him, that Heaven alone recognises, is a religion that is not the product of barbarism, that she is not absurd in her dogmas, ridiculous in her ceremonies, or despotic in her enjoinments, that she is not hostile to science and art, or adverse to all that is rational and beautiful, that she is not, as urged, ever striving to bring men into abject subjection to her austere and absolute will, and that she is not verily the chief impediment to their advancement in happiness and their progress in knowledge—on the contrary, that she is Divine in her teachings, sublime in her virtues, and imposing in her rites. Susceptible of all the charms of poetry and the amplitudes of rhetoric, she has an enthusiastic patronage for genius. She purifies the taste by her experience in the school of ages, and gradually expands the mind by her well-appointed studies. She stimulates emulation by her judicious encomiums, and bestows universal renown in lauding excellence wherever she meets with it. To Catholicity, indeed, as Chateaubriand sets forth, mankind is a debtor, from the roughest and the most primitive times to those of the most abstract sciences, for what they most cultivate and exult in by reason of the grandeur and utility of their results. Catholicity is truly the soul of society, and comprises within herself every honourable and beneficial state of life, and by her accessible education, and the diversity of her numerous sacred appointments, she opens a way for the gifted among the most lowly to celebrity and dignity.

But what is principally to be regarded and prized in Catholicity is that her tenets admit of no abbreviation, nor can her evangelical counsels ever become "dead" virtues. There is now, as in the past, the same unreserved and definite credence among her diversified millions in what makes the second lively joy of the Catholic mother, the spiritual regeneration of her new-born; in what confirms and invigorates the Christian in accomplishing the momentous and pledged purposes of his religious being; in what restores lost days to virtue; in what stills the temptations of the Christian in the final moments of probation; in what hallows with the sacred union in Eden; and, finally, in what makes a blending with the Divine attributes of that ineffable Being whose might made Satan's lightning fall from the abodes of sanctity. These several sacraments were all believed in, and respectively explained in the cathedrals that yet exist, as gigantic in their structure as elaborate in their finish, which testifies to the national zeal which, in ages past, raised them, and which seem to be preserved for the eventual triumph of a faith in which they had their elevation and their consecration. Within this Catholic faith, that stands in relation to society, as she does to reason, not as an enemy to thwart, but as an authority to regulate, the evangelical counsels, too, will be found to exist in all the vigour of their first heroisms—voluntary poverty, perpetual chastity, and entire obedience—not under any clear form as their several worths intimated to humanity before the Redeemer of the world made it known in so fervid a tone. In the evangelical counsels grace, which is defined, in Catholicity's Christian doctrine, a supernatural gift of God, freely bestowed upon us for our sanctification and salvation, chiefly develops its force and power. It is this aid which enables the just to preserve their innocence and their fervour, and the penitent by their sighs and tears to regain the friendship of God. In this alone, by co-operating with it, is the triumph of the Christian over disorderly passions, attachment to the senses, and over almost resistless pride. Without it our humanity could do nothing, and with its aid it has elevated our humanity into the third heaven, ere the tie of life between soul and body has been severed. The virtues that grace nourishes and invigorates subsist; they are as immortal as the truths on which they are grounded. In this vivifying period exist also within Catholicity the perfections of the past to the present day. This is now just adverted to, to be specially instanced in this empire, in which dire charges against religious houses are so fully contradicted, as well as in those kingdoms of an undisturbed faith of centuries, in the many convents and monasteries inhabited by fervent religious communities.

Heresy, which is ever denouncing tradition, that discloses but little appreciation of the vital attestation which it comprises, and is ever, in her varying interpretations upon Scripture, varying her errors, has not failed to meddle with the sound and conclusive reasoning of a great authority in Christendom upon the nature of grace—St. Augustine. This profound and patient thinker, one of the most influential doctors of the Church, even with the heterodox, who had his enlightenment from the same source as the Apostles, which enabled him to edify by his virtue as well as to illumine upon dogma, has fully vindicated what the Catholic Church has taught and decided as to this fundamental tenet of Christianity. This grace, which precedes all merits and perfects the Christian, and which effected in its great exponent a conversion approaching in the miraculous to that of Saul, is, as Fléchier details forth, in substance with the Fathers, "an invincible force which ensures acquiescence without infringing on free will, which acts without prejudice to the rights of Heaven or to those of earth, and without interfering with what belongs to God, or with what God has ceded to man." In the science of the firmament man may display a marvellous exactitude in his calculations, and astonish by his discoveries, but he will never shine with the uninterrupted glow of the heavens without the assistance and aid of grace. He may be as profound in knowledge as skilful in art, he may write and he may act, but we have the word of God Himself to assure the human race that its every endeavour is all in vain to extricate itself from the labyrinth of evil without the help of its light, or to reach with the prophet the centre of all good without the assistance of its strength. Magdalen wept and was forgiven, and Peter witnessed to his repentance by his tears. Both, under so consoling and moving a form, testified to the speedy efficacy of grace when responded to by an unhesitating and faithful co-operation. That conscience alone which is in due communing with this grace can secure the peace which mere humanity never yet found included in the most craved for of what is sublunary when ultimately possessed. For although man has lost by sin his claim to a sovereign felicity to which his innocence formerly entitled him, he has not, however, lost his desire to be happy. Born for God, nothing limited can content him. To be happy he must identify himself with the will of God through something meritorious, which can have no existence except through the aid of grace. The name of Christian is of small account unless grace is at hand to impart to it a worth which has its wide and ineffable expandings in the saint, and ceases only in him, in its vital operations, when, on his expiring, raptures are instantaneously realised amid the attributes of the Deity. In the sinner it dissipates the thickening terrors of the future, and sustains him in the great fight of the Apostle, "against the world, the flesh, and the devil." In this strife for a crown for which all must contend specially against "the spiritual powers of darkness," the hands that from time to time are uplifted, with the confidence of Israel's leader, for assistance, are sure to be strengthened unto victory in the steady succourings of grace. Defeat, and the forfeiture of eternal bliss, is only for those in whom grace becomes void by their cowardice and relaxed resistance, and too often the calamity is deepened by their siding with the dissolute, if not with the disbelieving, who will have their respective reprobation and anathema. This salutary grace, so far from being in opposition to intellectual progress, as hitherto dwelt upon by its light, lays open to view another world, which, in its contemplation, is realised an acquaintance with what, without grace, the philosophy of the past or the present could never have arrived at, and thus, in some respects, is conjoined the knowledge of men with that of angels. At this pre-eminent period of Christian self-sufficiency, grace may yet continue to be especially adverted to, displaying, as in Apostolic days, its wondrous workings amongst the erring and the prejudiced, of every sect, grade, condition, and capacity, in their final conversion to Catholicity, once as bitterly adverse to her regaining a position in this influential empire as the idolatrous Senate was to the spread of Christianity at Rome, or the Jewish Sanhedrim to its prevailing at Jerusalem. All this evinces that it is with Heaven, not with earth, to master fostered passion and to sway a perverted understanding, through, when adequately responded to, the medium of grace, purchased by the death of the Cross to ensure eternal life. "No man can come to me," declares the Divine Founder of Christianity, " except the Father who sent Me draw him." (St. John, c. vi., v. 44.) " Without Me you can do nothing."

Under the most heroic forms its action is also attested to in religious houses, both as to monasteries and convents (now so rapidly multiplying on every side), that were first raised and tenanted by the sanctity of the desert, and by those whose hearts were dissevered from the frail and fragile of this world. The high of rule, the rich, the avaricious, and the dissolute, in contemplating the serenity of feature that existed within them, have ultimately entered, to carry out what formerly begot instant revolt in thought, entire obedience, voluntary poverty, and perpetual chastity. Within these sacred asylums of a perfected Christianity, that " have peace placed upon their precincts " (Ps. cxlvii., v. 14), it is that a good conscience yields pre-eminently a continual banquet, and which does not condemn enjoyment when unmingled with fault. Its whisperings of peace to the tried in virtue might be compared with those of the gentle evening breezes which joyously apprised a yet unforfeited innocence of the approach of Him to familiar converse who gave to Eden its majesty and beauty in tree and flower. But no condition is incompatible that is of a legitimate character with the most sublime agencies of grace. From God, who is the Divine Author of Christianity, comes a varied stewardship as to state and possessions. It is not easy to believe that God has created the goods of this earth for the perverse alone, and that those were not entitled to the accumulation and use of them who strove to correspond in their conduct with the Gospel after the most edifying form. Saints are, as already adverted to, to be read of in history as being engaged in every diversity of lawful pursuits, and the Most High has recognised their diligence in His blessings here, and with a final admittance after their assigned task into the rest of their Lord. The Redeemer of mankind selected those for the chief part for His Apostles who had been engaged in some special occupation, and on them descended the Divine Spirit for the enlightenment and conversion of the world to Christianity. Religion, with its comprised spiritual aids, illumines and imparts confidence to reason; it gives a knowledge of duty, and stimulates man to its vigorous fulfilment, by the promise of future ineffable joys in the name of the "Giver of all good gifts."

Though from this intervening of grace, it is scarcely necessary to repeat, Christendom derives both life and merit, yet, nevertheless, it obtains but little consideration, and is as little implored, in a Protestant

Christianity. Nor is this surprising, since heresy is not in concert with truth, with which grace is allied. No one, indeed, is excepted from the assistance of grace; but how indifferently will it be co-operated with by those who ground their Christianity upon the teaching of some heresiarch that goes to impede the action of grace, or to leave for it but a very scanty respect in the extended right of private judgment! Heresy, in its full and perverse sense, equally anathematised with infidelity, will have its own modelling of virtue as well as belief; and her writings ever tend to impress that in Catholicity—in which a clear definition and a safe exposition of grace is alone to be met with—the Christian is marred in the development of his natural gifts, and in the enhancement of their value in society, in order to be in due co-operation with what is termed a vital medium of salvation. On this important matter the observations of Père Félix have a value, by unfolding in substance that Catholicity, as to spiritual doctrines, includes no straitenings upon the development of natural endowments—in fact, that an appreciation of them is heightened by an advancement in Christian perfection: "With moral progress all rises, all ascends, all advances, in order to the progressive conquest of destiny. Virtue by itself does not teach science; but it implants in man that which forwards him in science, in the sense of the true, and in the attainment of lofty thoughts. Virtue by itself teaches not the arts; but it yields that which forms illustrious artists—the sense of the beautiful, and an enthusiasm for great things. Virtue by itself teaches neither politics, nor legislation, nor administration; but it gives to man that which creates great legislators and true statesmen—the sense of justice and self-devotion in the cause of mankind." Elsewhere, in his "Conferences," Père Félix very sensibly remarks " that Christianity wills material progress as a means, she wills it not as an end; she wills matter as a slave, she wills it not as a sovereign; she desires the development of matter as a normal condition of life, she wills it not as a sovereign ambition of life. The possession of the uncreated as the end, the possession of the created as the means; before man, and above him God, as the goal; before man the material creation given to him as a means whereby to ascend to God, and in the midst man himself, carrying along with him mute nature to glorify God—here is the order, such as Christian preaching and philosophical reasoning proclaim it, and will defend it even to the last." In the above, then, it may be readily discerned that Catholicity has equally as sound as clear an answer to the foregoing subject, and which is in due correspondence with her origin and her mission, and which she will always be able to give, in whatever age science, art, or political economy have made signally illustrious.

Catholicity is only otherwise to this in conduct in what is unorthodox or sinful. But here she is with God, " who hath indeed delivered up the world to the consideration of men," as Scripture declares, yet, at the same time, the inspired Word affirms that He has established a Church in which His attributes, His revelations, His sacred mysteries, and His will may be surely known—in the knowledge of which there is nothing that tends to counteract what does honour to reason in its beneficial and solid results. A knowledge of mathematics may be combined with that of revelation without a fear for the Bible. Whatever God bestows there is an all-wise motive for the bestowal, and a never-failing Providence for the attainment of its sacred purposes. If it is here asked why there is so much insistence upon all this, it is in order decisively to meet the contentious and stern obstinacy of Protestants in re-asserting the contrary. It has its object at this agitated period of religious controversy to induce the resident and the educated of the universities of this empire of Catholic institution to consider how far foregoing affirmed matter is in agreement with the Christianity of the Wykehams and the Wainfleets. A Christianity which had truth for a triumph, and every achieved excellence for a joy. A Christianity which had a sedulous and systematic culture for reason in her schools, and the enthusiasm of steady progress in science and learning did not interfere with a zeal in carrying out Christian perfections. A Christianity which is now spreading far and wide in this land, as distinct in attributes as the gifts with which the Creator has endowed man, and which (to be again repeated) cannot but be in close confederacy, as having but one common Providence in the Founder and the Giver. This Christianity then may, being, as set forth, a sublime philosophy which demonstrates unity and order in nature without suffering any disparagement to affect or come upon what enlarges the powers of the mind and realises fixity of judgment. The many that have been converted to the Catholic faith, and have gained in the most renowned of universities public honours by their successful competitions in the highest departments of science and literature, did not experience any dissatisfaction, on entering as teachers into Catholic academies and colleges, at the existing educational arrangements therein carried out, whilst the most ample liberty was not denied them (as far as a prescribed course of studies permitted) of imparting their varied and profound knowledge.

If it is still urged that Catholic tutoring continues

to be in accordance with the despotic and superstitious character of Catholicism, how is it, then (it may be further inquired), that Ritualists, who have so spontaneously taken up with Catholic teachings and practices, which include, as alleged, so much arbitrary obstructiveness to intellectual acquirements, that a spiritual rule might be rendered more effective and absolute, have not, in this discussed matter, intimated a similar conviction with the great mass of Protestants? It is because the Ritualists, in gradually adopting so large an amount of Catholic tenets and rites, as orthodox and advantageous, once deemed by them as heterodox and superstitious, could not discover in progressive scrutiny any grounds for this charge against Catholicism, of a fettered education, to rest on, no more than for a host of other imputations and calumnies. As very aptly to be observed, the Christian in the Catholic Church yields an obedience prominently and exceptionally so to the thousand evangelical vessels of election within Protestantism; but it is an obedience to which reason and duty have a just claim, an obedience which is dignified through its religious action and its purity of motive. It is an obedience that is as constant as uniform, and best calculated to resist corruption, because disinterested. The worldling, in an insisted and necessary order of things, has to yield an obedience also with the

Christian; but with the Christian it is the man, with the worldling it is the slave; all is grovelling, nothing noble, nothing generous in conduct, ever vacillating as gain or advancement may diversely influence. If anything has pre-eminence in effectively precluding all this, it is Catholicity, to the fact of which history attests under the most tasking of trials, the most alluring of charms, and the most prevailing of impulses. She is a religion which has an exclusive dominion over her millions of subjects, in the firm conviction of her truths, and in the practice of her virtues. In her alone is to be found that tranquillity of intellect, and that peace of conscience, for which Heaven will substitute her joys in rewarding the merits of earth.

But what a vast spiritual dominion with the Papacy for a supreme headship, it is further to be observed, abides within Catholicity, from which is obtained so ready and fervid an obedience! In reference here to the immense extent of Great Britain's territorial dependencies, Daniel Webster sets it forth after a most ingenious and eloquent form. "She is a Power," he says, "which has dotted the surface of the whole globe with her possessions and military posts, whose morning drum, following the sun in his course, and keeping pace with the hours, circles the earth with one continuous and unbroken strain of the martial airs of England." Yet the temporal rule of the monarch of Great Britain cannot vie in magnitude with the spiritual rule of the Sovereign Pontiff of Rome throughout the Catholic world, in every variety of climate, and under every diversity of government, involving more than two hundred millions of souls, unanimous in their religious adherence, because undivided in their faith. The imposing testimonies of allegiance and homage, from all parts of the universe, during the life of Pius IX., have had the effect of making the successor to the Prince of the Apostles, as to his pre-eminently responsible and authoritative position, more widely known and more deeply revered.

But what a witnessing again to be remarked is there not in all this as to the marvellous inconsistency that the Ritualists are betrayed into, who, whilst professing teachings and adopting ceremonies as orthodox and legitimate, the gradual accumulated result of their patient and momentous reflection, should continue nevertheless to be estranged from the authority of the visible head of the Church, which both Scripture and tradition concur to establish as firmly as Ritualistic conviction upon so large an amount of Catholic tenets and rites, once so reprobated—an authority that resides in one "who," as St. Jerome lays down, "was constituted the supreme head of Catholicity, in order that schism therein might not have an abiding to confound"? With this pilot at the helm the Ritualists ought to be equally convinced, as they are of the profitableness unto salvation of what they have finally and confidently taken up with, that there can be no wreck of dogma, that from the hand which guides there can come no fatal swerving from the laws of God, the rights of nature, or the belief of antiquity, as remarks a celebrated polemic. However, though the Ritualists repudiate the immediate successor to the spiritual power of St. Peter, " the first who professed the faith, the first who filled up the number of the Apostles, the first who confirmed his faith by a miracle, the first who converted the Jews, and the first who received the Gentiles," they virtually, notwithstanding every conveyed intimation to the contrary, by their retained position in the Established Church, yield a spiritual submission to the Sovereign of Great Britain, a Sovereign indeed who commands respect as well as allegiance by her consistent and prudential conduct since her accession to a throne which has pre-eminence among the Governments of this world in influence; but this is one thing, "By me kings reign;" "Thou art Peter," is totally another, and especially for one against whose voice being heard in the Church, except in prayer and psalmody, there is the interdict of an Apostle. Protest will not justify here, a mere subterfuge, which, if acted upon in early persecutions, to appease conscience in offering incense to Jupiter Ammon, would have consigned few Christians to torment or death. All this goes fully to evince how incongruous and indefensible is the conduct of the Ritualists. Attacks on every side necessitate them now to form into somewhat of a closer phalanx, but the continuous and determined pressure of legislation will finally throw them into disorder, and in the dispersion there will arise divisions, either through the pusillanimity of concession or the infatuation of further resistance.

To Ritualists, the entire adoption, let it be again affirmed, excepting only one of Catholic teachings, cannot yield the invincible strength, the surety, or the perpetuity of Catholicity. God is as jealous of each of these teachings as of the whole which constitute His Church, and cannot become auxiliary to anything but what includes an entirety of truth. In assuming, then, this Church, as hitherto done, to be the same Catholic Church at the present as in the past time, when admitted to be in possession of the promise, and consequently of all truth, which it is impossible to prove that she could ever have lost, except at the certitude of affecting the being of Christianity itself, a single exclusion of any one of her teachings is, therefore, a severance from Him who declared,

" Without me you can do nothing." All is weakness. Man alone remains, with his competitive religious opinions, which, though in extreme opposition as to respective Christian holdings, the lamentable issue of Protestant Christianity, self-judgment, is a privilege, as averred, and must be upheld, vouched for in Holy Writ. This " sacred privilege" has given birth most indisputably to Protestantism, and sustains in its contradictory life a religion which, though designated Christian, is (as a judicious writer in the *Catholic Standard* remarks) " no religion in particular, but every kind of religion and irreligion." If a man says that he belongs to the "English" Church he gives you no clue to his belief. To be a Protestant is simply to be a person who claims the right of believing as he chooses, and certainly, as the same writer adds, " in the making of one's creed there is comprised the principle of indifference to every creed." " Protestantism," he further observes, "is, to believe what you like." Hence, in this country, the very listlessness of free belief begets among Protestants but little zeal in the attempt to ensure exclusiveness. It is only when heresy approximates to Catholicity, no matter in what degree Protestantism may be receded from as to her own vaunted tenets, that opposition starts into vigorous and determined action, as recently so especially evinced in the case of the sect of the

Ritualists. "Here battle was felt to be exceptionally necessary." To insist upon the orthodoxy of doctrines from Church of England pulpits, as severally involving salvation in their credence, that had been so signally and studiously selected out for dire anathema from among the doctrines of Rome, and also abetted and defiantly proclaimed too as orthodox by figured banners and emblematic vestments in sanctuaries consecrated by State bishops, that have, as occasion or Heaven demanded, been referred to with horror and execrated with vehemence, such innovations could never ensure a continuous toleration. Protestant prelates generally could not here, in reverence to their pledged episcopal duties, connive at these things for even a brief hour in their inferior clergy. What Ritualists teach and practise must deeply compromise "the pure and Evangelical Christianity" insisted on by the Protestant Defenders of the Faith in these realms, whilst they, at the same time, conspicuously fill ecclesiastical positions through the laws of the land, and thus securing through them a temporal provision and protection. It reveals on the part of the Ritualists a sympathy towards that ancient and venerable faith, in dogmas and rites, in which centuries can effect no change nor surprise into concession. It tends to make a nullity of the solemn asseveration upon the orthodoxy of the Protestant

Articles of Christian belief before the exercise of a Protestant ministry is permitted—indeed, a most incongruous legislative insistence in a religion of hallowed freedom of decision on all things appertaining to the reformed faith.

Yet, however anomalous it may appear to be, in trenching upon the liberty of judgment in a fixity of tenets, by the virtue of statute, the Legislature must be upheld and vindicated, that framed and established the Christianity of this empire. It is necessarily conservative and distinct upon a certain amount of belief and practices, hereby securing legal matter to operate on in maintaining the spiritual rights of the Crown and the mitre's administering; those who constitute the Government in this land may not be very sensitive about Christian teachings and doings, but they must be protective from their very office upon statutory clauses that preserve and aid the Church in federacy with the State. Between the two there is an identity of interests. Here the Ritualists will not prevail, though they may deem that they have an exclusive league with truth. They must cede to the omnipotent law, as Blackstone terms it, or retreat from an established Christianity to a ground where every upstart and heated enthusiast has a free field for building his peculiar Babel, and who is ever exclaiming, " The Bible, and the Bible only, is the religion of Christianity !"—a Christianity of his own devising, which he deferentially ascribes to the impulse of inspiration, and with the knowledge of which neither Luther nor Calvin were, before ending their Apostolical labours, supremely blessed. But before chivalrously venturing upon ground without the pale of the Established Church, and beyond the reach of the Legislature, where Synods, Convocations, and Acts of Uniformity are as much valued by the majority as the Thirty-nine Articles and the Athanasian Creed, with its concluding solemn and warning words, " This is the Catholic faith, which except a man believe faithfully he cannot be saved," it might be deemed prudent with the Ritualists to weigh well to what an extent their fortitude would be taxed by the riotous inroads which would be made into the midst of them, in taking up with free ground now unprotected through State mediums, by the visionary Gospellers of the day, and in supplying also the requirements of their yet costly ritual, by voluntary contributions. They might, indeed, be fully equal to every assailment and every need, in the fervour of a first sacrifice for conscience and Heaven, during a period; but it is only Catholicity that can hold uninterruptedly to these emphatic and inspired words, " This is our victory, our faith!" and which possesses a witnessing to this in history, in her continuous fixity and undiminished authority amid the rise and fall of empires, their grandeur and their ruins.

In Catholicity there is no retrocession which would be triumph for the assailing, nor within her could any urgency compromisingly interfere with tenet or rite, to ensure gain or help, however ample or advantageous. But Ritualism, in adopting the rites and tenets of Catholicity, does not thereby in the slightest degree share in the promises of God to His Church. She is still human, as hitherto declared, and if not so readily, is liable to a change as sects at large in teachings and practices, not possessing the sacred pledge of surety any more than the Lutherans or the Calvinists. She certainly, without comparison, presents a more specious and steadfast show of unity and strength than either of these two latter, but it is as with sticks closely huddled together, and not scattered, which may nevertheless be easily disengaged and snapped in two; but with Catholics it is, in the quaint language of Judge Haliburton, "as in compact bundles, tightly and securely bound, which have resisted every striving of hand and bend of knee to loosen or to break." Catholicity has never fallen off in her unity, though Protestants assert that she has forfeited the promises made in her regard. "It never can be proved against her," says Bossuet, "that she has evinced the slightest inconsistency or variation since the origin of Christianity." She has always, throughout ages, demonstrated that she has had her indestructible foundation upon a rock, firm and united in the principles which she has professed and evolved. An abiding Infinite Wisdom has never allowed her to become demented, as with Protestantism, which is forced to countenance every fresh vagary of the human intellect. With her saints and martyrs in the past, and with her millions of the immediate hour spread over the face of the earth, she can, without a falter in her words or a tremor in her voice, exclaim, " If I am deceived, Thou, O God, art the Author of my deception!" She can lift up her right hand with the angel in the Apocalypse to Heaven, and swear by Him who liveth for ever and ever, who declared, "Lo, I am with you all days unto the end of the world," that her faith, a faith " without which it is impossible to please God, shall be until time shall be no longer." (Apoc., c. x., v. 6.) To which of the thousand sects so confident of their creed and their Paradise could it be said, with any expectation of the doing, " Go thou and do likewise " ?

SECTION IX.

The near approach of the Ritualist party to Catholicity, by their adoption of all the external practices of religion, has, it must be stated, led to a most determined and reckless onset being made on them by a Protestant Episcopacy, which in its meritorious and transcendent doings hauled down the Cross with contumely, and smashed up the confessional into unsightly fragments, which acts have been considered with enthusiasm as services rendered to God and Christianity. However, in reference again to confession, which in the prostration of dying moments is so formally enjoined by what is authoritative in Protestantism, the question is apposite enough, why should it not be also spiritually profitable in the robust and perilous days of life? This is one of the prominent inconsistencies to be satisfactorily explained, which are quite as numerous in Protestantism as contradictions. It is also to be solicitously inquired, what is there so exclusively in conflict with ancient Christian practices in the elevation of the Cross within a

Christian temple? It directly and emotionally testifies to the sufferings and humiliations by which grace and redemption were secured. The sinner could scarcely gaze on it without some compunction for flagrant guilt, nor could the devout contemplate it without adding to the ardour of prayer. It signalled forth the triumph in the heavens of Constantine, and might be deemed to be as fully entitled to as conspicuous a position beneath a sacred roof as, already alluded to, the banner of the Turk in St. George's Chapel, which has been so often advanced, like the Roman ensign, to exterminate the Christian. "The Cross of Christ," says Montalembert, "has presided over all the destinies of the modern world; it is connected with all its adversities and its glories. It has served as the basis of its laws, and as the standard of its armies. It hallowed the most showy magnificence of civilisation, and the most hidden emotions of piety. It has sanctified the palaces of emperors and the cabins of peasants; in every age and in every country, mankind have placed under its shelter all their glory and their virtue." On this most absorbing of Christian subjects, it is due here to observe that the Ritualists are able to justify themselves, and at the same time to convict their adversaries of the injustice of the present action now taken against them on account of their demonstrations of respect and reverence in regard to the

Cross, inasmuch as with the Catholics it has a termination in the glory of Him who was attached to it for our Redemption—the Cross, which at first beholding must at once ensure the sympathies of the Christian with what was realised upon it, and if it fails to do so there cannot be much fellowship in Christian feeling with St. Paul, who constantly preached up the Cross of Christ, and never desisted from carrying it. He would not have hesitated to bow his head before the Cross on which his Saviour was designated King, and which it is surprising that most Protestant prelates would not do also, since they incline their heads on passing the throne in the House of Lords, even when not occupied by sovereignty. "I have often," said Bossuet, "represented to those unceasing wranglers who can discern nothing reasonable except what proceeds from their own judgments, the honour which is rendered in private as well as in public life to the Book of the Gospels within the Catholic Church. It is elevated, and lights precede it, in carrying it to the place where it is to be read or sung, then incensed; honour is also done to it by the rising of the congregation. At the termination of the reading or the singing of it, it is conveyed to the officiating priest, and presented to him, who reverentially kisses the appointed Gospel that has been read or sung. Here, though there is only ink and paper, honour is given to the Book of the Gospels, as comprising the words of Eternal Life. Yet, notwithstanding all this, I have never met," continues Bossuet, " with any one sufficiently insensate to place what I have set forth under the head of idolatrous practices. I have said finally to those vociferators of ' She is blasphemous in her worship,' ' What is then the Cross, in your opinion, otherwise than an abridgment of the Gospels ? The entire of the Gospel is represented by it, under one sign and a single character. Why then should it not be kissed? Why should it not be reverenced by an inclination of the head, and under other forms indicative of honour and respect, as well as the Book of the Gospels ? ' "

But in reviewing preceding matter in the aggregate, which has been treated on in these pages, what a majestic mien does not Catholicity ever present, ever preserve—the Church of ages, venerable in aspect, the Church of truth, unaltered in feature ? Her position is as august as pre-eminent in an authority founded by the Son of God in unity, exercised in the Divinely instituted primacy of St. Peter, and conserved in its integrity, as from the first, in his legitimate successors. She is as instant, as must be conceded by those who read and reflect with honest purposes, to anathematise errors as she is exact in their respective entries, that always remain to witness to the indefectibility in every doctrinal detail of her sacred mission. Her formal decisions in manifesting belief do not comprise novelties unheard of in tradition, nor contradictions that mar their orthodox purport with perplexing embarrassment. She is never without her heroic virtue, witnessed to from time to time by the miracle, which evinces its continuous abiding within her, as well as the Apostolicity of the faith that she professes. It may here be well-fitting specially to observe that whilst numbers who, as said, value themselves more upon their differences than their religion, are steadily retrograding from all that is Catholic, from indeed the very substance of Christianity, so as to bring it within a something of mere religious consideration, against which the grossest objections may be levelled without producing a startle, numbers, on the other hand, are identifying themselves more and more with Catholicity in what she teaches and what she enjoins. This, indeed, has been sufficiently heretofore expanded upon, as well as several other things, yet repetition may not always enfeeble the force of a suitable introduced remark. The immediate matter here demonstratively manifests in the extreme recession of one party and the closer approach of another to Catholicity a testification in her favour as to a fixity of teachings, as also the care of a Providence that is Divinely guaranteed never from her to pass away, and which Protestantism could not under any reference realise in her own regard.

But forcible as this ought to be, a very reverend Canon, a Vicar, a Rural Dean, and a Master of Arts, in the certitude of being "a faithful and true witness" (Apoc. c. xi., v. 14) on earth, as also afterwards to be proved in heaven, as to what the Apostles taught and believed, thus, in his leisure moments, sets forth a Church which early Protestant Reformers have admitted retains what is fundamental in Christianity for salvation, and from whence the Ritualists have alone been able to obtain materials to fill up, if possible, the unseemly gaps which the reforming on the reformed have effected in perfecting their Christian creed. "To sum up all in a few words," says this faithful and true witness, "on earth, to be also in heaven, the religion of our English forefathers before the Reformation was a religion without knowledge, without faith, and without a lively hope; a religion without justification, regeneration, and sanctification; a religion without any clear views of Christ or the Holy Ghost. Except in rare instances it was little better than an organised system of Mary worship, saint worship, image worship, relic worship, pilgrimages, almsgivings, formalism, ceremonialism, processions, prostrations, bowings, crossings, fastings, confessions, penances, absolutions, masses, and blind obedience to the priest. It was a huge higgledy-piggledy of ignorance and idolatry, and serving an unknown God by deputy. The only practical result was that the priests took the people's money and undertook to secure their salvation, and the people flattered themselves the more they gave to the priests the more sure they were to go to heaven." All this ought not to be taken notice of, as being the usual rapid and frenetic outburst of primitive Evangelical men, who would do away with every symbol of belief as adverse to the full exercise of the blessed liberty of the Gospel—men who would, as with the so reverentially designated "rubbish of Aaron," shovel away every vestige of imposing rite, as deforming the beauty of God's House, and as destructive of that singleness of worship so acceptable to a jealous God. But herein is a vouching for all the above, though so plenteously and coarsely alleged, in the high titles of Canon, Vicar, Rural Dean, and Master of Arts, that lay claim at least by their holding to some show of alliance with learning, prudence, probity, and veracity. Now, the Scripture declares, "The number of fools is infinite" (Eccl. c. i., v. 15), and it may be here well noticed that certainly, according to the Rev. J. C. Ryle, M.A., Christ Church, Oxford, such men, enumerated by himself, as Manning and Newman, Oakeley and Dodsworth, Faber and the Wilberforces, with whom many others may be associated, distinguished by intellect, erudition, and piety, and once also pre-eminently so by their persistent opposition to Catholicity, must have added to the multitude of the insane, under a very vital consideration of not being "wise unto salvation," in taking up in the entirety with the old faith. The state of those becomes still more desperate (who yet survive) by defending and propagating a faith, though, in which some of their most exemplary, learned, and gifted fellow-professors have died with confidence and tranquillity. Is it possible that Catholicity should have so conclusive a witnessing in her favour as comprised in the above celebrated men, seconded also in the main as to her teachings and rites by the convictions and practices at this immediate hour of several hundreds of most influential and highly educated clergymen, and yet possess no fundamental claim to be denominated Christian? It is quite possible in the vicar of Stradbroke's summary conclusions upon Catholicity, with whom the olden belief is something execrable in its entirety, and which had so blocked up the "blessed road" with mounds of rubbish as to render access to God an utter impossibility. In assuming this as a fact, Christianity, the life of the world, came then finally to a dead stand until the reformers were mercifully deputed, enlightened, and strengthened to bring down

and clear away every impeding and stubborn obstacle
in the approach to the throne of Infinite Love and
Goodness, and yet, nevertheless, though appointed
here to the doing of Heaven's work, such was occasionally the heat of temper as to what was orthodox
or devotional among the reformers that pickaxes and
spades might have become rather fearful weapons in
their practised and expeditious hands.

But however gross may be the absurdities, and
incredible the charges, which the vicar of Stradbroke (who appears to be more desirous to be uncom-
mon than just) has set forth, under so multiplied a
detail, against the olden faith, he will notwithstanding
have both the stout advocacy and the firm belief of
the chivalric and unstaid children of the Bible, with
their emphatic " Nothing but the Bible!"—and who
will enthusiastically associate him with the Apostolate
of Paul, that "withstood Peter to his face." (Gal.,
c. ii., v. 7.) But, on the other hand, it is almost
needless to say that numbers there are in Christendom
at large who, though differing in tenets among themselves, and in opposition to the Church, which has no
dissension as to doctrines within her, will not chime in
with those, in all their plenteousness of damning
epithets, who sedulously exclude from their thoughts
everything that antiquity reposed in and venerated,
who have their own opinions of to-day in the place of

the fixed decisions of ancient Councils, and hold as sad supersitions the acts which constituted the heroisms of saints, who range under the head of "higgledy-piggledies" (which Dr. Johnson interprets a mass of absurdities) the hierarchy of Catholicity, with its venerable chief, its ordinances, its decrees, and its canons, from which nations have derived both experience and wisdom in the framing of their laws, and in giving permanency to their enforcement. With Protestants of the most ordinary understanding, it must be something inconceivable that for centuries, among two hundred millions or more, there should be an united assent (and which subsists now) as to all the teachings and practices of Catholicity, notwithstanding their being of such an alleged preposterous nature as just given in detail. Certainly History cannot be proved to have been so calamitously and completely duped for ages, as to verity of matter, in all her eloquent and circumstantial discussions upon every proceeding and movement of Catholicity which she, in her pages, has had for her principal interest and chief praise.

Catholicity cannot but in all this yield a stronger motive for reliance and credence than ever-propounding and ever-differing Protestantism could, whose doctrinal confusions, that have arisen in the hitherto strenuous efforts made to put forward somewhat of an Apostolical and detailed belief, might be aptly assimilated to those of the clashing and breaking waves upon the wide, sterile sea-shore. Moreover, Catholicity, in spite of every test in the present, as in the past, that could be well applied by the profound in learning, the versed in science, and the subtle in intellect, to disprove her claim to a celestial origin and to a Divine promise for her existence, has retained, in a vast and pre-eminent degree, the confidence of mankind, notwithstanding all its alleged attendant and eternal consequences. This adds much now to the humiliating abashment of those who once thought that all would be lost for Catholicity, her sublime doctrines, her majestic rites, and her heroic virtues, in the forcible exposure of her true worth. . Yet repeated insistence upon this, as well as other kindred matter, may perhaps be deemed somewhat tedious. However, it may be justified by the reiterated charges, often in words as mendacious as audacious, against Catholicity, which Thiers, who was as conversant with Governments as with history, declared, it may be said, in the last hours of his lengthened and experienced life, " to be the Christianity that preserves the world from chaos." For however ingenious man may be in realising chimeras, he is totally unable to give a body to them; they will soon flit away, as well observed, to be succeeded by others, to puzzle and confound more deeply.

"Lots are cast into the lap, but they are disposed of by the Lord." (Prov. c. xvi.) It may be well here to observe that the unscrupulous allegations of Protestants against Catholicity, as interminable as their evanescent Gospel truths, have a purpose, equally with maligning Catholic teaching, in keeping up an aversion to the persons of the Catholic priesthood, conjoined with an insinuation of their utter inadequacy, considering the principles by which they are actuated, advantageously or safely to respond to any position of civil importance in society. Hence, even at this immediate and refined period, a charity boy can scarcely confront a priest in the street without a sneer upon his stolid features, or a matronly teacher in a primitive Christianity school without a lowering of her sedate brow, with a pouting of lip. But the priest of a Church who, through a varied duty, enters into what is temporal as well as what is spiritual, does not lose his citizenship in his ordination, nor does it unfit him for any secular and dignified offices, under the most responsible forms. He can feel as a patriot, and has a full right to pronounce upon what may be best considered for his country's good, as well as to reply to a Christian's conscientious difficulties in the transactions of ordinary life. His sacred character, if duly weighed by himself, would restrain him from party invective and party hostility, and from countenancing those who think to redress a wrong though violating a law. In some countries, especially in Ireland, former religious persecutions had in a great measure intertwined priests with people in politics, and it is not easy to disentangle this relationship, even when a revision of statute has left little for murmur. In most cases, to attempt to bring this about, no matter under whatever plausible plea, would be to expose the ministrations of the priesthood with the people to some embarrassment, and even when engaged in the most solemn and sacred of functions, scarcely could all risings in the breasts of the opposite in convictions be repressed or mastered. However, the priest, who, though, in all spiritual exigences is the servant of the Christian, is, in common with every citizen, free from every controlling as to siding with any opinion or party in what is of a purely political nature. Whether what has been now and hitherto urged in regard to the above in the defence of priest or Pontiff will lessen prejudice, or increase caution in entertaining accusations so constantly and recklessly brought against the members of the Catholic priesthood, it is difficult to say. Probably not. The readings of a Protestant education, again partially to be dwelt upon, readily unite credence with crime perpetrated by sacerdotal and anointed hands, and chiefly at early life, in the perusal of novels and romances, this belief commences, and strange yet true to affirm, the fictions fondly dwelt on in youth become facts with hundreds in after-times. This is doggedly evinced in those who can never give up one accusation without starting another, as also in those who have ever in store some reproach against the Catholic priesthood, no matter how estimable may be their lives in their deeds. If they quit the world to be removed from its temptations and corruptions, they are melancholy enthusiasts and useless drones. If in the world they raise themselves up against tyranny and oppression, they are meddlers, and step out of their own province to increase disturbance and add to trouble. If, in consideration of their ability and experience, they are entrusted with the administration of a national importance, they are intriguing and ambitious. The Pontiffs of a God of concord and justice are represented as continually abusing their authority, encroaching on the rights of others, and thwarting the advancement of every public good.

Nevertheless, Catholicity, so repulsively depicted, has patriotism in her priesthood, and possesses what is not to be met with without her precincts—obedience in her congregations and order in her hierarchy. Still within her prominent boundaries virtue has her ready succour, and truth her instant defence, in her ordained.

What feeling, it may also be suitably here adverted to, doth there not arise among her faithful, for the most part with whom Christian doctrine is of such an early and detailed acquaintance, in reflecting upon her venerable dogmas, so much akin with what is experienced in contemplating her ancient cathedrals and abbeys, within which, in centuries past, they were so solicitously inculcated and firmly believed? What emotion does there not also come into play among them in recalling to mind in subsequent life what was so sedulously read by them in the place of romantic tales and defaming novels, the history of saints and martyrs, which Protestants well-nigh prescind from in their Christian readings, for fear, as it may be surmised, that the Catholic virtues of past days might impart a dangerous estimation to Catholic doctrines in present times? Throughout all Catholic works of the most remote date a common sentiment prevails, to which, at this immediate hour, those of a religious complexion are all in full response. This—that does not subsist in Protestantism, but which is so obvious in Catholicity—results from this latter having truth for her basis, "that has her descent from heaven," as Massillon so impressively sets forth, and which of all things on earth is best calculated to engage and engross the thoughts of man. She alone illumines his mind and directs his heart—she makes the foundation of all his hopes, and mitigates all his sorrows—she alone is the source of a good conscience and the terror of a bad one. She alone immortalises those that love her, ennobles the chains of those that suffer for her, and secures historic renown for those who have died for her. She alone can inspire great thoughts, and form wise as well as exalted souls of which the world is not worthy. All the solicitudes of man ought to be centred in knowing her, all his talent should be devoted to making her known, and all his zeal employed in defending her. We can scarcely well comprehend her without knowing something of ourselves.

Animated by this truth, though opposing empires have successively ruled, Catholicity, identified with God's providence, has never been brought to a stand in her assigned mission. History vouches for this before Protestantism had an entry within her pages; and in a respective reference to the final decay and crumble of nations, history ever includes, in a minute detail of events, an august testimony to the indissolubility of the faith of ages. Except to Catholicity, which has her vitality in what is exterior as well as what is interior—"which is always to endure, and always to battle," says Pascal—and which, when apparently on the brink of destruction, has ever had her speedy rescue, that has made evident the intervention of an Almighty hand—the foregoing remarks could not be made applicable to any sect. Did Catholicity admit of what was absolutely antagonistical to an exclusive claim to truth, it would not then be totally incompatible for her to enter upon a little fondling acquiescence to satisfy the whims of the myriad wayward, and so to obtain peace for the hour, though at the depreciated worth of Christianity. But her mission is of God, not of man. "Lo! I am with you all days, unto the end;" and she manifests a Divine presence by her subsisting unity to this moment, as much as Protestantism demonstrates its absence by ceaseless divisions from its very commencement. "Without me you can do nothing."

Nevertheless, with serenity on his brow, and doubtless consolation in his heart, a venerable Doctor, entitled Archbishop of Canterbury, declared in Church Congress some time back that the present day was a bright day for the Protestant Church. It is to be, however, primarily observed, this was uttered as upon private opinion, yet the dignity of position, and the influence attached to it, warrants some comment. The Archbishop, as reported, proceeded, in his address to the Church Congress, to say: "Look abroad—what other country would they change Churches with? Look at home—which of the other denominations would they exchange places with? Look back—what age were they prepared to declare it would have been far more satisfactory for them to have lived in? For his part he thanked God, and took courage. The Protestant Church was a great historical Church, which had been handed down to them by the fathers of the Reformation. It was the Church of Hooker, Jewell, Jeremy Taylor, Barron, Cudworth, John Keble, Thomas Arnold, and Charles Simeon. A Church which was good enough for all these was good enough for them. A Church which had been honoured by the advocacy of so many saints of God would, he believed, go on flourishing in its Master's cause, waiting for the Lord's coming, and be found ready when its Lord came." [1] At the close of the above, delivered to a formal assembly, somewhat affecting ancient ecclesiastical congregatings, there was a manifestation that might be classed with enthusiasm —doubtless on account of the setting forth of a Protestantism by His Grace after so unhesitating and explicit a form. Certainly, if this address to the numbers congregated of fame and station could be divested of the marvellous, it could not very well be of the "prodigious"—prodigious in the broadness of its included challenges, and the venturous character of its affirmations.

---

[1] *Daily Telegraph*, October 10th, 1877.

But in the first place on foregoing polemical matter it might be incidentally observed that the brightness which gave a clearer view of things to the eyes of the Archbishop might have a very deceptive source. It might have proceeded from what is of a meteoric nature, to whose erratic and brief course St. Jude figuratively refers in connection with the first heretics, in whose opinion Apostolic teachings were not altogether free from the necessity of a mending, and which goes to prove that with them the miracle even did not add much awe to the words of the inspired. Probably it was from this not-to-be-disputed fact that the founder of the Reformation, so pre-eminently entitled to precedency among the Archbishop's Protestant teachers and Doctors, derived hardihood enough openly to avow that he valued not the Epistle of St. James a straw. But to proceed with the questioning of the Archbishop, and then to make a reference to it in a somewhat summary form. "Look abroad," continued His Grace—" what other countries would they change their Church with?" Not presumedly with the Catholic, or the so-styled Greek Church, is the reply, both being so deeply involved in Protestant anathema by reason of a close assimilation with a respective teaching, except as to the procession of the Holy Ghost and the Papal supremacy, nor indeed with any other phase of a Christian profession that should comprise, to some extent, what was of a fixed and definite nature. "Look at home," continues the Primate, with Evangelical exultation and an unfaltering voice— " which of the other denominations would they change places with ?" But what is Protestantism, it is here speedily to be rejoined, but a compound of denominations among which a claim is severally entertained to Heaven's special approval, for their peculiar construction upon what truly constitutes a pre-eminent Christian faith. In Protestantism nothing doctrinally distinct could be set forth. Search the Scriptures —that is, judge for yourselves—is an assumed right with all heretics, to be prized even with the Scriptural texts on which their judgment is founded. This has given being to conflicting Protestantism, ever in opposition to Catholicity, as from the first, and as it ever will be to the last, whilst her Christian unity is maintained among millions that have through it been best assured of the exclusive possession of truth throughout past, and which assurance will exist with them throughout future ages. There is no choosing within her, which, if countenanced, paralyses all authority in enforcing belief, as witnessed within Protestantism. She is the "one faith," "without which it is impossible to please God." His Grace proceeded to say, "Look back—what age were they prepared to declare it would have been far more satisfactory for them to have lived in?" It certainly could not, in reply, have been unsatisfactory for the appealed to to have lived in and believed with the first four centuries, since Protestantism admits that at these primitive periods purity of teaching, both as to tenets and morals, prevailed. Indeed, there must be an assigned date for the existence of the above in Christianity, or otherwise Christianity would be left fully open on all sides to be demolished by infidelity as a fiction of man's devising, which had no framing in a Divine hand that was also pledged to sustain it. "The Protestant Church," concluded the Archbishop, in his address to Congress, "was the Church of Hooker, Jewell, Jeremy Taylor, Barron, Cudworth, John Keble, Thomas Arnold, and Charles Simeon." But why not have witnessed to his Church as an Apostolic Church, by declaring it to be the Church of saints and martyrs who taught and edified in the first four centuries, which assented to the decrees and observed the ordinances of General Councils which were severally held during the early and genuine Christian periods—the great historic Church, the Church of Irenæus, that anathematised the Valentinians; of Polycarp, that anathematised Marcion; of Zepherinus, that anathematised Sabellius; and of Athanasius, that anathematised Arius? Certainly, among the paraded names with which the Archbishop of Canterbury identified his Christianity and his salvation, not one could be selected, though in high repute as the writers of volumes many, that superseded in the vastly the gifts, the erudition, and the piety of a Gother, a Faber, a Newman, a Dalgairns, and others also that still retain the religious estimation of those they have separated from, and who are now visited with no shudderings upon the very dubious nature of their ordinations, which they occasionally experienced in carrying out their ministerial duties when Protestants. The Archbishop might have no misgivings for his virtue at the coming of the Redeemer, but certainly he might experience a few as to a Divine approving of so indefinite and chequered a faith as that of Protestantism.

Luther said, which may very fitly succeed to foregoing archiepiscopal convictions upon the Christian sureties of a present Protestant faith, "We are forced to acknowledge, Protestants as we are, that in Popery there are the truths of salvation—yea, all the truths of salvation—and that we received them from Popery, for it is in Popery that we find the true Holy Scriptures, the true baptism, the true sacraments of the altar, the true keys which pardon sin, the true preach-

---

[1] Luther's works published, to which Suger, in his "Plain Talk," refers.

ing, the true catechism, the true articles of faith, and moreover I say that in Popery true Christianity is to be found." But perhaps it may be urged that when Luther advanced the above, under such a distinct and comprehensive detailing, there had not yet come upon him an enlightenment with the fulness of the illumined evangelist, and that incidental visits of traditional insistences surprised him, and rather largely, into very astounding admissions. However, they might be deemed the last conscientious deferences paid to the teachings of the Catholic Church before all became reckless and then desperate. Audin narrates what has an intimate connection with the above as follows, that Luther, whilst in the company of the seduced one, contemplating during the hush of a serene night the glowing stars in the firmament, that are made in the inspired Word so impressively to symbolise forth the glory of the elect, avowed that it was not for him ever to hope to shine among their splendours. When earnestly entreated by Catherine to return to what he had once professed if now assured that he had grievously erred, "Too late, Kate, too late!" was the sad, sad reply. And what were the last moments of Luther, so terrible to nature and so portentous to him, when about to pass into the hands of Him where all is life, where all is action, where nothing ever relaxes or lessens in vigour? Not a supplication for mercy passed from his lips, not the slightest manifestation was to be witnessed of religious rite. He departed, and his eyes were closed in silence. And what kind of a Christianity did the great heresiarch, the new evangelist, of so felicitous a temperament and so restrained an appetite, bequeath to the universe for its peace here and happiness hereafter? From what has preceded in discussing the character of Protestantism some judgment may be formed, not very indicative of its Apostolicity.

The spirit of confusion, so manifestly and eminently prevalent among the leaders of Protestantism, had a vast influence in bringing about the thorough conviction of Henry the Fourth of France as to the Catholic Church being alone the true one. In compliance with the intimated wishes of this monarch a conference was held at St. Denis to examine into the respective worth of the two creeds, the Catholic and the Protestant, at which Henry in person was present, together with an equal number of divines on either side to carry out the discussion. In the course of the proceedings the King, in addressing himself to the Protestant theologians, said, "You are all then of one accord in admitting that salvation is to be secured in the Catholic Church?" "Certainly," rejoined the ministers appealed to, "provided that a man leads a good life." Thereupon, turning to the Catholic divines, he asked, "Do you consider that I can work out my salvation whilst remaining a Protestant?" "It is our profound conviction, Sire, and we as unhesitatingly as solemnly declare it to you, that having once known the true Church, you must enter it, and there is no safety for your soul if you continue a Protestant." On receiving this frank and definite reply, Henry again addressed himself to the Protestant ministers, saying: "It is then the height of prudence that I should profess the Catholic faith, and not your belief. For you proclaim, with the Catholics, that in their religion I can be saved; whereas in yours, it is true, I can secure salvation as to your opinions, but it is otherwise in Catholic convictions. In conformity, therefore, with common sense, I must take up then with the surer side." Henry became a member of the Catholic Church, and manifested his sincerity in so doing by an unswerving adhesion to her every teaching. "We have our faith from our forefathers," said one day to him a learned Doctor of the reformed belief. "And we have our faith," was the speedy rejoinder of Henry, "from God, which we have learnt from our forefathers."

SECTION X.

THE foregoing matter will have afforded sufficient and convincing evidence to the mind of every unprejudiced and thoughtful inquirer that there is only one way, as the profound Bossuet declares, "to become a Christian, and that is by becoming a Catholic." There can be only one Christianity, and if Protestantism is Christianity, it cannot be so with Catholicity. But whence does Protestantism get her Christianity, except from Catholicity? To reject her authority, or even to impeach her ancient vouchings, is to affect the very being of Christianity herself. The institution of Jesus Christ, as Suger, in his "Plain Talk," very forcibly remarks, cannot be made subject to the caprice of man, who sets about framing a faith in conformity with his own whim or whims. In this there cannot be the genuine Christianity which our Lord imparted to His Apostles, and which He enjoined them to spread over the face of the earth that He has so mercifully and lovingly redeemed. It follows from this, as Nightingale very conclusively observes in his portraiture of Catholicism, that in a Church which upholds an unrestricted right of private judgment no authority can dwell. She may, as he asserts, issue her orders of Synods, Convocations, and Acts of Conformity. She may enlarge or curtail her Thirty-nine Articles. She may even pronounce sentences "of God's wrath" and " everlasting damnation" against heretics and schismatics, but so long as the Protestant Church admits that the groundwork of the Reformation is the right of private judgment, though she expend her strength in fulminations and her skill in devising new terms of salvation, she will be only laughed at by the discerning Christian, as inconsistent and intolerant. Things for the most part within Protestantism must take their course, under the influence of a privilege proclaimed as sacred as the Heaven that restored to Christendom through the Reformation its first purity. And what does all this, so closely in response with what has gone before as to the Reformation and the proceeds of its extreme phases, commonly terminate in? *Indifference* or *infidelity*. However, as to these two principal and generally confident results of free judgment, the Puseyites or Ritualists must be admitted as largely in the exceptional as to the foregoing usual terminations of Protestantism, by the action which they have taken. Eventually, startled at the appalling risk of making further advances with the reforming, they halted, reflected, and then withdrew from a road in which they had so complacently hitherto journeyed—the thronged and broad road to eternal ruin—and took up that which, though rough and tasking in its course, if persevered in, infallibly brings into sight the august and prominently elevated Church of ages. But here, in briefly referring again to the two most frequent terminations of Protestantism, indifference or infidelity, it is to be observed that they are not so very wide asunder as to calamitous endings. In respect to the latter state, it has been sufficiently expatiated upon in order to make known its deadly nature. In regard to indifference, it may be said that it is a lethargy of the soul, which the voice of religion is scarcely effective enough to arouse into something of a meritorious religious purpose. With numbers it would appear that a blast from the last trumpet could alone be adequate to the bringing about a prompt arousing upon matters of everlasting moment. Hence the great majority of Protestants—"so enamoured are they," as the late Rev. F. Garside observes, "of the tideless dead calm on which their minds float without moving, that if an angel were to stir the waters, they would almost complain at the interference."[1] Nor will sectarianism ever be able to

---

[1] The Prophet of Carmel, p. 101.

make head against these two preceding terrible evils, whatever unexceptionable logic may be uttered from pulpits, combined with pilfered rites to procure consideration for sanctuaries. The stately-moving Irvingite, with broad stole and of emphatic delivery, in fraternity with angels and communication with archangels, will fail to arrest the attention of the listless or the incredulous, unless under a brief wonderment or a transient curiosity.

The Church, again to be asserted, that God has established, and which has invariably triumphed over the powers of darkness and the powers of this world, alone identifies herself with the promise. In her heroic virtues the worth of her sublime doctrines is discovered, and which, in their exercise in the days of penury, squalor, and chains, gave her a fixed influence which thrones had not then attained in wide dominion. Into whatever contrast she may be brought abashment is not hers, as to an inferiority in any admitted and prized excellence. Nor is it for any description of Christians without her boundaries, in solving or elucidating, to vie with her as to what in the inspired Word may be hidden or obscure. A greater wisdom than that of Israel's King resides within her, that is one with Him " who did all things well." Let the civilised world pass through every form of legitimate government, Catholicity will not be affected in the soundness of her ancient ministrations, nor will the grades of her hierarchy be disturbed. Whilst expanding the intellect she does not contract the heart She fills it with emotions that do not corrupt, but purify. She alone possesses the peace that was imparted by the ascending Saviour to His assembled chosen when environed with a glory surpassing in splendour that which suddenly chased away the gloom of the sepulchre, and evinced the fulfilment of the promised Resurrection, that made all finally conclusive for the Divineness of Christianity. Conscience in her alone has an unruffled calm, in a firm conviction of the orthodoxy of her teachings, and should this be troubled by the commission of sin the ready and efficient means exist within the Church of the Ambroses and the Gregories to regain the forfeited quietude, in those holy institutions which extend help to the perfect as well as tranquillity to the guilty. "Lo! I am with you all days," to sweeten the yoke and lighten the burthen. In a religion of fitful opinion this is not fully understood or appreciated, and hence arises a most accommodating and lax form of Christianity in doctrines and precepts, to give it currency, and which is not very persistently defended when its stirling value is doubted and contested. With regard to the prevailing of truth it has its confirmation here, in modern as well as ancient times, under the most unquestionable of forms, in the re-establishment of churches, colleges, convents, and monasteries, which "to-day as yesterday" are the same in tenets, rites, and discipline. She still constitutes the matter of the most absorbing events on record, which will retain their freshness and their surpassing importance, in their very imposing and cherished details, when the renowned of the past shall possess but a very curt historic entry, as the mighty of old who held in derision those who comprised in themselves and within themselves the Providence of the Most High, for the preservation of mankind, of an immediate belief which was in its entirety figurative, and of a future faith which was to include within itself the realisation of all that was typical in the old law. Truth, says Pascal, in alluding to what preceded the new law, was founded on figure, so that the truth is now distinguished by the figure. This is obvious in that Christianity alone in which is revealed a faithful fulfilment in response upon response' of what was prominently figurative in the Jewish religion, and eminently so in the holy sacrifice of the altar, that comprises the real presence—the eternal bread, as Gerbet sets forth so demonstratively, which nourishes our souls, languishing for the everlasting truth, the celestial drink which slakes within us the infinite thirst of love. The immolation of typical victims was the most solemn act of a primitive worship; mankind doomed to die sought even in the bosom of death salvation and life; immolation still remains, but the period of figure having ceased on Calvary, Christ Himself becomes the Victim. Here, in connection with the above and foregoing doctrinal and ritual matter, a question may not be very incongruously started as to the final conversion of many of the Jewish race, to which St. Paul makes so special an allusion, whether it would be through the medium of Catholicism and Protestantism. Certainly not through a Protestant medium, which, as heretofore remarked, has been well lopped down to a very questionable stump, but through that Church is conviction to be brought about that existed before Protestantism was, and after whom the Jew has ever carried his Bible under his arm, finding only in her the fulfilment of every figure that could possibly bring about a firm conviction that she is one in creed and holy in deed. Yet still it is the Bible, and with it an assurance of future bliss.

The Bible only is the true religion of the Protestants, affirms William of Chillingworth. "Very true," says the judicious Hooker, in his "Ecclesiastical Polity," "but then you must submit to receive your Bible from the hands of the Church of England men." "Certainly, by all means the Bible," adds the learned Margaret Professor, " yet the Bible is nothing without the Book of Common Prayer." "Nay, nay, the Bible is not the thing you want, unless you discover in it all the great and precious contained in the Assembly Catechism, and can submit to the wholesome discipline of the Directory," replies the pious and sober Presbyterian. " No, no," says the zealous Methodist, " it is the Bible collated with Mr. Wesley's and Mr. Fletcher's checks that is the religion of the Protestants." " And thou mayest read the Bible and the checks likewise till doomsday, friend, to no purpose, unless thou hast the light of the spirit," exclaims the modest Quaker. " A truce with your spirit," cries out the Swedenborgian. " Why don't you read the works of the illuminated Baron, wherein are answered all questions, be they as high as heaven, or deep as hell?" " You are all right, and all are wrong," rejoins the Rev. Dr. Sturges, Prebendary of Winchester, "provided the magistrate chooses to say so, for it is his province to decide which shall be the national religion." In all this, which sounds prodigious in its utterance, Catholicity is not permitted to have a voice with even the Swedenborgian or Wesleyan. She is not to be credited in her interpretations on the Divine Word, though from her Protestantism received it, since she is imbued with the most deadly of teachings.

Through this Catholicity brings, as so solemnly averred, the direst anathemas of Holy Writ upon herself, and she is designated by an epithet that must, if it were possible, cause a shudder amongst the martyrs and saints in heaven, who saluted her as mother on earth, and who died for her doctrines or confirmed them by their virtues. However, victory has never departed from her faith, though it is alleged that God has done so, by those especially who are utterly incapable of defining their creed, that with each of them has an exceptional acceptance with the God of Truth. Catholicity, in whose orthodoxies there are no betterings, as with the perfections of the Deity, and however severe may be the scrutiny which she may have to undergo, has no tremor. The ancient Roman tribunals, with philosophy for their counselling, could not bring the members of the holy Catholic Church into public contempt upon convicted falsities. Catholicity has taken her stand at the most inimical tribunals, and has counted triumphs with their number. Perhaps under a judicial consideration nothing is more generally commended than the equitable conclusions come to in the Judiciary Courts of Great Britain. Rarely is a matter to be heard against the probity of her judges, and as rarely is their adequacy questioned as to learning, experience, and ability in the discharge of an office to which the Scripture extends such majesty to give force to reason and weight to decision. One or other of the many subtle influences and motives that so frequently and busily beset humanity may incidentally sway the hand to tamper with the poise of such immediate and serious consequence in the transactions and ministrations of nations; but a momentary advertence to that oath which is solemnly taken before occupying a seat upon a judiciary bench—" I do swear that I will do right to all manner of people, after the laws and usages of this realm, without fear or favour, affection or ill will; so help me God!"—must on the instant steady the hand; and in a true righting of the beam Heaven receives its just due. Were the judges presiding over the diversified Courts of Judicature in this kingdom assembled together to adjudicate upon the respective claims of Catholicism and Protestantism, as to the holding of a belief that should be best pleasing to God, is it possible that the judicial summing-up could be with Protestantism, to the exclusion of Catholicity's one revealed faith, which can alone ensure agreement in Christendom, as the one determining Divine action in harmony with the creation? Such a summing-up, if arrived at, would be constituted, in an aggregate of witnessings, as confounding as that which bewildered the High Priest of the Jews, and compelled him to interrogate the Divine Prisoner himself, so misrepresented in His words, and so maligned in His purposes, in order to arrive at certitudes. It is not credible that the judges of this land, who so deliberately enunciated words that implied, "May God so help me with His wisdom to discern what is just, and aid me with His power in maintaining it!" could rest with a composed conscience in the above decision, that was founded upon nought but what was as uncertain as fluctuating, as presumptuous as wild, and as contradictory as assertive.

In the supposition, however, that so formal and so absolute a decision had a place in favour of Protestantism, together with its exclusive acceptance as a Christian belief with Heaven, therein would be discerned something in close and kindred keeping with the conduct of an infatuated sculptor who should, in most artistically executing the figures of the three chief reformers, to evince his profound persuasion of the Apostolicity of their mission, surmount them with the representation of an angel, with trumpet at mouth, and displaying expanded wings, as if despatched in lightning haste from Heaven to confirm and announce to the earth their evangelical and Godly errand—"Hear you them!" But on a sudden let it be conceived that an excited and dense crowd of people, brought together by the unveiling of a work of rumoured excellence, are thrown into consternation by the fierce and rapid utterance of epithets, proceeding as it were from the several reformers, and addressed to each other, of the most gross and reviling description. Surely in all this there could not be much attesting, much response, to the sacredness of their mission, though proclaimed as such by the winged from on high for the speedy and merciful diffusion throughout the universe of the restored Christianity first propagated by the Apostles, and to subsist with time. There could be but little edification or confidence most assuredly to be derived from those among whom there was no common doctrinal agreement, and who virulently vilified one another in proportion to a respective opposition among themselves as to what was to be definitely declared as orthodox, and entitled to be classed with inspiration's worth. There is in the foregoing a manifestation of as little charity as unity. Without the former all is "sounding brass and tinkling cymbal;" without the latter there cannot be the one faith that is alone acceptable to God. If it is to be observed that all here is supposition as to the voices severally proceeding from the ably finished pieces of statuary faithfully representing the three first reformers, which, however, might indeed have been effected by some gifted and adroit ventriloquist, it is, nevertheless, an historical fact as to the foul and repulsive epithets with which they fraternally saluted each other in their frequent vehement disputes to which their broad differences as to Christian verities gave rise. "Dog, hog, devil, and bedevilled," passed as freely as cordially from their purified lips in the fulfilling of their alleged Divine commission, that went beyond in hallowed purport that of Isaias. If there was a showing of some prominent accord among a few of the principal abettors of Protestantism it had its source in the fearful avowal that so absolutely tended to forward vice and to impede the progress of virtue. Now, the most lax and ranting of present preachers, whose Evangelical simplicity tolerates only a white neckerchief in the discharge of their most important conventicle duties, could scarcely possess the scandalous effrontery to utter from their pulpits what so vitally affects sanctity, "Sin boldly," as long as these words remain in the inspired page—" Be holy, as your Heavenly Father is holy." It would be rather difficult to find among the most wanton of the early heresiarchs one that went beyond Luther in an as-you-like-it licence of Christian expoundings, that not only mystified faith but undermined morality. The virtues comprised in this latter principally aided the broad spread of Christianity, and on which the Apostles and Evangelists dwelt with such solicitous instance. They had their charms, if miracles had their wonders. An eloquent man, though not a Catholic, thus fervidly expresses himself upon this immediate and all-important matter—" Turn to the virtues formed to connect, to blend, to associate, and to co-operate, bearing the same course with kindred energies and harmonious sympathy—each perfect in its own lovely sphere—each moving in its own more contracted or wider orbit with different but concentrating powers, guided by the same influence of reason, and endeavouring at the same blessed end—the happiness of the individual, the harmony of the species, and the glory of the Creator."[1] Had these ardent words come under the supervising of impetuous Luther probably there would not be much left for a further obliteration. He had very little solicitude for anything except for what gave its joy in eating or drinking, of which he both boasted and exulted in boisterous clamour. When not complimented with a very speedy and unqualified submission to his own well-pondered Evangelical constructions upon the heads of those who failed to render this ready assent the most opprobrious terms were quickly heaped, which were not figuratively very expressive of the burning charity of " a vessel of election " towards the offending. But He who said, " Let there be light," has not enlightened

---

[1] Sheridan.

the Protestant Church through Luther's so-pronounced Biblical and indulgent expoundings, who, with the Apostle, affected to glory in the Cross. All is confusion, all is contention here, as when in the days of Saul darkness had fallen upon the inimical Philistines, in contrast to a Church entitled Catholic and to which the following may be so well applied—

> "But thou shalt flourish in immortal youth,
> Unhurt amidst the war of elements,
> The wreck of matter, and the crush of worlds"[1]—

the Church that is not established in opinion, nor could any true Church have an existence in a thing of such a fickle nature, no more than that a Church could become heterodox which, as admitted, had received a Divine pledge of being preserved from all false teaching to the end of time. Few names have a greater repute for ability, learning, and integrity than Grotius, who, at the end of his most celebrated work, "The Truth of the Christian Religion," says, "Though an angel should descend from heaven we are not to receive any other doctrine than that of Christ, confirmed by so many testimonies." Whence, however, is this teaching to come but from a Church of unity, for truth admits of no division, the Catholic Church,

---

[1] Addison.

the Church of Christ, confirmed by evidences to which no complexion of Christians can lay claim without its prominently defined precincts, which have over them the same vigilance of watch as that which witnesses the "fall of a hair from the head as well as that of a sparrow"?

Grotius, though gifted with so acute an intellect, enhanced by so profound and varied an erudition, could never deduce from free judgment anything of a positive nature which might realise conviction. He could only realise it in Catholic unity. The learned Jesuit Petaud (Petavius), who was on the most intimate terms of friendship with Grotius, testifies that towards the close of this great writer's life, he became, notwithstanding the many passages cited from his works declaratory to the contrary, perfectly satisfied that authority and conviction could be attained only within Catholicity. So strong was the persuasion of Petaud on this point that when he heard of the rather unexpected death of Grotius, he offered up the Holy Sacrifice for the repose of his soul.[1] Feller, on the above, judiciously observes, which he was so fully justified in doing, considering the many surprising conversions that of late have taken place in this land among those who sought for something stable in

---

[1] Biographie Universelle, Art. Grotius.

Protestantism to rest their hopes on, yet could not discover it, that Grotius's variations, his incertitudes, and even his increasing errors, coalesced to bring so righteous a mind to an ultimate understanding of the truth. He could alight on no fixity of doctrine but within the Catholic Church, that exclusively defines and insists with authority upon belief. "The necessity of believing in the Holy Catholic Church appeareth in this," says Dr. Pearson, the learned Bishop of Chester, "that Christ has appointed it as the only way to eternal life."[1] We read at the first that the "Lord added to the Church daily such as should be saved." And what was then daily done hath been done since continually. Christ "never appointed two ways to heaven," nor did He build a church to save some, and make an institution for other men's salvation. There is no other name under heaven given among men whereby we must be saved, but the name of Jesus. And that name "is no otherwise given" under heaven "than in the Church," as none were saved from the Deluge but such as were in the Ark of Noah, framed for their reception by the command of God; as none of the firstborn of Egypt lived but such as were within those habitations whose doorposts were sprinkled with blood by the appointment

---

[1] Exposition of the Ninth Article of the Creed.

of God for their preservation; as none of the inhabitants of Jericho could escape the fire or sword but such as were within the house of Rahab, for whose protection a covenant was made. "Lo none shall escape the eternal wrath of God which belong not to the Church of God." When we profess to believe, he summarily continues, in "the Holy Catholic Church," every one is thereby understood to declare thus much—"I am fully persuaded, and make a free confession of which, as of a necessary and infallible truth, that Christ, by the preaching of the Apostles, did gather unto Himself a Church, to which He daily added such as should be saved, and will successively and daily add unto the same, unto the end of the world, so that, by virtue of His all-sufficient promise, I am assured that there was, has been hitherto, now is, and hereafter will be, as long as the sun and moon will endure, *a Church of Christ one and the same.*" Thus does Bishop Pearson in his exposition on the Ninth Article of the Creed express himself as to unity in faith, and its absolute necessity. The question now to be asked is immediately consequent upon foregoing matter—in what sect, congregation, or Church is this one faith necessary to salvation to be found? Who among Protestants will enter upon the inquiry? Who will hope to give a definite reply with the holy of the past when questioned upon their faith? Dr.

Pusey has recently alluded to his one faith, which he has been pleased to federate with Apostolical, but his language is so qualified and ambiguous in regard to Ritualism as to make it quite certain that an attempt to prove his belief to be an Apostolical fact would be as difficult as to disprove that he received through the medium of Catholicity the inspired Word on which he grounds this belief. But under what form does Protestantism, considered at large, present herself at this immediate period, opinion upon opinion, error upon error? In adducing here another forcible witnessing upon this matter in Dr. Johnson, "It is destruction joined with reformation, resulting from men who, resolved not to stop short, have generally gone too far, and in lopping superfluities have wounded essentials." Nor will truth upon truth adopted from Catholicity check effectually the progressive dire Christian calamity whilst prescinding from Catholicity, that alone comprises the faith which Nightingale, in his portraiture of Catholicism, avows "has ever been the same in all times and at all places."[1] And to this may follow, " I must and do freely profess," as writes Thorndike, of such authority among Protestants, "that I find no position necessary to salvation prohibited, none de-

---

[1] P. 250.

structive to salvation enjoined, to be believed by the Church of Rome."[1]

Protestant writers may depress with fears the well-disposed towards Catholicity by subtleties upon historic advancements, often, for the most part, of their own concoction, but He will not refuse to give peace to those that have recourse in their troubles to Him, who, whilst He stilled the storm that threatened instant wreck, at the same moment dissipated the attendant haziness that deepened confusion among the bewildered within the staggering and reeling vessel. It is for doubting Protestants to omit a little of their Bible-reading and psalmody-singing, and to elevate their voices to heaven in earnest supplication for enlightenment—" Behold, he prays "—and then they may expect that " the scales will fall from their eyes," and that they will see with the conviction and the joy of Damaris. Once in possession of Catholic certitude, that has been so studiously and conscientiously sought after, it is not probable that harassing doubt will again come upon the possessor, since it is but to ring, as well said, the genuine against the counterfeit, and however skilfully this latter may be executed, and however closely it may approximate in weight to what is sterling, detection will be as im-

---

[1] In Epil. p. 146.

mediate as assured. But what a gladsome day indeed it must have been for those who, after travelling so many devious ways—"For there is a way," says Solomon, "which seems to man right, but its end leads to perdition"—had got upon the right way at last that conducted to "the one fold and to the One Shepherd"—the way of the Cross for many truly before they came to such a happy close, before they could exclaim: "This is the day, the day of triumph, which the Lord, co-operating, has made. Let us be glad and rejoice therein." An education which has imparted and nourished prejudices into the most stubborn persuasions, a belief which does not include many terrors for conscience, nor much insistency upon precept, must create a difficulty to be mastered with regard to Catholicity that comprises the violence by which heaven is to be gained. Few, it may be justly observed, have been aware, in connection with foregoing matter, of the strength of the bonds that were upon them, because, as if wreathed with flowers, they have not felt their pressure until aroused into an effort to release themselves; they have then sorely experienced what strenuous and continuous efforts were required to effect it. In this all-important struggle, which involves in the future an eternal joy or everlasting woe, perseverance can alone attain the calm of Catholic convictions, and give serenity to dying moments. To these every step in this life brings us nearer and nearer. We may wish to rest and loiter on the road, but we cannot; the decree, as so impressively exclaims Bossuet, has gone forth, and we must advance; an invincible power constrains us to do so without ceasing. We are necessitated sometimes to precipitate our steps, even to run. Feelingly convinced of all this, how pathetically does not a young lady, a convert to Catholicity, express herself in the following Litany for a happy death: "O Lord Jesus Christ, God of goodness, and Father of mercies, I approach to Thee with a contrite and humble heart; to Thee I recommend, at this final hour of my life, the decision of my eternal doom. When my feet, benumbed with death, shall warn me that my mortal course is drawing to an end; when my face, pale and livid, shall fill the beholders with pity and compassion, and make known my approaching farewell to all; when my ears, soon to be for ever shut to the discourse of men, shall be open to the irrevocable decree which is to separate me from the number of the living; when my eyes, dim and troubled at the approach of death, shall fix themselves on Thee, my last and only support; when the enemies of my salvation, the spirits of darkness, shall endeavour to cloud my imagination, and to make, if possible, Thy tender mercies less visible, and to plunge me into despair; when my poor heart, enfeebled with frequent struggles, shall feel the immediate pressure of death; when the last tear, the forerunner of my dissolution, shall trickle down my cheek, receive it as an expiation of my sins. When my sorrowing friends shall invoke Thy clemency in my behalf; when the world shall at last have vanished from my sight, and my soul have departed, leaving my body cold and lifeless, and I shall appear in Thy Divine presence, merciful Jesus, have pity on me, reject me not, but receive me into Thy bosom of goodness and love." In the utterance of these impressive and affecting ejaculations, undisturbed now by the fitful intrusions of preferential Christianities, yet not without a misgiving of a mingling which might somewhat disparage the deeds of the heroic, and make even fear for an Apostle, nevertheless, confident in the teachings of her Catholic faith, she tranquilly surrendered her spirit into the hands of Him that framed it, and which were raised to bless His chosen in its propagation. On the instant of quitting this world she beheld the Shepherd of the one fold, who ever recognises His own by the unanimity of their belief, and whose glories brighten in accordance with the merits of their virtue. The wilful in dissenting from a Church of unity, and the persistent in an iniquitous doing, whatever may have been their learning or their science on this earth, even unto wonderment, now seeing through the light of God, will exclaim, "We fools, it is we that have erred!"—too late to be deplored.

Sectarianism, with an erect head and a defiant eye, and a Bible under arm, may have a passport to palace or to cottage, but the Gates of Paradise will not fly open even upon its sacred pressure, however strong that might be, or vehement the accompanying cry, "Lord! Lord!" for not every one that thus exclaims "will enter the kingdom of heaven." The Bible, which contains many things hard to be understood, and which people may wrest to their own destruction, whatever extravagant interpretations may be put upon it, utters not a word. But the Church speaks, from whom Christendom received the inspired Word, and which Christendom is Divinely commanded to hear—not Luther, not Calvin, not Zuinglius—and he that will not hear this Church, as with Luther, Calvin, and Zuinglius, let him be unto you, it is said, "as a heathen or a publican." Nevertheless, Protestantism or Sectarianism has a broad and potent existence. This must be admitted, yet at the same time it must be conceded that random and differing opinions, though in the myriad, can never be made the constituents of truth.

Were Catholicity, with its sublime teachings and

august rites, to have an end, and that voice be no longer heard that kings and rulers have ever listened to with interest, and heretics and Deists not without some attention, what description of Christianity would remain in the future for history to record and descant upon? What would barely remain worthy of Him, who alone is great, but the silent architecture of the cathedrals of the past that torpid and dreary Protestantism has possessed herself of, and from which she has so sedulously excluded all that which dignifies the throne and ought to create reverence for the altar? But where truth abides, and this is with Catholicity, a close communication can alone, as already sufficiently dwelt on, be effected with the Deity, and which ever realises a suitable impress, as upon Israel's legislator, and ensures a grandeur of feature throughout the telling details of the religious services of the ancient faith. But all this, and the varied vital controversial matter that has preceded it, will not prevail much with many in favour of Catholicity, the one, the unchangeable, and the olden faith. It will have its immediate contradiction. This, however, can hardly give place to surprise, since the Creator Himself, within the sacred boundary which He had planted with loveliness, and where He seemed to dwell with innocence, was impiously confronted with a denial that death would be consequent on eating what was forbidden; and the deluded, ennobled as they were with the Divine image, were induced to exercise their own judgment and to partake of what was interdicted, yet "delightful to behold;" then, on the instant, mortal guilt had its existence, and Paradise began to droop and to wane.

In drawing to a conclusion it may be well to make some brief reference to the Communion of Saints, which has its prominence as an article of Catholic belief in a Creed that has ever had an enduring and an undeviating tradition for its recognition, with the warranty of inspiration for the entirety of its orthodoxy. Theologians, in defining this most comprehensive Christian dogma, make it to consist in the union of the Church militant, triumphant, and suffering—that of the saints in heaven, the faithful on earth, the suffering in purgatory, constituting one and the same Church, having Jesus Christ for an invisible and the successor of St. Peter for a visible head. In this Communion is included complete unity in what is doctrinal and in what is moral. It conducts to the source of both, and that is Divine. It must, at least, be admitted that the term Communion has a more congenial blending with the unanimity which must always have a place where truth prevails than with vague and discordant protest, which in the virulent exceptions upon the most ancient teachings, that is always in the ratio of a more abbreviated dogmatical credence, imparts a greater prominence and authoritativeness of character to one of the most venerable of Christian registrations. In severing from this Apostolical harmony, Christianity at once becomes federated with incertitude. "Old Catholics" even, in such an event, assume new features, not to be recognised by Him who, when the books shall be closed, when forgiveness of sin shall no longer have an entry therein, when all shall have arisen with the instantaneousness with which light had a presence in the Creation, will declare: "I know you not. Depart from me; you who were not with those of my fold who knew me, and I knew them." "Come, enter into the ineffable joy of the Lord," will be addressed to those who counted their victories in obeying a bidding that is to exist with probation, and which no edict of the triumphant can control or thwart. Invincible ignorance may, indeed, plead for many that have been reared in the most preposterous and opposite of beliefs, without being favoured with even a transient intervening gleam of enlightenment, to induce a suspicion of error as to their several special Christian safeties, yet when this is so, and the intimations of conscience are not disregarded, the mercy of God is not excluded. But what is to be said to those who have read much, thought much, and argued much on Scripture evidences, but who nevertheless, in upholding the right of private judgment, virtually fraternise with those who by their countless differences have turned Christianity, as Babel, into tumult? That there is but one Church exclusively enjoined to be listened to—"He that heareth you heareth me"—and which teaches that the faith is one, as truth is one, and without which it is impossible to please God. With regard to others who indeed believe, but who are not within the one true fold, they do not make one with the Communion of Saints; they falter at some sacrifice which it is imperative to make to effect an entry within the boundaries of truth. Reserves never made the heroisms of Christianity. All must be in subserviency to the requirements of truth, without which the conquest is not complete. When this unreserved submission, so devotedly rendered by united martyr and saint, is yielded, then there is identity with the Church, that is One, Holy, Catholic and Apostolical. He who has so recently filled the Papal Chair exclaimed, with those before him, from the depth of his fervid convictions, "God is with us," and His pledged Divinity will make this as certain as it is evident to the end of the world!

FINIS.

W. W. HEAD AND MARK, PRINTERS, FLEET LANE, OLD BAILEY, E.C.

www.ingramcontent.com/pod-product-compliance
Lightning Source LLC
Chambersburg PA
CBHW051721300426
44115CB00007B/419